A Spy's Diary of World War II

A Spy's Diary of World War II

Inside the OSS with an American Agent in Europe

WAYNE NELSON

McFarland & Company, Inc., Publishers

Jefferson, North Carolina, and London

Library of Congress Cataloguing-in-Publication Data

Nelson, Wayne, 1912–1986.
    A spy's diary of World War II : inside the OSS with an
American agent in Europe / Wayne Nelson.
        p.   cm.
    Includes index.

    ISBN 978-0-7864-4548-6
    softcover : 50# alkaline paper ∞

    1. Nelson, Wayne, 1912–1986 — Diaries.   2. World War, 1939–
1945 — Secret service — United States.   3. World War, 1939–
1945 — Underground movements — Europe.   4. United States.
Office of Strategic Services.   5. Spies — United States — Diaries.
I. Title.
D810.S8N45   2009
940.54' 8673092 — dc22   2009031127
[B]

British Library cataloguing data are available

On the front cover: OSS civilians and military officers aboard the SS
Darbyshire during Operation Dragoon; American Navy Torpedo Boat
(MTB); French Croix de Guerre medal (left) and American Bronze
Star medal

Manufactured in the United States of America

McFarland & Company, Inc., Publishers
  Box 611, Jefferson, North Carolina 28640
    www.mcfarlandpub.com

Table of Contents

Prologue: The Fever of War   1

Preface (by Kay Shaw Nelson)   5

Introduction: The Briefcase (by Kay Shaw Nelson)   11

1. The SS *Evangeline*   15
2. Algiers   21
3. La Maddalena   32
4. Corsica   67
5. Operations from Bastia   86
6. Interlude   108
7. Dark Moon Ops   121
8. Operation Dragoon   134
9. France: The Vosges Region   154
10. Courageous Women and Men Spies   173
11. Bordeaux Pockets   186

Epilogue (by Kay Shaw Nelson)   196
Index   203

Prologue: The Fever of War

War is like a fever. Once it's started, it must run its course. Over one year into our part of the war, for those of us who have been dubbed "Donovan's Cloak and Dagger Boys" by a recent *Time* magazine, it's been a long, hot spell with no sign of breaking.

Armistice Day seems an appropriate date to review the bidding so far. When Colonel William Donovan was given the directorate by President Franklin Roosevelt to design a centralized intelligence agency, he rounded up quite a cast of characters to operate in the Mediterranean theatre. Some were recruited from behind Ivy League walls, but others volunteered from every corner of our country, from different cultures and with multiple languages. It's fair to say that nothing before has been attempted like it, and we can just hope that somewhere in the process of recruiting, training, landing behind enemy lines, propagandizing, and being as creative as the most gifted playwright, we are making a difference and laying some groundwork for those who will come after us.

I understand that our little gang is earning a reputation for some of our exploits.

When I first started writing this diary, I had in mind the outline of a magnificent play that would be eventually acted on the stage. Now, through a clearer fog of war, I see that the policy planners and historians and academicians will have plenty to analyze and study in the years ahead. But where are those to memorialize the anonymous shadow warriors who are setting the stage for those who will see the victory? Certainly, history will study and analyze for decades to come Churchill and Roosevelt and MacArthur and Donovan. And the enemy. But there are other heroes that we have spent our time recruiting and training and sending out to near certain death behind enemy lines. That, I believe now, is why I've kept the diary. So that there will be at least one hands-on-account of the Joes. They are our boys, of course. And the enemy, of course, of which there'll be a lot more later on.

We should never forget Vierin who was stranded on the Mediterranean Island of Giglio and barely missed capture and certain torture or death by Germans who patrolled within inches of the mouth of the cave that served as their hide out.

We should never forget Pierre who was in Algiers, after he had come back from Morocco, having been sentenced to death and just saved at the last moment (after all he had risked before D-Day).

We should never forget Blesio who had been with the Garibaldi Legion in Spain and as a result was put into a concentration camp in North Africa from which he was rescued after a long battle.

We should never forget the little guy coming to Sinety — a wilted flower and the way he was so grateful when I tried to talk with him in the three or four words of French I had picked up at the time, when no one paid any attention to him, and the way he began to brighten up, to bloom, and after only a few weeks, to fill out with more food, and then go off to fight against Fascism having been in the thick of the 5th Army fight.

We should never forget Primo, the chap here who is sort of major domo and waits on "us officers," who was in the Spanish war, who came into Sardinia in June and again in July, and was captured and was between the artillery fires and was sentenced to the firing squad and saved in the nick of time, and who asked if I wanted him to go to Giglio with me the other day, still eager to go on with the fight.

We should never forget young Jiminez who is about 23 or 24 and has known nothing but war since he was 16, and who was in the Spanish war, did missions behind the lines, who landed with our boys at Salerno and was radio operator on the beach when our outfit set up and was tapping a telegraph key when the 88's were firing so close you could see the muzzle flashes.

I was green as Pollyanna when I first came to the theatre, hoping like anything to go to the front lines and into the war. Now there are days when I question everything — the policy, the fight. But I keep going because I can never forget the faces and the thousands of incidents that prove the same general policy of trying to protect an outmoded pre-war status quo — then I hope to God I never get through the darned war and that I never write a play that sees the stage.

One other possibility is that the fight will go on. That there will always be a fight during my lifetime and that there will be no chance, no time, to sit down and reflect. And the people who are my friends now will be sold on some other prejudice that I will be fighting.

It's going to be an interesting world after this war — or after whatever truce is made that ends this part of the war.

But the diary begins at the beginning that, for its purposes, is last year in January 1943 when Henry and I, as the first civilians to go overseas for the Office of Strategic Services, prepared to board the troop ship SS Evangeline. It was to be the first trip overseas for the old relic and for me to another kind of stage in the Mediterranean theatre.

Preface

by Kay Shaw Nelson

Soon after the Japanese attack on Pearl Harbor on December 7, 1941, and the United States' official entry into World War II, Wayne Nelson wanted and tried to get into one of the military services and hopefully go overseas to serve his country. Although he was 29 years old and had full vision in only one eye he had high hopes for succeeding.

On December 22, 1941, Allen Dulles, a corporation lawyer in the prestigious Wall Street firm of Sullivan and Cromwell, wrote a letter to Lieutenant Raymond Lisle about the possibility of Wayne's joining the Navy. It stated:

> In connection with your inquiry some days ago, I am writing to recommend as a man who might be very useful to you, Mr. Aubrey W. Nelson. Mr. Nelson has been working with us here in the office as night stenographer for some years, and in effect fills the function of a court stenographer. Further, he has assisted me in the preparation for trials of important cases and in this has rendered very unusual services.
>
> He has an excellent education, is extremely efficient, capable and self-reliant.

Wayne was not accepted by the Navy and it is not known if he made any other specific attempts to join a military service but by the spring of 1942 he had gone with Dulles to join the Coordinator of Information (COI), established in July 1941 with Colonel William J. "Wild Bill" Donovan as director. Dulles was made head of the New York office in Room 3663 of the International Building of Rockefeller Center and soon built up a staff of experts on German and European affairs.

By the summer of 1942 Dulles was seeking an overseas assignment with the Office of Strategic Services (OSS) that had replaced the COI and Colonel Donovan offered him a position in London where he would work with David K.F. Bruce, the lawyer-diplomat and later OSS chief in Europe, and British intelligence. Dulles, however, had other ideas and suggested that instead he should be sent to a "less glamorous post, but one where I felt my past experience would serve me in good stead." He had served as an American intelligence agent in Switzerland during World War I and liked the idea of returning there.

With Donovan's approval, Dulles began making plans to leave the New York OSS office for Berne, Switzerland, to serve as the OSS director's "sounding board for occupied Europe." He requested that Wayne go with him, which the young man was happy to do. He had great respect for Mr. Dulles and enjoyed working with him. By mid–October Wayne had made the necessary preparations — had a physical, taken his shots and been issued a special passport, along with visas for Bermuda, Portugal and Switzerland. Then the only route to Switzerland for an American was flying to Lisbon, and from there traveling overland through Portugal, Spain, and Vichy France.

Unfortunately, Dulles' departure was several times delayed because of difficulties with the State Department about his cover and status. It was finally decided that he would be an assistant to the minister and Dulles departed for Switzerland on November 2.

The veteran traveler, however, was lucky to arrive at his destination. Traveling by train through Vichy France he just missed being nabbed by the Gestapo and barely made it to Switzerland before the French closed the Franco-Swiss border to respond to the TORCH landings. He later wrote, "I was one of the last Americans to do so until the liberation of France."

There was no way that Wayne could join Dulles and he was very disappointed. But he persisted in his effort to get overseas.

North Africa had been a constantly recurring theme in the history of COI and OSS and Wayne was well acquainted with most of the events and had met or knew of many of the people working in the area. He set his sights on an assignment there.

Sometime before this, on October 10, 1941, Donovan had presented to President Roosevelt a plan for undercover intelligence in North Africa as "a concrete illustration of what can be done" and since then he had presented his views about the importance of the Mediterranean in World War II.

In *The Armies of Ignorance* William Corson states:

According to Wayne Nelson, who authored the portion of the *War Report* dealing with Donovan's mission:

Donovan felt that many people were prone to think of the Mediterranean as an East-West channel for shipping. He believed it should be thought of primarily as a no-man's land between Europe and Africa, two great forces or potential forces, facing each other from the North and South. Germany controlled either directly or indirectly most of the northern "battle line" of this front on the Continent of Europe. It was imperative in Donovan's view for the British — or the British and the Americans — to control the southern front along the Mediterranean shores of Africa.

In February 1941 the United States "agreed to send certain essential materials and supplies to North Africa," and in the summer of 1941, Donovan's twelve "control officers," ostensible regular vice-consuls, were sent to North Africa to be stationed in Casablanca, Algiers, Oran, Tunis, and Rabat to collect intelligence. They were responsible to Robert D. Murphy, a Foreign Service career officer, in Algiers.

Later that same year Lieutenant Colonel William O. Eddy, USMCR, a former college president who had wide experience in Africa and spoke Arab fluently, was appointed by Donovan to be the COI's man in Tangier.

In July 1942 Prime Minister Winston Churchill and President Franklin D. Roosevelt met secretly and gave their approval for an invasion of Axis-held northwest North Africa. Operation TORCH was the code name for the tremendous undertaking placed under the command of General Dwight D. Eisenhower, soon to become supreme Allied commander in Europe. This was America's first major offensive of the war.

The Allied landings, with troop convoys sailing from the United States and Great Britain, were made on the Atlantic Ocean coast of French Morocco and on the Mediterranean Sea coast of Algeria at Oran and Algiers on November 8, 1942.

Operation TORCH provided the first major test of OSS in which all branches took place and according to the *War Report* the Joint Chiefs of Staff thus "had before it, not only the paper record of committee discussions, but the concrete example of accomplishments in action."

By the time the plan for Wayne's assignment to Berne had fallen through he was working as a personnel assistant to Donovan at the OSS administrative headquarters in the Central Building, one of the limestone and brick structures previously occupied by the Public Health Ser-

vice at 15th and E Streets in a northwest section of Washington called
Foggy Bottom. It had a view of the Lincoln Memorial, the Potomac
River, and an old brewery.

(Wayne first went to work for Donovan in April 1942 when the latter was laid up in the St. Regis Hotel in New York after his limousine
was in an accident in Washington and he refused to go to the hospital,
returning by train to New York and was driven to his apartment in the
hotel. According to reports on April 2 Donovan had to cancel appoint-
ments and for the next six weeks while recuperating directed the COI
from his bed.)

In 1942, while living in Washington and working with Jimmy Murphy for Donovan, Wayne at age 30 had unarmed combat training,
learned about mandatory codes and ciphers, all in preparation for an
overseas assignment. Plans were underway for him to go to North Africa.
A cable sent from Donovan to Eddy in Algiers stated, "State Department has given us tentative approval for the appointment of Aubrey Nelson as clerk-secretary at the Legation in Tangier for service to you. At
one time Nelson was asked for by Robert Murphy."

In a cable of December 11 Donovan notified Eddy that Aubrey Nelson's assignment to Tangier had been approved finally by the State
Department: "When Nelson arrives in Tangier, you can arrange for his
transfer to Algiers locally. He should remain an OSS employee. However, we approve of your lending his services to Murphy. He is an SI
man and has had SI training. He expects to leave in a few days: he is
awaiting air transportation."

For some reason the plans for Wayne to fly to North Africa were
changed. A cable of January 4, 1943, informed Eddy that "a group of 4
officers, 20 enlisted men and 2 civilians in charge of Captain Sage are
leaving tomorrow for North Africa by boat.... Included in this group are
the training instructors which you requested, Aubrey Nelson, communications men and 2 other groups going under training cover. Captain
Sage knows the details...." (Although his proper name was Aubrey
Wellington Nelson, as an actor he took the stage name of "Wayne" and
was known by it ever since.)

A cable from Donovan on January 13 listed Sage's manifest of supplies and equipment, office equipment, medical kits to have a total weight
of 23,260 pounds. It also stated that "Sage's ship and his party were still
at port of embarkation but expected daily to leave."

The "boat" did sail on the next day, the fourteenth. Wayne Nelson was finally on his way overseas heading for North Africa.

Far away in Casablanca, FDR, Churchill and members of their military staffs were opening a significant conference to plan 1943's war strategy. And in New York *Variety* reported that the most popular current songs were *Had The Craziest Dream*, *There Are Such Things*, and *Moonlight Becomes You.*

Introduction: The Briefcase

by Kay Shaw Nelson

"I remember seeing Wayne keep these diaries. As I recall, he kept them in some sort of esoteric shorthand. I also recall that he had several volumes in various shapes and sizes. The reason for my comment is that these diaries would contain some very interesting material, particularly if Wayne expressed his candid views as he was apt to do."

— Letter from Peter Karlow, January 8, 1992

Over the years, since I first met and married Wayne Nelson, an OSS veteran and CIA intelligence officer in 1950, he would talk about in considerable detail and with great enthusiasm his experiences as a spy for our country, the United States of America, in World War II. From our very first encounter at a Georgetown, D.C., party he regaled me with fascinating tales about the heroic people he had met and the faraway places where they lived and fought for their freedom and ideals. Ever since that evening the stories about his wartime encounters continued not only to entrance me but everyone he knew. As one friend stated, "Wayne is a born raconteur."

I recall particularly one summer evening in Washington D.C., when Wayne and I were working for the Central Intelligence Agency, and meeting regularly for dinner and weekend social events. It was shortly after the shocking news that Communist North Korean forces had stormed across the 38th parallel invading the American-supported Republic of South Korea. Suddenly the Cold War was hot and we were all spending long hours at the office.

While dining at an outdoor café and talking once again about his exhilarating experiences Wayne suddenly handed me a few typewritten pages and said, "Here is an article, The Brief Case Story, that I wrote and want you to read." He added, "Remember when I told you about my diary, scribbled and written in my self-taught shorthand on odd pieces of paper at all times of the day and night wherever I happened to be. You know I'm a fast talker and addicted writer. As soon as I heard about my going overseas to serve with the OSS I decided to write a chronicle of my experiences and because of my unique script that nobody else would be able to read what I wrote. Hopefully after the war I would write a play about them and it would be on Broadway."

He went on: "In order to capture the emotions and reactions focusing on daily events, the excitement, disappointments, accomplishments, and frustrations, you have to inscribe them as they've just happened, lest you forget. I wanted to be sure to remember how we planned and executed operations and survived day-to-day, the exhilaration, fear, and camaraderie. What I did and how it happened is in these diaries, my personal memories, and I want to share them with you." I was deeply touched.

Ah yes, the diary or diaries. I had heard about what was in them as Wayne often spoke about his rubber boat operations in Corsica and Sardinia, the Allied invasion of Southern France (Operation Dragoon), sending agents across enemy lines in the Vosges Mountains, and traveling with the Reparations Commission to Moscow and Potsdam. But I had never seen the diaries. Did they actually exist? Where are they now?" I wanted to know.

"Of course they exist, in my Mark Cross briefcase, a farewell gift from the office of Sullivan and Cromwell where I worked with Allen Dulles, and I carried with me throughout the war. It's the subject of the article I just gave you. Although pretty beaten up now, having traveled many times from New York to Washington, across the Atlantic Ocean to North Africa, surviving air raids, trips aboard all kinds of ships, and even a beachhead landing, it was my secret storage carryall, " Wayne enthused.

Later, in Wayne's article I read with considerable interest the story of the briefcase where the diaries had been stored and their travels. They'd had quite a journey and some memorable experiences, especially landing at St. Tropez in France. As the Brief Case relates about August 16, 1944:

We hopped into the Higgins boat and buzzed off to the beach. I might remark that I had landed ahead of Nelson, since he had to swing me in front of him in order to get on shore. He set me down on the sand while he lit a cigarette, and I must say that I felt pretty good. How many brief-cases have made a beachhead landing?

A few minutes later I was piled on a truck with a lot of musette bags and bedrolls and we rolled off to St. Tropez. (I was chuckling all the way thinking of Nelson — he had to walk.) There were still snipers in St. Tropez when I got there, but we managed to rout them out, and had things well under control by the time Nelson arrived a couple of hours later.

And as the Brief Case adds: "I carried your C-rations, your dirty laundry, your lousy liquor and your cigarettes as well as some pretty important papers. Some of them were marked Top Secret."

One evening at Wayne's Washington apartment I finally saw the diaries, pages and pages of single-spaced, typed data carefully placed in files in the infamous briefcase.

"You see," Wayne explained, "all the time I was overseas the hand-written pieces of paper, stored in the briefcase, would be sent whenever possible to my apartment in New York. Then in the spring of 1944 when I flew back to New York for a brief home leave, before returning to Corsica, I brought a lot of the diaries with me. It was not until much later, after the end of the war, that I translated or deciphered my shorthand into English and typed all the diaries on these pages."

"This must have been quite a task," I commented while stunned at the thought. He nodded in agreement.

Later, while traveling and living overseas on assignments with the CIA I lost track of the briefcase and the diaries but I am sure Wayne knew where they were. In 1959 when we bought and moved into our home in Bethesda, Maryland, a suburb of Washington, D.C., the brief-case resurfaced and over the years Wayne would occasionally look over the diary contents and reminisce about them, recalling in detail fasci-nating lively and daring operations.

For me it was a great pleasure to accompany my husband to some of the places, especially Italy, Corsica and the Vosges region of France, where he had served with the OSS, and to try to comprehend the significance of his wartime experiences. I also had the good fortune to have met General Donovan on a few occasions and to meet some of Wayne's legendary colleagues, today considered heroic intelligence oper-atives, and listen to them recall their remarkable exploits, remaining in awe of everything they said and enjoying their expressions and pride of having served with unquestionable valor, often against considerable odds, in the OSS.

Although Wayne never realized his dream of turning the diaries into a play, he did express a desire to have them given to an intelligence library and this will be done.

Since Wayne's death in 1986 it has been a pleasure and privilege for me and our daughter, Rae Nelson, to review and edit the diaries' contents. We know that her father, the author, Wayne Nelson, would be happy that his personal account will be published.

As the widow of a former OSS intelligence officer and the mother of a lineal descendant, I, along with Rae, often attend the programs and social events of "the Office of Strategic Services Society that celebrates the historical accomplishment of the OSS during World War II — the first organized effort by the nation to implement a centralized system of strategic intelligence, spearheaded by the legendary General 'Wild Bill' Donovan — and educates the public regarding the continuing importance of strategic intelligence to the preservation of freedom in this country and around the world."

The Society publishes *The OSS Society Journal* that includes news items, book reviews, photos, and wartime memories. The Society offers research assistance in response to requests from historians, writers, media, military organizations, and descendants of OSS veterans. It also provides speakers to a wide array of organizations. The president of the Society is Charles T. Pinck.

1

The SS *Evangeline*

An OSS cable of January 4, 1943, informed General William O. Eddy that "a group of 4 officers, 20 enlisted men and 2 civilians are leaving tomorrow for North Africa by boat." Included in this group was Aubrey Nelson, one of the civilians. A cable of January 13 listed a manifest of supplies and equipment and stated that the boat was "still at port of embarkation but expected daily to leave." The boat did sail on the next day, the fourteenth.

SS Evangeline
January 13, 1943

This will be the first trip overseas both for myself and the troop transport, the SS Evangeline that bears the convoy number "609."

Approaching the docks in New York with the long-anticipated adventure of crossing the Atlantic finally at hand, I had imagined we would board a ship along the lines of the Queen Mary. Instead, the SS Evangeline turns out to be a former Eastern Steamship Lines coast-wise steamer that used to ply the waters between Boston and Nova Scotia.

Henry Leger (experienced ocean traveler), my roommate, remarks, "Good God! This tub will roll and buck." We finally find our bags and get more or less settled in our stateroom with upper and lower berths, washstand (hot and cold water three hours a day), and a wooden seat, three or four feet long. Then we inspect the ship's armament. There are two three-inch guns at the bow, two more at the stern, and a five-inch gun at the stern. Six 50-caliber machine guns are also on board.

We lie at the dock overnight (some people had been on board for five days). Then in the morning we pull out. All that day we are still clearing the environs of New York.

The ship's captain is a hard-bitten old seadog. About two months earlier he was on a ship that was torpedoed in the Caribbean and spent twelve days in an open boat before he landed on a beach. He mentions to us that he found Horlick's malted milk tablets a great help in trading with the natives, particularly the native girls. He advises that in the event one is forced to abandon ship, someone should immediately ration the water (probably two tablespoons per day, per person) and constant guard should be put on the water supply.

After two days on board, the order is issued that no one can go on deck without a helmet. I have none. (My roommate and I are the first civilians to go over by transport for the outfit. As a result of our experience, those who came later were issued army equipment.) The transport officer lends us old-style World War I helmets that we later persuade him to let us keep as souvenirs.

Four nurses are the only women on board. There are about 150 officers and 1300 enlisted men.

The distinction between officers and enlisted men shocks one at first, but as the war goes on I suppose one gets used to it. The officers are reasonable guys, of course, but so are the men. The officers' mess is adequate with only two meals a day provided at 6:30 A.M. and 6:30 P.M. The officers, of course, are quartered in staterooms and the enlisted men are housed in the side passageways and rear lower decks. The men eat out of mess kits and the food suffers, at least by comparison with that of the officers.

Our contingent of 29 enlisted men is on the lowest deck in the stern, next to where the ammunition is stored. Water trickles down the stairways from the upper decks where a porthole leaks. On the way it gathers orange peels, bits of paper, and other throwaway elements. It sloshes around with the roll of the ship. At times it slops over the men in the lowest areas. Complaints are made and, after several days, the situation is cleaned up only to recur within a short time.

Any officer who has any real feelings is ashamed when he returns to his cabin after being below decks. Those officers who have convinced themselves of the natural superiority that accompanies the mere facet of rank view it as a natural condition, however, and claim that such distinctions are necessary "for discipline."

One of our sergeants, Adam Leavengood, a teacher at various American universities, started some classes to teach the officers French every evening for one hour. There is much singing of French songs while the ship bucked and rolled with occasional interruptions by an alert. At night the singing is rather forced with self-conscious gaiety, everyone trying to avoid thinking of the possibility of submarine attack.

For thirteen days, one spends a lot of the time standing on deck or sitting on rails with ships all around — low freighters, grace liners, other one-stackers like the Evangeline, destroyers, the cruiser and the comfortable view of the battleship's stern.

During the nights at sea one begins to realize why many writers began their careers at sea. The sky and the sea stretch into eternity. A mere man and a ship seem small against this backdrop, but he is also large, for no other men intrude upon his view. A paradox somewhat like Voltaire's situation in "Micromegas."

There are various maneuvers the convoy goes through during the voyage. Sometimes almost all of the 24 ships are spread out fan-wise; at other times, they form a triangle, or a long line of paroled ships with one or two bringing up the rear like a backfield in a football game. Always three destroyers sweep ahead of the convoy, flashing back blinder signals constantly. The battleship is in the center, waddling along like an old fat lady. Off to starboard is the cruiser, with two or three planes that are used for patrolling. In our convoy, the battleship is the "Texas," the cruiser is the "Brooklyn" and nine destroyers accompany us.

There are unsettling moments on a troop transport when something goes wrong with the engines and the ship stops. The rest of the convoy continues, signal flags are quickly hoisted and the formation closes up. A tin can (destroyer) rushes in from the flanks to the halted vessel with blinkers flashing. The cargo (officers, men, Wacs and nurses) wonders what's up. Most don't say much, just watch the convoy forging ahead. Some interest themselves in the destroyer, now within a hundred yards while others try to make jokes. The bridge and poker games continue.

On our ship, the engines are fixed in about 45 minutes, and we have caught up with the convoy and taken our usual place in the formation within three hours. However, the next day another transport has engine trouble. There are probably 2,000 troops on board her (she is only slightly larger than our vessel). While waiting for repairs, she lies there, making no progress, rolling gently. It is late afternoon, and we stand on deck watching her drop below the horizon, until she is lost to sight. The convoy simply zigzags on. Few of us say anything about it.

The next morning the ship has been repaired and has caught up with us. It waddles along in its usual place, about a quarter of a mile to our left (or should I say "to port").

Off Gibraltar the convoy splits up. About a dozen ships (including ours) are going in to Oran, the rest will turn south to Casablanca. All the U.S. naval escort goes to Casa, and our part of the convoy is escorted through Gibraltar to Oran by elements of the British navy.

The Mediterranean is a wonder when we enter at night. The Gibraltar side is complete dark, but gay lights sparkle on the Tangier side. Practically everyone is up on deck around 11 P.M. to see the first vague silhouette of land after thirteen days of nothing but water and sky. A cloud hides the moon; there seems to be more stars than anyone could imagine.

On arrival at Oran, one imagines how menacing the hills around the port would have been if manned by hostile cannon. Later I learned when I talked with Leland Rounds (an OSS officer under Vice Consul cover) that they had been. The hills form a horseshoe with cliffs about 60 feet high.

The convoy forms in a single line while entering the port. The corvettes and the destroyer bustle around. French tugs close around and the crews beg for, and receive, American cigarettes that are tossed down to them from the decks.

When we dock, French rowboats go to the outboard side of the ship, where the soldiers lower canteens on ropes that are filled with vile wine from dirty old barrels in exchange for cigarettes. An officer, prompted by sanitary motives, stops this promising trade — not increasing his popularity with the men.

In the harbor, we see other ships that have made the voyage — some half-sunk with just the smokestacks protruding above the water. Some are lying at the docks with huge, gapping holes in the bow or stern.

Our enlisted men have had a hard voyage, for, in addition to the natural discomforts of their position and surroundings, they were on the lowest deck next to the ammunition magazine.

Further, the plates did not seem too strong down there, and whenever a depth charge was dropped within one half mile of us, the plates groaned and strained and seemed about to crack.

We finally tie up at 7 pm, instead of 4 pm. (Dick) Crosby, Adam, Pinky (Harris) and I stand on the forward deck watching the men working on the dock below. An American lieutenant is urging them to work faster loading oil drums on trucks. His French vocabulary seems confined to a repetition of "Allez! Allez! Mes Enfants! Vite!" in varying degrees of annoyance.

The following morning we disembark. Pinky, Henry and I decide to find the Consul, Leland Rounds, and contact Colonel Eddy through him. We leave our luggage at the dock and go into the town. The Army finally provides us transportation to the Grand Hotel, Rounds' headquarters. I know Rounds by name from reports before the invasion and we are cordially received.

The first disillusionment comes when Rounds tells me those hills were manned by guns on D-Day and that the other side fired point-blank at our ships entering the harbor with a great number of casualties resulting. I ask what happened because the plans had seemed so perfect, and though little of the real situation in North America was known in Washington, the impression I had gained was that everything had gone smoothly.

Ridgeway Knight and Leland Rounds had handled the Oran preparations. I was told by no greater a trusted source than Leland that he had gone to London to reenter with the first troops and Knight had stayed behind. The kingpin of their plans turned "chicken" at the last minute and so a rushed message at our radio station at Gibraltar had not gotten through in time. As a consequence, the troops landing directly at Oran walked (or sailed) right into fire. Landings near the port were successful, however, and the situation was brought under control in a couple of days.

I learn subsequently that Algiers went smoothly, although the troops were ten hours or more late. (The Chantiers de la Jeunnesse — a Petainese youth group — held vital points for us for ten hours and there was a bad fighting at Casa [near Fedala], but on the whole the advance preparations were a tremendous success).

Tomorrow we are off to Algiers, but today Henry and I head back to the Evangeline in an old horse-drawn cab. We have lunch at a little restaurant that has a sidewalk café and it is then I first realize (the Pollyanna I am) that in war you can't get everything you want. On the boat, the two meals a day, though of good quality, hardly kept me satisfied. So I had been thinking that when we got ashore, several of us would have a fine lunch — perhaps a steak, a fine wine — perhaps a Martini before hand. Then in the evening a handsome dinner, someplace where there would be gay lights, an orchestra and a floorshow. Instead, for lunch we had some three or four hunks of some sort of meat, probably very old mutton, accompanied by brownish-gray bread, and some pasta. All cooked in what seemed to me particularly vile and rancid olive oil. (There's a lot of Spanish influence in Oran.) Ordinary wines were an extremely reasonable six to eight francs a bottle, although the presence of Americans would soon send prices skyrocketing.

Leland goes off to some engagement or other, and Henry and I take a walk. I say I've always wanted to sit at a sidewalk café in a foreign country and sip and drink and just watch the people go by. We find one that has comfortable wicker chairs around small round tables. My request for a Martini met with shocked surprise by the waiter. They have no cocktails. Well, I'll settle for a whiskey and soda. The waiter looks at me as through I were crazy. All they have is sweet vermouth and watery beer. I take a vermouth and proceed to enjoy the feeling of being overseas. Here we are, at last, nearer to the stage in the Mediterranean theatre.

2

Algiers

Wayne Nelson served as cable officer in Algiers, January to September 1943 — processing and controlling all ingoing and outgoing cable traffic.

January 1943
Algiers

I've met a lot of the heroes of pre D-Day since arriving in Algiers. It is like coming in contact with characters from Olympus. The list includes Leland Rounds, Pittman Springs, Boyd, David King, Kenneth Pendar, Robert Murphy (I'd known him before), Frank Knox, James Doolittle, Depax (Pinkeye), Edmond Taylor, Clark. These are some of the band of twelve vice-consuls who outwitted 300 or 400 German and Italian agents before D-Day — an amazing aggregation and people who have done an incredible job.

Just to illustrate how anxious I am to get to the front and be part of the war, to my eyes the first air raid we witness appears to be a beautiful show. The port and a good part of the city spread like a huge amphitheater before us. Planes are coming over the hills to the left of us and sweeping down over the harbor. The red tracers form crazy lines in the sky and occasionally whole portions of the port are lit up by heavier fire. Searchlights play hide and seek with the planes all over the sky and the bullets leave red, green, yellow and white trails. Then the angry red-orange glow and ominous rumble of bombs lends a tympanic touch.

Three German planes are caught in the crossbeam of four dancing searchlights that attempt desperately to hold onto them as the air ships seem to sail slowly over the port. The tracers start toward the planes, but peter out in red, green and white streamers that curl and fold before reaching their objective. White puffs appear in the darkness of the sky around the planes and yellow flashes spark (as if connected to some distant lightning bug), but the German planes ride it out and disappear in the blackness. After a few minutes, all that is left is the heavy silence and cold darkness of the blacked-out night.

I have heard it remarked that air raids in Algiers have a theatrical dimension nowhere else to be found. Although I have no basis for comparison, I am inclined to agree and am exhilarated thinking "I'm finally getting close to the war." A man allows himself the illusion that he's at least doing something if he is near gunfire, though he may be standing motionless, useless and idle. I remark to a companion that this was "some raid." The response is that "it wasn't so hot." On the verge of sarcasm, I retort "I suppose you've been through this sort of thing." I'm humbled when out of the darkness the man replies flatly that he was in Berlin when the British raided it, in Paris when the Germans raided it, and in London during the blitz of 1940 and 1941. I'm humbled when talks for a while about the London raids when the hell was so great it seemed impossible that anyone would live through it.

March 1943

Have I mentioned that the Germans booby-trap their own dead, as well as ours? They do.

I've also learned that certain Moroccan troops (Goums) still get paid according to the prisoners they bring in or those they killed but only upon their bringing in the dead man's papers and one of his ears that they cut off. I also learn that the Germans booby-trapped a wounded Italian. One of their Allies! This seems worse than booby-trapping one's own or the enemy's dead. I heard that the British counterpart of our outfit, if a man turns sour, take him up in a plane and drop him by parachute — coincidentally the chute does not open. We've also learned from one of our fellows who is "in" that some British agents near him were caught. One of them had his fingernails torn out.

April 1943

The war from Algiers becomes monotonous after a while. At first it gives one a kick to be anywhere near the war but then the sight of air raids and the sound of planes buzzing become as ordinary as fireworks at the World's Fair.

The first casualty we have is when a ship bearing one of our men goes down. It is a Corporal Boyd, who was escorting some radio equipment from America. The ship was torpedoed in the Atlantic and several hundred were lost. We begin to feel even more lucky that we got through all right. Another corporal, Shairey, who was in the same convoy with Boyd, arrives safely with the equipment he was escorting. All he knows is that Boyd's ship was in the convoy one evening, and the next morning it was not. We are informed by the military authorities that the ship is to be considered lost with all aboard.

Jerry, Ross and Dick go up to the Tunisian front. It seems they are to train foreigners, Italians and French, to go through the enemy lines and blow up bridges, set booby-traps, etc. Then Carl Coon, a former Harvard anthropologist and Arab specialist who was in North Africa long before the invasion, and more recently has been up at the Tunisian front, comes back to Algiers. I have never seen a man so close to a nervous breakdown. He has been out on patrol in enemy territory, strafed by the Germans, besieged in a lighthouse at Captain Svuerat while booby trapping in enemy territory. When I saw him it seemed impossible for him to stand or sit still for even one second. I should judge him to be about 42 or 43, a swell person, with a marvelous sense of humor. Bawdy and coarse at times, he likes to challenge one with bawdy jokes to test if you're Puritan enough to act shocked. They wanted him to go to a hospital for a ten-day rest, but he would have none of it.

After a few days rest he went to Tangier and when he returns he relays that Jerry is missing. It seems Jerry was intent on retrieving a tarpaulin that had fallen from a truck and told a sergeant (Steve Byzek) with a jeep to go back to get it at a time when our forces were retreating. He had not been heard from for three days, and Coon expressed the view that he was quite possibly captured. I was puzzled at this view (one of our men captured? A fellow I knew?), and in view of Coon's nervous state put it down to over-dramatization and imagination spurred by frayed nerves. A couple of days later we heard that Jerry was all right. This brought things back into proper focus again. I had been right — over-dramatization.

One of the grimly amusing footnotes in this war is an invention of Carl's "Coon's Exploding Turds." As an anthropologist, he was sent out to study the rocks around the Tunisian front so explosive imitations could be manufactured to place on the roads to booby-trap enemy tanks.

He didn't find any rocks, but did find a lot of camel and mule dung. He collected a lot of dried samples and sent them back in a diplomatic pouch, probably the first time that such a pouch has carried literally what it has so often carried figuratively. Pretty soon artificial explosive versions were being manufactured (listed as "Coon's Explosive Turds: specify Donkey or Camel"). Meanwhile, he constructed some homemade samples to stop German tanks. He'd dig a hole in the road, sink a condom filled with plastic into it, place a pressure switch on top and cover it all with a dried piece of the real thing.

Colonels Eddy and Huntington go up to Tunis two days later on an inspection trip. The next day we receive word from him that Sergeant Milt Felsen has been wounded and both he and Jerry have been captured. This time, it's for real. This doesn't seem possible. Jerry had come over on the boat with me and we had played bridge about every night on the boat and gotten drunk together. We were never close friends but, with the possibilities inherent in capture of one of our organization, I suppose I'm getting some sort of vicarious adventure out of just knowing the guy.

It seems that Jerry was on a patrol between the lines with a group of men. The Arabs in the region spotted them and lit signal fires for the Germans. The Germans opened up with 75s. Milt Felsen was wounded twice by the first two rounds. Jerry and the rest tried to drag Milt to the jeeps some distance away. The Germans sent armored cars into the little valley and our men took cover. The Germans spotted Jerry's bright leather jacket in the brush and called upon him to surrender. He stood up and they asked where his comrades are. Jerry convinced them that he and Milt are the only ones. The Germans thereupon take them away and Steve and the others get back to the jeeps; he prevents them from starting the motors until the jeeps have been pushed a sufficient distance to prevent an alarm. And they make their way back to our lines.

A few nights later, Warwick, Dostart, Henry and I are sitting at dinner in Villa Sinety, a rambling house built around a patio. The French doors to the terrace and the window are blacked out and there is just a dim overhead light. Suddenly a face shows through the panes of the doors. It turns out to be Ross (a particular pal of Jerry's) who has just returned from the front with two of Rucker's parachute sergeants. He is very drunk. Ross is only about 29 and was a promising doctor in Cleveland, or some place. He is the doctor for Rucker's parachute boys, but has already made twelve jumps he was not required to. He's very good-looking and a captain. Warwick's reaction is sympathetic. Dostert's is reserved and a bit cool. Henry is sympathetic. My sympathy is tinged with curiosity. It is no ordinary drunk he's in and I think at the time he's suffering from a mental shock of some sort. Henry and I take him out of the room to give him some cold water to douse his head in, and then he comes in to the table to eat.

He keeps muttering, over and over: "You've got no idea what it's like up there. I'm a medical officer, but does that mean anything? Hell no! They see a captain's bars and they say take this patrol out and burn that Arab village. You give me some Americans, I don't care if it's only four or five, and I'll invade the damned German lines. But they give me twelve Frenchmen and Spaniards. They don't talk English and I don't know their language, and they say, 'Go out and burn this Arab village.'" It seems the Arabs in a village eighteen kilometers beyond our lines were suspected of trafficking with the enemy — giving information and sending people through our lines to get it. So Ross took these guys out and burned the village. That wasn't all — he had to conduct his medical work without proper equipment. I'd run across a bottle of Hair & Hair Gold Label Scotch that afternoon, so Ross and I went home and drank it, while I probed him with questions. I wanted to get his replies and reactions before he had time to rest and recover. The general situation seems to be that one goes to the front and guys get killed and shot up and it does not seem real at the time. The enemy appears as dolls or puppets — cloth and sawdust. Then when one at some distance the realization that they were not inanimate, but real human beings, asserts itself. This comes in the form of a shock to any one with imagination and feeling,

The next morning, Ross is suffering from nothing more than a hangover. He may remember our conversation way back in his mind though, for I think that under the professional detachment that he wears today, he's a pretty sensitive guy with something eating his insides.

Pinky goes up to the front a day or two later. He's a type who is not at all sensitive. He's a tall, red-headed Marine lieutenant who is out for adventure, and I don't believe he would spend much time trying to analyze anything. After he was there a day and a half, he was instructed to go to the town of Sbeitla, which the Germans had left, to clean up. Steve, an English captain, and Pinky were apparently having the type of time that the hot-blooded, redhead loves. They go to a house and Pinky throws open the doors calling inside to anyone there to come out. Steve sprays the inside with a Tommy gun and they search the place for booby traps and go on to the next house. They were returning to the jeep when Pinky got a piece of casing through his forearm and Steve caught it in the back, arm, both legs, scalp and one piece pierced his lung. During this time, I realize that I am not really close to the war at all. I seem further away than when I was in Washington and want to get to the front. I wonder how close one has to get to be satisfied that one is a part of it.

May 3, 1943

After four out of eight of our men are casualties in a period of four weeks, all the front business stops and I still haven't had my chance ... at least for the moment.

May 5, 1943

Heard about one of our men who had been a big hero in the last war. He settled into a country club life in Chicago and was Vice President of a bank with a wife and three children. Finally, when this war came, he was anxious to get into it. He'd heard about our outfit, so he got up one night at 3 am, told his wife he could not stand inaction any longer and went to Washington to get into our organization. His wife took it fatalistically and said she always knew she would lose him if war came. He will probably be set down in the Balkans.

Monday after Easter 1943

The French lieutenant comes to stay at the apartment. He is working for us. He is a fellow who should be a footnote to history in that he assisted General Clark on his submarine exploit. He then was slapped by his commanding officer in front of the regiment's officers for this — after D-Day. We drive to his home at Cherchel for lunch on Easter Sunday. It is a beautiful day and we pass by some old Roman ruins. He has a nice wife and child and, except for the language and the unbelievably landscape, one might well imagine we are in a small suburb in America.

May 17, 1943

Donald, Sheila, Dewitt and I sit on the balcony one evening with some brandy I have managed to get on the black market. We have been working hard all week and the last couple of days have been going through clothes, aging and forging papers, etc. As we sit there at dusk, we see a sub carrying our men going out of the harbor. We lift our glasses and silently toast them and wish them well.

May 20, 1943

A few notes. One of the devices we used before the invasion was to spread a rumor that it was coming. The rumor would spread and the exact day and hour would be named. Then nothing would happen. This happened many times so when it finally came off, the whole German and Italian force was caught unaware.

The German Armistice Commission (from Oran) that was captured and taken to England to be interrogated denounced one of our local (alien) agents in Oran as having worked for them. The Frenchman who was a collaborationist and who is still in charge of police at Oran, is sore at Leland. The local man is put in the French army, arrested and sent to Morocco where he is condemned to death. The British did not check with us before giving the French this report. We just get him off in time.

We have some wild rides to Matifou at night in a jeep going 70 to 75 miles an hour. Particularly one night when we get word that the Gestapo is on to one of our nests of agents and we have to get word to them to move. We receive word at 7:30 pm, leave dinner, go to the code room, code the message or warning, and hop into the jeep — then it is ready for the next contact.

May 26, 1943

We have a car now that will only start on a hill being pushed and that provides amusement in the mornings. There is a gang of little Arab kids — all between the ages of four or six and seven — and they make a daily big show of pushing us manfully to get started. They always come up and say "John choomgum" or "Johnny BomBom." We give them some chewing gum or candy. As we pass by on the street, almost any place, there are often cute little Arab kids who come to attention and salute.

May 13, 1943

Yesterday was my birthday and we had not had any raids for a couple of weeks. The campaign in Tunis had just finished and we were all thinking that there would be no more excitement of that nature. Sheila persuaded the cook to make me a cake and they went out in the country and got some chicken. We were just finishing dinner when the guns began to pop. There had been no alert, or, if there had, we had not heard it. We went up to the roof to watch. It was a heavier raid than usual and there were many cracks about Hitler and Goering providing the "floor show" for my birthday. We saw a couple of planes go down in spiralling paths of flame. Planes were coming over the hill near the house and fragments were falling around. I got one that landed near me for a souvenir. A 20 mm. shell hit the side of the house and knocked off a good bit of the tile above the window.

May 16, 1943

I heard a good story the other day. An American aviator was over occupied France. He was up very high when his plane gave out and he bailed out by parachute. He passed out on the way down and the next thing he remembers is dangling, head down, from a tree. His hands were frozen and he had no feeling, but he managed to get his knife from his pocket and cut himself down. Finally he got into the resistance chain and was passed from farmhouse to farmhouse. In one there was only a young widow. She spoke no English and he no French. He was tired and sleepy and there was only one bed. He wanted her to leave him there to sleep, but she couldn't understand his words. Finally, he pointed to the bed and pantomimed that he wanted to take off his clothes and go to bed. She nodded that she understood. He began to disrobe; so did she. After three days, he didn't want to go home. Finally, he did through the rest of the chain and wound up at the hotel "The Rock" in Gibraltor where, dressed in French peasant clothes, he wound up sitting next to a friend of mine in a bar. The aviator asked for a whiskey soda. My friend said, "Where did you learn to speak English?" The aviator replied, "In Brooklyn," and proceeded to relay the story, with many admonitions that it was secret.

June 6, 1943

An ominous message came through the other day on our radio station at Matifou — "strange fist on _____ this morning." We keep sending messages and, after a day, we know that our man is captured and someone is operating it for the Germans. Then we get a message from another part of the resistance chain that the station was blown and the operators captured by the Gestapo, including a girl. We have just gotten direct contact with my old friend at Berne (Allen Dulles), so we send a message asking him to discreetly get organizations there to try to prevent her from being tortured.

Mid-June 1943

I had lunch with Douglas Fairbanks, Jr. today. He is a Lt. (s.g.) in the Navy and seems to be a nice, regular chap.

July 1943

I spend some time in rendezvous at night teaching a young Frenchman the things he must know to go in. The meeting is held clandestinely in a little, shabby room. There is a process to rendezvous with agents at various places in town. We drive by, for instance. Then the agent walks down a street and a couple of blocks away we stop, see if we are observed and, if not, pick the guy up. We talk as we drive, exchange money or messages and leave him in a suitable place.

July 23, 1943

The Axis sabotage school grads started really going to work the beginning of July. On July 3, the ammunition train at Maison Blanche blew up. It was parked next to a train of Italian prisoners and killed between 200 and 300. Then a train at Sidi Feruck, two days later, blew up. In the meantime, down near Oujda there is a series of four incidents in a week. Then up here in the harbor a ship blew up, set off another one beside her and then the ammunition on the dock started blowing. It was at Villa Magnol, 3 or 4 miles from the explosion — which shattered some windows in our villa there. I was sitting by an open window when I noticed my chair begin to tumble at least a second or two before we heard the sound of the explosion. We could see a huge column of smoke billowing up — over in the direction of the port, a moment after the deafening blast. We rushed to a car and drove on the hill near the port to view the scene. The burning ship was towed off to the side of the port (a wonderful and courageous job for whoever got the towline on her) where it burns for three days.

While watching the scene, I look up casually behind at a very poor-looking house where a shabbily dressed woman is viewing the scene with a pair of shiny new field glasses. I notice a similar scene in another nearby house. I point this out to my companion who notes, "They must pay well for info around here."

August 2, 1943

There have been systematic desertions from Girauds to de Gaulle's army this summer, Leclerc men were coming back to Algiers, and a de Gaulle pautsh was planned. It failed at the last moment.

Donald, Art and I sat down the other evening to discuss whether I can go to Oujda, which would mean a chance to go in with the Fifth Army at Salerno. The conversation began to get heated when Donald, in a momentary lull, pulled a condom out of his pocket and blew it up into a balloon. The next thing you know I was batting the damned thing around with one of the best secret agents in the world and a lieutenant colonel with all of us cursing the one who should let it fall to the floor. Eventually it lodged in a lighting fixture and in a few minutes exploded, startling us to no end.

August 20, 1943

We have news that P was captured. The story seems to be this. P went out with two teams. Two men were on one team, P and another were on the second team and a single G-1 (Sam of G-2) was to be the radioman for both. They wore peasant dress over their uniforms and had a native as a guide.

One team passed completely through the lines. After an appropriate interval, P and the others started through, not knowing the Germans were observing them. One of the men with P stepped on a landmine and the racket caused the Germans to attack. Sam received three slugs in the back near the base of his spine and the group put up a battle with small arms for about half an hour (all they had were .45's). The man with P, Tony R., set off the land mines purposely to keep the Germans away. They destroyed part of the radio and Tony R. swallowed the signal plan.

The team that had gone through, returned with information about the German lines and defenses and numbers of troops that led to an American attack which drove the Germans back.

P and Sam and Tony R. had, of course, surrendered finally. On retreating, the Germans abandoned Sam (they had limited transport and he weighed over 200 pounds). They left him on a litter in an open field and the Americans picked him up later. Tony R. was taken by a German lieutenant in a command car with a driver. Tony R. had been searched, but they didn't discover s small pen knife in his watch pocket. At a stop, the driver was sent on an errand and Tony R. somehow got the knife from his pocket and slit the throat of the German and, when he was dead, got out of the car and ran like hell for an hour. He made his way back to American lines and provided extremely valuable intelligence. He's been recommended for the Silver Star.

A few days later we get word that a part of seven of our men with the aid of a couple of PT boats and a few PT armed seamen, have gone to the Island of Stromboli and procured its surrender. They returned with 45 prisoners, a half-burned Italian code, and important documents.

Late August 1943

Did I mention we finally got direct contact with AWD (General Donovan). I slip in a message "Regards from Wayne." His next message says "Best regards to Wayne. Still hope he comes here when Italy is cleaned up." Maybe I can still have a job in Berne if I get in a scrape here. AWD is doing a grand job and everyone wonders how he manages to accomplish all that he does.

October 10, 1943

Carl Coon is back from Corsica. He relays a trick the Germans pulled in leaving Bastia. They left their food and other supplies on the docks and the civilian population ran down to get them and a wild scramble ensued. Then the American planes (not knowing the Germans were out) bombed the port and were hitting the French population.

I understand my chance to get in the real action will come at out next stop — La Maddalena in Italy.

3

La Maddalena

*Wayne Nelson was a SI Operations Officer in Sardinia from October to November 1943. An OSS operations base was at the naval port of La Maddalena, a remote and beautiful island, fortified during the war, located at the eastern approaches of the Straits of Bonifacio, between the Mediterranean islands of Corsica and Sardinia.**

October 1943

On October 22 Frank (Tarallo) and I departed on a plane from the Algiers airport (Maison Blanche) for Palermo, Italy. We flew over Tunisian battlefields, saw battered houses and pockmarked fields where bombs and shells had fallen, and stopped in Tunis briefly. Then flying across the Mediterranean to Palermo where we went to a house and met Max (Corvo) and then with Frank and Tony we ride through the war-torn streets, past shattered buildings, shell and bomb holes to the docks. There we board a British LST 323, and I go up, not without trepidation, since I had never climbed one of the damned things before, and this was not the most auspicious situation for a first try. We were on our way to La Maddalena.

Max and Tom (Stonborough) have a cabin with only two bunks; Frank and I sleep on the metal floor. The boat is filthy. C rations are all that is served for all meals in the officers mess. An American Ack-Ack crew is also on board. Sometime that night we pull out.

October 22, 1943

The day is again calm. The corvette is about ½ mile ahead. Then comes our ship. Then the other LST, about 500 yards behind us. We

*OSS Field Report

don't sight a thing the next day. Traffic is still pretty much confined to the African coastline this far east — the Germans bombed a convoy just off that coast about ten days ago and got several ships.

October 23, 1943

About 5 in the afternoon we sight the southern tip of Sardinia. We proceed up the coast. The following morning we are in the straits of Bonifacio. The men shoot crap and play poker. Some wander around the boat. Others just sleep. That night we pull out, and the following day, it's very easy but coming up the coast of Sardinia we are getting into real operational waters. As one of the officers remarked: "This tub is really a floating mine; what with all the ammunition and gasoline we have on board."

While in the Atlantic you have submarines, but little likelihood of anything else, here there is a possibility of submarines, surface craft (operating from Italian coastal bases from Spezia south), plenty of mines, and German airplanes from any of 100 bases.

La Maddalena, Sardinia
October 28, 1943

There is a lot of joking among ourselves about how we have out-flanked Rommel (we are far north of the German-American lines in Italy at the moment).

Maddalena is the place where they hid Mussolini, and from which the Germans took him. It is also the place where Garibaldi spent his last years.

We heard yesterday, October 27, the day after we landed, that the two LSTs we came in on were hit shortly after leaving the port yester-day. They were set upon by German planes. (If they'd gotten the intel-ligence earlier and hit those with the explosive load we had on board, I and the others would be little bits of hamburger for the fish right now!)

The A/A crews that came in with us get set up, and the day after we arrive there are a couple of alerts. Apparently these are only recon-naissance planes. However, there are only about 800 Americans on the island, plus a few British navy personnel, and the PT's (there are about six PT's at any one time).

Max and I drive around the Island in a jeep on October 27 and the view from the hills is wonderful. Shaggy hills slope into the water and there is rock, rock, and more rock. The verdure here is a rich, deep green and the water is clear and blue. The sunsets here, as they are everywhere, are beautiful but they seem to be set off more here. We can see Sardinia, of course, and further off the northwest, brown-gray in the distance, there is Corsica. The greens here are oil colors — as opposed to the water coloring of Algiers and North Africa generally.

Max and I go up into the hills to the Italian coast gun emplacements. There we are surrounded by Italian soldiers and have a lot of fun kidding them.

Some of the boys come back from the town that evening with a rumor that the Germans are going to return and recapture the Island. If they choose to do so, it should not be too difficult. According to the boys, the Island is still full of Fascists.

We have quite a character here by the name of Joe Sicalzi. He's a little fellow, 48 years old, who used to be Al Capone's chauffeur and bodyguard. "Haven't you got someone I can kill for you?" "I can get you gin. The good stuff." "Why you no let me take the jeep and get gin?" "There is a whorehouse here: American soldiers everyday from three to four. One girl, she is beautiful like the pin-up girls. 15 lira (15 cents) was the price before the Americans came. Now it is 60 lira." (Max tells him to get the beautiful girl out of the whorehouse and he will set her up in an apartment, let her dry out for a while and train her as an agent.)

This town was pretty badly hit, apparently by our planes. All around the docks there are bomb craters in the roads, and almost all the buildings have at least some damage. In and around the PT base the damage is more noticeable. In the hotel we have taken, Tom's and my room is on the third (European second) floor, and just looks over the rooftops of a low building nearby. We look out on a piazza, and all the buildings have sustained some damage. In our hotel it is windows and plaster only; in the building about fifty feet across the way, whole walls are out.

The view of the rooftops gives a quite artistic atmosphere to the place. They have some sort of moss growing on them, and thus, from the original terra cotta pink, have turned yellow and red.

I think I've mentioned "C" rations before in these notes. "K" rations are really something. One meal and pork and veal loaf in a little round tin (about the size of a small can of lobster); one has scrambled eggs and ham mixed in this tin. Another has a wonderful American cheese. Little rectangular biscuits come with each and they are swell, even by themselves. There also are three lumps of sugar and bouillon, coffee, lemon powder or cocoa. Included are four cigarettes and a stick of chewing gum and with each one is a bar of chocolate, fruit or malted milk and dextrose tablets.

I made up a parody after three days when the facilities would not work and we had to get water from three miles away, even to wash. The tune is "I'm Dreaming of a White Christmas."

> I'm dreaming of a white bathroom
> Just like the ones we used to know,
> Where the fixtures glisten,
> And nothin's missin,'
> No matter when you have to go.
> I'm dreaming of a white bathroom
> With every letter home I write —
> May your days be cheery and bright
> And may all your toilet tops be white.

La Maddalena, Sardinia
October 30, 1943

We went out to Capraia (a nearby island) yesterday and saw the home of Garibaldi and his tomb. It is now a museum and a shrine. The surrounding country is characterized by huge, stony crags and wide expanses of sea with little villages, such as La Maddalena, in the distance. The rock islands fall or roll into the sea.

We acquire some Scotch from an Italian sailor. Six bottles of "Special Club" Scotch — apparently a British Navy ration — for 550 a bottle. This sailor is a thin man with a tic in his eye that moves spasmodically occasionally. He apparently is a slick article and claims he can get anything we want. His expression is always pleasant, but not a grin or a smile — just a reserved pleasantness. He will be useful if he can continue to get his liquor and other supplies.

Three of the PT officers came up to see us this afternoon: Commander Barnes. Lts. Muddie and Mannicky. We break out the Scotch and Barnes tells Frank what he wants. The Italian Admiral Brevonesi has apparently been screwing the Americans (the PT's and we are the only Americans beside the A/A battalion). We have heard that he is a Fascist and probably still in contact with Rome. Barnes is being kicked out of part of his base because the Italians want it. (As he says, it is the policy of the Allied High Command to keep Fascists in power as long as they cooperate — my question is how you can prove they are not cooperating if they are clever to cover up their tactics.) Barnes wants to know if we have any proof on the Italian Admiral so he can go to the British and force the issue to keep his men in their present quarters. Frank says that we will try.

We then discuss the Giglio job. This is a little island off the Italian coast on the main north-south convoy lines of the Germans. There are no German soldiers on the island, according to reports, but they visit the island every few days, apparently to get provisions. He wants a man with a radio put there to watch convoys and notify us when convoys pass. Thereupon, the PT's will go out and intercept them — but with this information they can throw their whole force at a large convoy and practically destroy it completely. (We all get quite enthusiastic about the possibility of this — Frank, Tom and I also are thinking that our men can tell us the times the Germans come, and we might hop over there if we could get a PT and capture them. None of us believes the Germans really come there for provisions, but feel that it is possibly an intelligence relay center.)

The PT officers and we sing a little snatch or two of Gilbert and Sullivan and they leave.

Frank immediately calls one of the boys in and plans are laid to get some dope on the Italian radio station on a little island off La Maddalena. This may tie in with the Admiral. Frank, Tom and I visit the Italian officers' club and try to find out who the Admiral's girl or junior aides are, and see what we can learn. We find out that a certain captain plans to spend two hours with the admiral this evening and will travel to Sardinia tomorrow. We will have him followed for we have word that a certain Italian officer in a Sardinian city is in touch with a Japanese agent there. The plans are laid, maps provided, and a fake pass drawn for our man who is to do the trailing.

Operation Giglio

"On November 2, a two-man mission requested by Commander Barnes was landed on the island of Giglio. Wayne Nelson, conducting officer of the mission, described its objective: to put two men with radio on the island of Giglio, located nine miles off the Italian coast and approximately 30 miles north of Civitavecchia, for the purpose of gathering and transmitting intelligence to our Maddalena base, with particular reference to German shipping and convoy movements along the Italian coast."

THE O.S.S. IN ITALY

This was a "rubber boat" or Motor Torpedo Boat operation under the orders of Commander Stanley M. Barnes, skipper of the U.S. Navy's MTB Squadron 15. This was the so-called "Ron 15" which carried some fifty operations on to Italian and French territory during World War II. Wayne Nelson

La Maddalena, Sardinia
October 31,1943

The afternoon of October 31, while I am in charge of the gang doing rubber boat and pistol practice, a couple of the boys come out to get one of the men to go on a mission. This is a real mission and will be conducted close by — not like those we imagined in Washington where

The pioneering American Navy Torpedo Boat (MTB), known as Ron 15, that carried some 50 OSS operations onto Italian and French territory.

the real impact of any plans is across the ocean and thousands of miles away. Here, when a man leaves it may be only sixty miles and he will be in enemy territory. The man selected is older — about 45 — and his name is Vierin. His son, about 24, is also with us.

I travel back to Maddalena because I have to see Frank about deciding on the security of the spot selected for actually holding the boat practice. (If you go to the sea from the clump of trees, you can be seen by Italian soldiers at the gun stations on the rocks above).

When I get back to town, Frank asks how I'd like to go on a PT run that evening (night of October 31 — November 1). I say, "Hell, yes." The job is to put the older Vierin and a young radioman onto the Island of Giglio, about ten miles off the Italian mainland. Their job is to stay there, get in radio contact with us and report on ship movements along the Italian coast. If they spot a convoy, they are to give us the number of ships, the time they spotted them, the types of ships, and their direction. Then the whole PT squadron can go out and waylay the convoy. I put the lining in my overcoat, put on a pistol belt with three clips, helmet, field jacket, cigarettes — and we're set. Naturally, I go through everything carefully to see that there are no documents on me in case of capture.

Commander Barnes, Lt. (j.g.) Sinclair, Frank, the two boys, another naval officer, and I have a final conference with the Italian captain of a barge that has just escaped from the Island in the last few days. The captain of the barge points out two possible sites at which to land. He tells us that Germans are not stationed regularly on the Island, but that they go there periodically.

The landing points are selected. The best one for this evening is called Allume Cove. Signals are arranged in the event the boys have to get off the boat or if we order them off, and the naval officers and I go to the Navy Officers' Mess, while the boys and the equipment to the boat where they will eat with the crew.

Needless to say, I am getting a tremendous kick out of all of this!

About 6 o'clock we go to the boat. Sinclair shows me to the officers' quarters and they are quite adequate. We leave in heavy weather with a driving rain and running sea. The boat kicks around like hell. We run into a terrific jam (it is now dark) at the submarine nets. No one can understand what the Italian barge master is saying, so one of our men translates — a four-way job from the older Vierin, then to Joe and then to me and finally to Sinclair. Then we clear the nets and head east for nine miles. We run through two heavy squalls. Joe gets seasick and throws up. I'm not nauseous, but when a bunch of the Mediterranean slaps me in the face and I swallow a couple of mouths full of seawater, I came close. The boat hops around like a rough airplane ride — only this is continuous, not intermittent, hopping.

After proceeding east for nine miles, we head northeast. We lose the accompanying PT (ours was the 212, the other the 216), and have to retrace our steps to reconnect with it. Soon we come into comparatively clear weather. The sky is filled with stars; it is fairly cool but not really cold. Of course, the water washes all around us. We sight a light on the horizon at one point and think maybe it belongs to an enemy ship. We stop the motors and wait for about fifteen minutes before it is ascertained that it is not.

When we cleared the original mine fields, we saw flashes on the horizon that looked like a bombing — either directly on Maddalena or a point north of Maddalena. (When I came back in the morning I found it was not Maddalena, so it must have been a bombing some place in Corsica.)

I discover on this PT what a real blackout is. No cigarettes are allowed even below decks. The PT also is equipped with radar that is a marvelous thing. It is a circle, with a streak of light half the diameter, which moves constantly around the circle clockwise. The center of the circle is the position of the boat. The radar covers a range of seventy-five miles around the boat and anything on the water — islands or boats — appears in this circle in its correct dimensions and shape. *C'est formidable!*

I have another observation while on this trip that relates to hunting convoys. I've been on convoys as the hunted. Now I am with the hunters. And how happy we would be if we could get a troopship! (*C'est la guerre vraiment!*)

At 11 o'clock we sight the dark shape of the Island on the horizon, about fourteen miles away. We continue, and 7½ miles from the island. Then we idle in. The other boat stands off about five miles to cover us. The supplies for the men are stacked at the rear of the PT — a radio in a suitcase, battery, three cases of rations, three barracks bags, two musette bags. They carry canteens, pistols (.45s with sixty-five rounds each,) and GI regulation flashlights.

I talk with the boys to ensure they understand their primary job is to cover the convoy movements. But I let them know if they want to get any additional information such as where the Germans go when they visit the island or the movement of German troop movements etc. I go over with them the signals and plans in case they have to be taken off.

We go to within about 100 yards of the shore. The cliffs rise steep for about 100 feet, but at the innermost point of the cove there seems to be a little beach. We can discern trees on the sides of the cliffs, so assume there must be a way out of the beach up the hills. Joe is worried about this, so I tell him that when he goes in on the rubber boat, to look for a possible way up the cliff before he gives the signal to retrieve the boat with his flashlight. (The rubber boat is let in on a rope while they paddle and then the rope being used to pull the boat back to the PT when they have landed and signal it is okay.)

I tell him that if he does not feel certain that there is a way off the beach, to come back. They get in the boat. The equipment and supplies are handed down to them. I say good-bye — "hope I'll be seeing you in a couple of weeks" — and they start paddling — in the wrong direction. We can't make any noise and so can't call to them, therefore the rope is used to pull them back, and I call softly to Joe, who does not hear me. Then we haul them back to the stern, face the stern toward the proper point of the shore, and they are off. (The motors are revved up very slightly for a moment to give them a start.) The boat was launched at 12:20 A.M.

At 1 A.M. we leave the vicinity of the island. Sinclair tells me we are going patrolling to look for prey. We are to proceed southeast to the Island of Giannutri, then between that and the mainland, turning south toward Civitavecchia. He says there has been a minefield sown here recently, but no one knows exactly where it is, but we hope to skirt it. Apparently we do so, for the rest of the trip is uneventful. Finally, sighting nothing, we start for home. At about 5:00 A.M. I curl, or rather twist, myself into a ledge in the pilot house, rather than the officers' bunks, because the radar is there and I don't want to miss anything, just in case. About 6:00 A.M. dawn has broken and I go topside.

It is a beautiful dawn, cool and brilliant streaks of color in the sky, offsetting the craggy beauty of Sardinia and adjacent islands, which we are now approaching. We dock in Maddalena at 7:45 A.M.. Sinclair invites me to eat breakfast with the Navy officers but, feeling it is just about time Frank and Tom will be eating, I take a rain check on it and go to the Ilva to eat with them. Barnes will be at the mess, so I don't go over there to ask for transportation (as he would probably ask me to stay) but walk from the PT base to the hotel (about 1½ miles) and am pretty damned tired. When I get there, Tom is just sitting down to breakfast. We grab some K ration ham and eggs and coffee. Then another drive, and at 10:15 A.M.. I'm writing this. (At least this will ease my mind on the subject of a report for most of the facts are here — though of course there are some which for security reasons can't be put down.)

So that is my first operation! Not much, it is true. But interesting as hell to me. (At least I can say I've been in enemy territorial waters — the lines are now along the Voiturno.) Perhaps the next will be more interesting. Hope so.

La Maddalena, Sardinia
November 4, 1943

Still no word from the boys I put in. Frank is now trying to get the PT's to send a boat to find out where and how they are. I've made him promise that I will take one or two of the boys along as interpreters and be in charge of finding them, since I put them in. My idea is to have a PT drop us one night and pick us up the following night.

Yesterday and today I have been making up a training schedule of subjects for the fellows. Since I'm handling all SI training — I wish I could speak Italian, but I am picking up some useful phrases.

Today went out to the camp on Capraia (a small island) for some pistol practice. Pete Durante was directing rubber boat practice for the four teams that have been working out together. When they finished I got in a boat with Pete and paddled about 25 yards. Did all right, too, Pete says. First time I ever got in one of the things — interesting, but I imagine it gets pretty tiring over a longer distance; they're damned slow.

After they were finished with the boats, two of the Italian civilians went swimming and caught a small octopus (squid) — the tentacles were, I should judge, about fifteen inches long. And I'll be damned if those guys didn't start eating it raw! I'll be stewed, screwed and tattooed if it isn't the damndest thing I ever saw. Apparently it is fairly ordinary practice in parts of Sardinia and Southern Italy to eat octopus — raw! Whew!

Heard some of the boys talking about the whores on the island this morning. Every morning they are driven to the quarters of the Italian officers about 9:00 or 9:30 A.M.. Then back to the brothel. Then there

Harbor scenes, La Maddelena, Sardinia, and Bastia, Corsica, January 1944.

are separate hours for the Italian soldiers, American and British soldiers and sailors, American and British officers — I don't know where the local civilian population fits in. At any rate they finish about midnight. Quite a day's work, if you ask me. One of the Italians says they had prostitutes up within five miles of the front for the Italian army.

La Maddalena, Sardinia
November 7, 1943

Still no word from the boys on Giglio. I've been trying, both yesterday and the day before, to persuade Frank that I should go back with an interpreter and be put in one night and picked up the next, using the intervening time to find out what their condition is. The British Navy knew we put someone in, and told the Italians — and I don't know how far you can trust the Italians in power here. The Italians made an expedition up to Giglio Wednesday night with two small boats to get some people out. Commander Barnes, when Frank and I saw him yesterday, was loath to allow anyone to go back to Giglio again for fear the Germans may have come to the Island and "it would be throwing good money after bad." We found that a certain doctor from the Island had come out with the American aviators who escaped with the boats and spent 24 hours there. Since we were worried about the fact that we have had no radio contact with our boys, Frank and I went to see the Italian Admiralty about getting information from the doctor. We were told by a suave commandant that he would introduce us to doctor if we would come to the Italian Officers' Club yesterday evening. Frank could not go, so I went with Tom.

I found the Italian Liaison Officer there, and he introduced me to the doctor. I found that there was indeed a good possibility that the Germans are on the Island, but the doctor did not think so. It seems well established that they do visit the Island frequently, though at irregular intervals. They came and took twenty hostages off last week (because the two American aviators got away), and the black shirts (Italian fascist militia) watch on behalf of the Germans and are in radio contact with them.

Well, the way it stands now, the PT commander may say "okay" at any moment and I will be off with one guy and a couple of guns. It seems funny the way things happen here. In Washington things are planned and then you wait for years, it seems, before anything actually happens.

Yet look at my experience here. I leave Algiers at 10:00 A.M. one morning expecting to be stuck for weeks, or months, in Palermo. After a 500- or 600-mile plane ride, I am in Palermo at 4:00 in the afternoon. By 8:00 P.M., I am getting into a landing barge, which then scurries through the harbor to an LST.

Then in the darkness of the blackout I am climbing a Jacob's ladder to the LST and for two nights sleeping on the floor in a cabin so crowded that there is not even room to stretch out full length, and literally not enough room to turn around. (Incidentally we have learned since that we were lucky to get through at all because some of the mine fields were not charted, in addition to the German ships, submarines, and planes.) Then I am in Maddalena sleeping on ration boxes — not a hell of a lot better than the floor. Then, about three or four days later, after expecting not to get out for weeks, or months, I have my first operation and a trip near the enemy shore and am on patrol with the PT's. Now, perhaps in a few hours, perhaps in a day or two, or perhaps never, I may have a trip actually into enemy territory. Sometimes I don't recognize myself as the guy who thought he would not get a chance to even get a smell of this war.

Later, November 7, 1943

We met with the fishing boat captain from Giglio and he promised to return with the doctor to give us more intelligence on the Island. Then we found that our men had not tried out the radio's battery that was sent in with the boys. I went to see Barnes again and asked if we could go back to the Island. Frank had suggested getting there at dusk and rendezvousing again sometime after midnight, so my idea of 24 hours or more on land is apparently out. So I saw Barnes and gave him the dope we had gotten. He said the moon was bad just now, but the next time he had three boats going out on patrol, he would take two of our men along and drop them, and come back for them some hours later. Sinclair was in on this conference (as he would apparently do the same job this time). He suggested he would drop us, go on patrol, and return. The earliest they can get us there is about 10 o'clock. They would therefore have to rendezvous at 1:00 or 2:00 A.M. I still think 24 hours would be better, but if a few hours is all that can be done, it is all that can be done.

It is presently planned that Joe Sicalzi go with me. He will put on civilian clothes and contact the people whose names were given to old Vierin. I will wait by the landing spot in case Vierin and Joe are hiding but watching that point. If Joe can't get any news of them or they do not contact us at the landing point, we are screwed. Then it is a question of whether I can break orders and stay longer on the chance of finding them in the daytime, thus risk being observed by the militia or the Germans. We would take an extra battery with us and a supply of food in case we find Vierin. If the battery really is what is wrong with the radio, then we leave the stuff and return. If something else is wrong with the radio, we bring back the whole works — men and equipment. If they have been taken prisoner, I don't know what we do. If we are surprised at the beach, we try to shoot it out and get off shore with the rubber boat, depending on the PT picking us up.

If we are caught — there you have it!

Incidentally, as I believe I have mentioned before, Joe is the fellow who used to be Al Capone's chauffeur. He was deported from America in 1935 (after a five-year prison term), but has helped us considerably since he was freed by the British from an Italian prison in Sicily. He is a character and good for a lot of laughs. This should prove very interesting if it comes off.

November 9, 1943

Today, I went down to the Italian Admiralty and had a couple of radio batteries requisitioned after the usual song and dance. Joe will pick them up tomorrow.

Young Vierin is now scheduled to go with Joe and me on the Giglio pick-up attempt. About 5:00 P.M. this afternoon we got the fishing boat captain in and spent an hour and a half with him getting every bit of detailed dope we could. The exact location of the house of his friend, how far from the observatory tower of the black shirts, how many stories, a recognition sentence, where the doors, gates, windows are. We traced a copy of the map of the island and got the location of every structure between Allume Cove and the vicinity of the friend's house and beyond, distance in point of time and kilometers (time to walk it by day, by night, etc.). Every other detail that I could imagine. Then Frank and I had dinner. I got young Vierin and Joe together, told them my plan and asked if they had any other or further ideas. They did and some things are accepted after discussion, and I draw what I consider to be as final a plan as can be drawn at this stage — leaving plenty of room for flexibility in case of emergency. We all have a drink and are ready to go when transportation (PT) is available.

Then from about 9:30 to 1 A.M. Frank and I listen to Joe talk about his experiences in California. With a female newspaper reporter, etc. Funny as hell — whether exaggerated or not.

After fifteen days on floors of dirty, little steamers and packing cases, I take Max's bed for the night, since he is in Brindisi. This will be the first night's sleep in a bed in sixteen days. And I'll be dammed if those Germans don't pick this night to raid. I had just gotten about an hour into a comparatively comfortable sleep when at 2:00 A.M. the alarm sounded. You could hear people running in the street in about fifteen seconds on their way to the shelter. We had the windows and shutters shut, so could see nothing. Frank finally got up after the guns started and we heard a couple of bombs in the distance.

I was going to stay in bed, but in about ten minutes one came near enough to rattle the windows, so I got up. And this was the first night's sleep in a bed in sixteen days (and the next night I am probably going off to that island and will get no sleep there either).

I put on trousers, shoes, shirt and overcoat, get my helmet, and Frank and I stumble downstairs in the dark. Most of our guys go to the shelter (we think some of them do so because the prostitutes from the house up the hill about three blocks away will probably be there) but Frank and I and about five others stay in the small lobby by the door to the street. The firing ceases. Most of it has been down near Capraia, by the PT base. After about five minutes it commences again. This time the guns on the hill near us open up, but the direction of the fire is not toward or over our building.

The firing ceases again for a few minutes. Then it really opens up and can be heard moving nearer us. We hear the motors of planes — hear those motors clearly; flying low, not diving. From my experience in Algiers, where when I heard the motors of the planes bombs fell from 100 yards to 500 yards away (in other words, too close for comfort), I feel a bit of disquietude, especially knowing we are only one block and a short one at that, from the docks. I go to the door and peep out. The line of fire of the A/A is coming to center directly above the building, the roar of the planes' motors mingles with the sound of the fire. The building shakes slightly. Must be a bomb or two about a quarter of a mile away. I can't distinguish the number of planes. I hope to hell I'll hear other bombs fall before they get far beyond our building, for the bombs fall in a slanting line and would arrive after the planes had passed. I hear the motors pass over the house, the A/A line of fire follows them. Both Frank and I realize this is close and I hold my breath for five or ten seconds to see what will happen.

Nothing happens. The fire ceases. There is silence. I release my breath and walk over to where Frank is standing in a little inside archway: "That was close, in case you don't know it." "You ain't kidding," he replies. Someone in the darkness says, "Guess it's all over. I'm going to bed." He moves toward the stairs and the firing commences again. He moves back to his previous position. Then the bastards start diving. Now they are fooling around continuously near our part of the island. Three more phases of this raid, and then they stop. The last three times were enough to make me hold my breath. When you hear a plane diving nearby, it is not pleasant, and always too close for comfort. I go upstairs and get a cracker with both apple butter and peanut butter on it, smoke a cigarette with Frank, and we go to sleep. It is 3:30 A.M.

November 10, 1943

In the morning we find that last night's raid was not the big one we have all been more or less expecting, but it was damned uncomfortable. It was a rainy night, and the A/A did not have a chance to spot them as they ducked from cloud to cloud. Talking this morning with a lieutenant from the PT base, he said they were pretty far off to the north (that being a ½ mile or so). Until the latter part of the raid when they came near us, they did not apparently get too close to the PT base. However, if last night is an indication of the shape of things to come, we should have some interesting evenings — and perhaps days on this island of Maddelena.

This morning Joe is to get some fake dog-tags made for me. I'll probably use Frank's old captain's bars on the operation (since he is now a major), and have the tags made with a fake serial number, etc. My only identification is a Special Passport that says I am attached to the Legation at Tangier! That would be fine to have fooling around the Island of Giglio, ten miles off the coast of Italy and about 100 miles or more north of our lines in Italy around midnight!!! They should have damned well made sure that all civilians had appropriate fake identification. Well, maybe they will put my commission through — it would certainly make things a lot easier in many respects; however, with Frank's bars and fake dog-tags, I should be all right.

Well, I've been in a rubber boat once in practice and then only fooling around. Perhaps tonight (this is written about ten in the morning and we are subject to one hour's notice from Barnes to be ready to go) or perhaps tomorrow night, I can get one for keeps.

Some gang we have here. Many of them have been former gangsters — like Joe and a couple of others. One guy ran a restaurant in the Village. One guy was a former news photographer in Connecticut. One guy worked with the Purple Gang in Detroit. Joe worked with about every mob in America in the twenties and early thirties — he was deported in 1935. Most of them have been on most dangerous missions. Two went into Sardinia a couple of months before the invasion of Sicily and were caught. They were told they would be shot if they did not reveal the signal plan and how to use the radio. They all shook hands that night and expected to be free in the morning. Tacquey, the lieutenant in charge of the three Italian agents — all were young men between the ages of twenty and thirty — told them, after the proposition was put up to them, that there was something more important at stake. Thousands of soldiers might be killed if they allowed the radio to be operated by the Italians and there was an invasion of the island, and so they agreed not to talk, but to face the firing squad.

The Italians, however, did not shoot them the following morning, but they expected to be killed at any time over the next several days while they spent five or six days in solitary, with the Italians coming around every day to tell them one of the others had talked, etc. One of the chaps here was loaned to the British for a mission and was imprisoned on this very island when captured. He had been caught with a detachment between the lines — mortar and 75 mm fire from both sides.

This is really quite a gang. And only symptomatic of the rest of the whole organization. The trouble is that everyone back in Algiers or Washington thinks I am doing a desk job and, by God, I'm out here in the asshole of the whole war, or the world, for that matter, being an operations officer, if only in a small way. This Giglio Island thing has been put in my hands by Frank and I only hope we can find those boys tonight, or whenever we get up there. If we can, I think even I would say, "Thank, God." Young Vierin's going with us to look for his father is a nice, if somewhat hammy, dramatic touch. When we were planning what to do last night it was a real mélange of languages. Young Vierin speaks only Italian and French. Joe speaks Italian and English. I speak a couple of words of French, fewer words of Italian picked up at random, and English. Occasionally I would explain to Vierin in French up to a point where I could not express what I wanted to say, and then tell the rest to Joe in English, who would give it to Vierin in Italian. I think we have it all worked out as much as we can. If I find them through the contact or at the beach, swell. But there is always the real dilemma — what if we find no trace of them? Well, we just have to wait and see, and make the attempt anyway.

La Maddelena, Sardinia
November 10, 1943

The Gerries came back at 2:00 P.M. today. No bombs dropped, so it was probably to see what damage they had done the night before. No electricity today, except for government (Italian) buildings, which apparently have their own power plant. Also no water. What a hole this joint is! (I am really getting a kick out of it, though — or I will when it's all over and I can look at it objectively.) Had some trouble with the Italians in getting a battery for the boys. They were inventing delays and I raised a bit of hell. (Frank was sick, so I had to run the works, what with Stoneborough away gallivanting around Sardinia). I am becoming quite an executive, perhaps. If we can keep the lieutenant colonels away, this will be what I wanted when I was in Algiers — a small show with young guys who can run it their own way. Except you run into such damned interference from Italians, British, etc. But lieutenant colonels would be too much to add to this. (By the way, "scuttlebutt" is a slang term around the Navy for rumors.)

November 11, 1943

I was talking with Frank yesterday evening about the air raid. He had some intelligence reports coming in about various people who had left town the night before and thought one or more of them might have passed intelligence from Sardinia to the Germans by radio. I am thinking in terms of Algiers where the German planes were at least 500 or 600 miles away and took hours to get there, said he should check up on those leaving several days ago. He reminded me that here we are only anywhere from 60 to 200 miles from a million German air bases and it would take only 30 or 40 minutes to come over. Even before I looked at a map, I knew he was right!

I went to see Barnes once again yesterday. He says the moon is bad for clandestine landings these days (as a matter of fact the moon is so bright it seemed like daylight most of last night). However, he would tell us when he was ready to shoot. He has some idea that the 5th Army is moving fast these days and may be opposite the island where Vierin and Ferrarra are soon. That is fine from the standpoint of making the question of convoy routes academic and from the standpoint of the convoy intelligence that Barnes wants. But our consideration at the moment is the safety of those two fellows, so I certainly hope he will be giving us a boat to go up there soon.

A good example of the harassing tactics of the Italians came up yesterday and the day before. We need a battery to take to the two men to the island. So Joe Sicalzi went down and found out that the Italians had some batteries, but it was necessary to have a requisition signed by the Italian Admiralty. Therefore, as an officer of the detachment, I went down to the Admiralty to fill out a requisition form in Frank's name (of course, the Italians were not told for what we needed the batteries — we asked for two). The next morning when I sent Joe down to get the batteries, he returned with the requisition, signed by the Italian Chief of Staff, but with the signature crossed out and the information that Frank's name was not recognized for requisitioning and we had to have Barnes' signature. So I went down and got Barnes to sign it and returned to the Admiralty myself and had the requisition signed by the Chief of Staff. I spoke in English to the lieutenant while looking at the Chief of Staff (who did not speak English). "I certainly hope it has been signed appropriately this time." The lieutenant looked uncertainly at the Chief of Staff, who lowered his eyes and shrugged his soldiers, whereupon the lieutenant smiled suavely and gave me the signed requisition. (The Chief of Staff had apparently wanted to see who was getting it.)

Then I returned to the Ilva, thinking the matter settled. Frank was sick and Tom and Max were away, so I was the only one of use in working condition. Joe went down to get the batteries. After fifteen minutes he phoned me. He said they had told him he could have the batteries in four days for it would take 86 hours to charge them ourselves. He said "okay" and hung up. Five minutes later he phoned and said it would

take a day to make the cases for them (apparently the two six-volt batteries were in six pieces). I told them to translate carefully to whoever
was there that he was merely repeating the words of the unofficale Amer-
icano: "Tell them to give you those batteries, and take the measurements
for the darned cases. Tell them to send the cases up here the first thing
in the morning and we will put them in the cases. And tell them I want
you back here with those batteries in ten minutes or I will raise holy
hell!" Joe was back with the batteries in seven minutes.

But that sort of thing shows the way they are trying to hold us up.
We learned just yesterday that one of the high Italian officers had sent
all their trucks over to Sardinia — obviously so they could not be used
by the Allied forces on this Island. We're working now to block them
from sending away the smaller vehicles they have here.

November 11, 1943

This is Armistice Day — well well!

Frank is still sick — the boys have gone out and practically bartered
their souls and gotten him a chicken and three eggs. Last night, because
Frank was ill and I was sleeping in the same room, and because there
was no water or electricity (which, it is said, were knocked out by the
air raid), I got the first really good night's sleep in God knows how long.
Nine hours! Incidentally, I'll cross my fingers and knock wood, but I'm
not so bad on this health business so far. All I've had is that one fever
for a few days in Algiers — which I cured by the simple expedient of getting out of bed and going out and having a great dinner and I didn't run
for doctor either. Lucky — so far.

It is funny to stand by the window of our hotel that faces the square
and the damaged and demolished buildings. It was not long before we
came here that the place had been practically completely knocked out
by our air raids. And most of the civilian population had left the island
and gone over to Sardinia. So we saw practically no civilians when we
first came — except elderly people who could not move well or were too
tired to care, and some younger people who didn't know enough to move,
and then, of course, the inevitable Italian sailors and soldiers. The Germans haven't yet come to do the real job, but they probably will when
we get it sufficiently repaired from our own bombing to make it worth
their while (we were among the first Allied troops to come here).

Just a few moments ago, I was watching an Italian soldier. His uniform is old and torn, he has a black patch over one eye, and carries one arm stiffly. He is with a woman, probably his wife, her dress is old and worn, but she is wearing a fur coat that is quite good looking. He is an officer I notice as they advance across the square. He is pointing out to her the bombed and damaged buildings. Then here come two girls across the square. And two men in civilian clothes that look comparatively new, about like the average person in New York. Such clothes are a definite sign of well being. Yes, the civilians are drifting back to their homes. Then, just a few minutes ago there was an alert. The siren, harsh and blatant and ominously whining, spurs the slow-moving people to quick action. They do not run, so much as "scurry," across the square, toward the air raid shelter. Although it seems all of them have gone to the shelter, more and more come from around corners. There is a woman of about 30—she has on nothing but a fur coat—as can be noticed when she runs and her coat blows up a bit. She is probably from the brothel up the hill. (This is at two o'clock in the afternoon, too!)

La Maddelena, Sardinia
November 12, 1943

Still hoping the job to get the boys off Giglio develops. Heard from one of the PT officers today that no patrols have gone out, except one under an English lieutenant commander. He got on board one of our boats, and had two British gunboats (MTB's) and a couple of other PT's with him. They spotted the largest merchant vessel our boys had yet sighted in these waters. It was about 8,000 to 10,000 tons and was protected by three gunboats. Now, our boys would have gotten this vessel between the moon and them and idled in on the side where the opposing gunboats were not and given the ship a couple of torpedoes, or, rather "fish."

These are tactics, I understand, which we ourselves learned from British MTB experience. But this English lieutenant commander follows the tactics Bulkley used in the Pacific, but which are not good under the circumstances existing in these waters (shore radar, shore batteries, planes, surface craft, mines). First, he goes up moon, and comes down full speed in the moon's light, following its path, clearly silhouetted. So they are challenged with blinkers two miles away; the Britisher only says "more speed." And they are fired on before they are within a mile; they loose a "fish" from a mile, which does nothing at all, and one man gets severely wounded, the PT gets several twenty mm shells in her, and then they return without getting the German ship. Christ!

This is about 3 P.M.; I went down to the PT base this morning to get all the intelligence they had on the Genoa region — particularly shore installations, OB, etc. They had some, but not enough. I'm going to wire Algiers for all the latest dope we have down there. The PT intelligence officer will be interested in anything we get, and he will share with us any info gotten by a man they have in Bastia now securing such intelligence. At the present time (3 o'clock) Frank is down talking to Barnes, trying to get him to send a boat up to look up the fellows on Giglio. It has been bad weather and a full, clear moon — but we are getting more and more anxious.

La Maddalena, Sardinia
November 12, 1943

A typical day at this stage of the game would be:

8:00 A.M. — Get up and Frank, Tom and I have breakfast together. It is served by Primo, with the assistance of a local kid who cleans up, shines shoes, etc.

8:30 A.M. — Shave.

9:00 A.M. — I go to see some Italian officer about something that has been done that should not have been done, or something that hasn't that should, or something that is being done but should be done sooner and faster.

10:00 A.M. — Back at the hotel. General talk with Frank and Tom about how we wish Max would give us the plans and let us get started on something.

10:30 A.M. — Down to the PT base. Talk with their finance officer about money matters, see their executive officer about pouches to Bizerte and the reverse, talk with their intelligence officer about what dope they have that they can give us and what we have or might get that would be of interest to them (at this point, generally, there is condemnation of British bastards). Also drop in to see Barnes and ask if we can pull off the pick-up try soon.

11:30 A.M. — Back to the hotel. Get bed made up a bit (this consists of blankets and bedroll. My mosquito net is inside the bedroll pocket to serve as pillow).

Noon — Lunch.

12:30 P.M. — Go out to the camp on Caprera. Training men on general intelligence needs. Pistol practice.

3:30 P.M. — Back to the hotel. Joe will have spotted something we can get if a requisition is forthcoming. So he will have made up an appointment for one of our officers with the British or Italians. Carry out this appointment.

4:00 P.M. — Work on training course back at hotel, such as preparing German divisional insignia for recognition training in OB, devising field problems (on a rainy day when they can't go to the camp because they have no change of clothing, the whole day will be spent lecturing to them, mostly through an interpreter, but sometimes in my own half-way Italian).

4:45 P.M. — Get the Italian grammar out and a have bit of study.

5:15 P.M. — Get out the bottle of Cinzano and Tom and I have a drink. We will then join Frank (who can't drink because he has been ill) and chew the fat generally.

6:00 P.M. — Dinner.

7:00 P.M. — If not going out to the Officers Club or some clandestine meeting, Tom and I will play a few games of chess and gin rummy.

Sometime between 11 and 1 A.M. — bed.

Typical menus, now that we have gotten a bit better organized:

Breakfast — Fruit juice, coffee, cereal (which is like paste with canned meat). A piece of fried spam. Bread and more coffee.

Lunch — Soup. Fish. (How they cook things with oil and garlic around here!) Bread, coffee, wine, crackers and apple butter and peanut butter. String beans.

Dinner — Soup. Spam. Beets. Bread. Apple butter, peanut butter. Wine. Coffee. (While the two bottles Tom and I picked up last — liqueur.)

All in all, it is not going to be so bad. At least Frank, Tom and I don't have bosses sitting on top of us. (Even though we are powerless to start on some real operations until Max gets the word from Palermo.) Our complement is 28 or 29 Italian agents and 9 GI's.

La Maddalena, Sardinia
November 16, 1943

A few little bits of news that we've gathered concerning past events:

1. In the raid the other evening there were sixteen German planes. Some were hitting mines in the harbor. One was shot down (this was a reasonable piece of work — the range was 9,000 yards and it was done without seeing the plane, purely by radar). The A/A officers are certain the Germans will return in *real* force — and, let me tell you, that should be an experience when it comes.

2. We've learned that when we came up here on that LST, loaded with ammunition and gasoline, the ship passed through an uncharted

mine field. It was just sheer luck that we got through. Frank, Tom
and I all shivered when we heard that. And I'm not kidding! A miss
is as good as a mile, but uncharted minefields in an LST loaded as
that was, ain't hay!

3. Max has wired us from Palermo to be very careful on the Giglio try
    because he has definite word that the Germans are there. (Wish he'd
    tell us his source, and how the info came in, damn it!) The weather
    has been too bad for the PT's to go out for the past week. I'm try-
    ing to get some fake dog tags made, in which event (as noted above)
    I'll probably use Frank's old bars for the job. If I don't get any
    identification it might be tough if something should happen. I tried
    to get the Italian fishing boat for the job, but even an LCT from
    Palermo had to put back after starting out yesterday, so I guess the
    only thing we can do is wait for decent PT weather. The only bad
    (rather, the "worst") possibility is that the Germans have captured
    the boys and will be watching the pinpoint. We know from the doc-
    tor that the Germans were not on the island about November 4 (three
    days after I put the boys in); therefore, there is a possibility that their
    capture might have prompted the Germans to occupy the island
    (which would coincide with Max's report). Well, we will see.

La Maddalena, Sardinia
November 18, 1943

The day before yesterday Tom and I had a rather interesting tea.
We had gone on November 15 for a walk up to the Villa Weber, the house
where Mussolini was kept when he was here. An Italian naval lieutenant had met us in the long drive leading to the house and after a bit of
polite conversation (he spoke French), had asked us to come for tea the
following afternoon. So the day before yesterday up the hill we went at
four in the afternoon.

This lieutenant (Sansonetta, who commands the Italian MAS boats —
Italian equivalent of PT's — and who took the two boats up to Giglio
when the doctor went back) sleeps in the same room where Mussolini was
kept. We saw the room and the house; very beautiful from the outside.
It sits just below the crest of a rocky hill. There are many trees and a brook
runs through the grounds. The house faces Sardinia and Corsica and both
of these islands can be seen from the house and grounds. Above the house
are only shaggy, bare rocks but down the hill and all around it trees min-
gle with the rocks. The beautiful, deep green of the trees makes them all
flesh on a body, of which the rocks are the bare, bleached bones.

Sansonetta talked of the battle of Matipan, in which he participated and in which his father was an Italian admiral. He has a peculiar face — the lower half is aristocratic and sensuous; eyes and forehead have a weak, rather sensitive appearance. All in all, he's quite handsome and about thirty-four. We were joined later by his senior officer. This man, probably about fifty, is clean shaven, with a Lodovico Sforza face. Thin, cruel lips and eyes that are fiery behind the frustration of defeat. He had spent many years in China.

Both of them were most sensitive about the defeat of the Italian navy. At one moment the older man said, "If we had the proper equipment, the Italian navy could beat the British navy any day." We sympathize with them and put in a few remarks to the effect that it was a shame the Germans didn't give them material, but instead had sort of left the Italians in the lurch.

These fellows have been indoctrinated. They will render us lip service if necessary, but would, I'm sure, help the Germans just as quickly and turn on us at the slightest provocation.

The tea was interesting, however, particularly in view of the surroundings, and we walked back to the Ilva in good spirits.

The A/A fellows have nicknamed one German reconnaissance plane that comes over almost every day "Photo Joe." This Photo Joe, we suppose, will come over every day on aerial reconnaissance. He will keep tabs on how the place is coming — how much shipping is in the port, how rebuilding is coming, etc.; and our boys will shoot at him when he comes within range; then, when they feel it is really worthwhile — bam! Good old Photo Joe! And the people will scurry to the shelters; then they will drift back to their homes; and all the while prices go up (wine has gone from 20 to 40 lire a liter since we have been here).

Slight friction between British and Americans as evidenced by a row in the street the other day.

The Italians have put a shadow on our place in the form of a couple of thug-looking guys who just observe. I spotted them the other day, and we will arrange for some of our people to tail them and find out exactly who they report to.

We have gotten info from Sardinia that when the Germans got out they left 200 Germans dressed as Italians who spoke Italian well. (Sort of the same thing as our racket.) These guys were to do sabotage and intelligence. We will have to keep a pretty good lookout for a while, I guess.

(Incidentally, the hit of "Stage Door Canteen" was the Benny Goodman number, with the girl beginning "Get Outta Here and Get Me Some Money Too." The Katherine Cornell scene drew jeers and laughs. The only spontaneous applause was for Kay Kyser on his first appearance. The best numbers, in my opinion, were Ray Bolger and the Benny Goodman number. The boys got a terrific kick out of the Xavier Cugat dame. The general opinion was "a terrible picture, but it features some good bands.")

N.B. By now, I've been at the houses of two rather opposite figures of Italian history — Garibaldi, the great democrat, and Mussolini, the "great" fascist. Tiens!

La Maddalena, Sardinia
November 18, 1943

I am sitting in a jeep at the PT base. To the right is a pile of bricks and stones that once was a building. Off my port are 3½ walls of a building, with boards hanging at crazy angles. Straight ahead are two buildings, both with the roofs off and one with a full wall blown out. To the back of me is a semi-circle of other demolished buildings.

Some sailors are playing touch football where a building once stood. A half-destroyed, half-sunken destroyer is in the water at the left. Beyond the pile of bricks at the right there is one good building left (no windows, but otherwise all right). This building is full of torpedoes and ammunition. PTs, rescue boats, and crash boats are to the left beyond the destroyed building. Beyond the half-destroyed low machinery buildings — across the docks to the left — are the craggy rocks of Capraia with the white Garibaldi house in a patch of dark green on the side of a hill, surmounted by tan and gray rocks pointing into a blue sky with a sprinkling of fleecy white clouds.

The alert sounded just a moment ago and the Italian people are running around for shelter. There are six planes over back of the Capraia hills (over my left shoulder). Some of the guns have started blazing away at them over there — probably D battery of the 167th A/A (90s and 40s).

The planes do not turn from their course to come in our direction. Their objective is probably Sardinia.

La Maddalena, Sardinia
November 20, 1943

Yesterday afternoon while we were having lunch, one of the PT sailors dropped by to say Commander Barnes would like to see the "party" at the PT base at 2:00 P.M. At last! So I got young Vierin (the son of the older man now on Giglio) fixed up with a borrowed helmet, pistol, belt, canteen, raincoat, etc. I got my .45, borrowed a box of cartridges, filled three clips, gave Vierin three full clips, got about eighty K rations in a musette bag, four packages of cigarettes apiece, a flashlight, a compass, checked my pockets to see there were no papers. Then I take the fake dog tags I had made (and what a lousy job!), borrowed Frank's first looey bars, fix them on my uniform, and we're ready to go. I revive my notes on Giglio, and review the plan with Vierin:

We will land and conceal the inflated rubber boat as much as possible. If we are not approached by the fellows, we will strike out almost due north to find the Carbino house (the fisherman friend of the Italian fishing boat skipper who had been given to the boys as a "safe house"). I will wait by the gate on guard. Young Vierin will go in and knock on the door to waken the man. When asked who is there, he is to reply, "Sono un amico di Scotto Sirio, Capitano del Rex." Then he is to seek information discreetly and may go inside if invited. If anyone approaches, I'll cough loudly and Vierin is to come out with gun ready.

If by chance there is a guard at the pinpoint, we try to shoot it out and get away. We are to have four hours on the island, after which we rendezvous with the PT. When we land at first the PT is to wait for me to flash a signal in Morse with a GI flashlight: M (..) wait a few minutes; U (. .), okay — make rendezvous in four hours; D (_ . .), we're coming out to the PT (this after the "wait" signal or at time of rendezvous); C (_ . _ .), something's gone wrong and we can't come out to the PT — we'll watch for someone to come for us every night between 10:00 P.M. and 2:00 A.M.

Vierin and I go to the PT base at 2:00 P.M. Tom comes along, driving the jeep. We go to the Operations Room and clear the signals with George Steele, the chap who will command the PT; Sinclair's PT is at Bizerte for repairs. That set, George says he will leave about 5:00 P.M., and we go over to the Navy Officers' Mess, where Tom and I play a game of ping-pong. Then we have some coffee. Then we play bridge until 4:30 P.M. Finally, I grab my things, and young Vierin (who had a lonesome time of it, since he only speaks French and Italian) grabs his. Mine consist of a helmet (which I have fixed with adhesive to indicate a first lt.), belt with .45, two extra clips, canteen, compass, first aid packet, overcoat, flashlight — that's the works. Vierin has all of the above, except a flashlight and compass, and he carries the musette bag.

We go to the boat (PT 215) and have dinner on board as we are pulling out. (Damned good, too: steak, boiled potatoes, peas and corn, bread and coffee) It is raining like hell. (Tom, of course, went back to the Ilva about 4:45 P.M.) We get outside the first submarine and mine nets. The boat is rolling wildly. The water slaps the bottom like a ton of bricks. George decides we'll have to go back. I break the news to young Vierin. The kid must be incredibly stoic and he feels the news all right. I would be glad to have that guy with me on any operation. We sit in the crew's quarters. The sailors are kidding around about how much money they can send back and who won the last crap game, who can steer the boat best, etc. They are sore that we even tried to go out at all because now they will be back too late for the movie. One of them says, "Are these two guys on the island Americans?" I tell him that one of them is, and that both of them are sticking their necks out for America as well as to help win this damned war. He shuts up. Somehow, with young Vierin sitting there thinking of his father who is on Giglio, and our returning now, even though Vierin can't understand the remark of the sailor, I feel sort of guilty on behalf of myself and all Americans. We came back to port. I say to Barnes, "Shall I get in touch with you tomorrow?" He tells me he will get in touch with us.

This afternoon (which is the day after the above), one of Barnes' officers comes up to say the weather is too rough to try tonight. Damn! It's now about twenty days, and those guys only had ten days worth of rations! Let's hope it will work out for tomorrow.

(I guess this job, if I ever get to do to it, will seem pretty interesting when and if I get back. It will only be my second time in a rubber boat—and the first was a very sheltered 25-yard ride in broad daylight). Since the lines of the 5th Army are still far below Rome, Giglio seems pretty well up into enemy territory. There is the possibility that the Germans are on the island (particularly in view of Max's cable).

If I had looked at anything like this a year ago and imagined myself doing it, I would have wanted to, but I would probably have been pretty scared. (Well, a little before a year ago, because I had gotten into the training school one year back and had a bit of the fever—though I must confess that even then I could occasionally scare myself thinking about the things I might sometime be doing). Now, somehow, the mind refuses to think enough to be scared. Things which would have seemed frightening as hell back in the States have become part of the normal routine of existence, though I imagine they will seem still different a few years from now. I told Tom, just as I was getting on the PT yesterday, that if anything happened to my operation, I had this little notebook and two other notebooks in my briefcase.

I sure hope this Giglio Island job can be pulled soon; it's beginning to get me down from a personal standpoint, even aside from the point of trying to get back the two guys. I imagine my first operation a failure. And two men lost if we can't get up there to get them, and perhaps lost even if we do get up there now. And then this damned waiting, and telling young Vierin "any day now" (indeed!), and turning back.

This apparently has had some rather amusing aspects of which I was not conscious. Three nights ago Tom was awakened by sounds from my bunk in the middle of the night, as though, he says, "someone were strangling." It was dark as pitch, so he grabbed his gun, lit his flashlight, and got out of bed. And, according to him, there I was in my sleep, snarling and gasping. I wasn't dreaming (so far as I know, at least), and it is possible that sub-consciously my mind may have been on this Giglio job, as it has for the past several weeks.

Rubber Boat Rescue

La Maddalena, Sardinia
November 24, 1943 (Thanksgiving Day)

On November 20 we were again informed that the weather was too bad to go out, but that Steele's boat (the 215–212 that made the first trip) would take us the next day, weather permitting. On November 21 at two in the afternoon Steele dropped by and said we would probably go out at 5:00 P.M. I said we would be on the boat at 4:30 sharp. The same preparations as before — and we were on the PT on time.

The boat pulled out at 5:00 as planned, and we started along the same course as on November 1. The weather was clear and cool. We sighted no ships even in the radar, but the radar indicated several planes nearby. I was assigned a .30 caliber machine gun on the starboard side and fired about forty rounds with all the guns in test firing. (The boat that accompanied us let off a five-inch anti-personnel rocket that whooshed past us about ten yards away as the boat swerved.)

About 8:o'clock Steele told me that the plans had been changed and that we would patrol first and be dropped on the island afterwards. If we met anything, possibly we would have to scoot for home and not try the pick-up. I wanted the pick-up that night.

We passed four miles off the north coast of Giglio and went into San Stefano. Passed Giglio about 10 o'clock. For four hours we patrolled the coast of the mainland, never more than three miles off and generally within two miles. We returned to Giglio about 1:30 A.M. and idled in. Steele said he could give me at the most three hours on the island and this was sure cutting the time to make the contact pretty thin. He did not go in as far as Sinclair did, but stopped about 200 yards off the point of the cove. The night was pretty dark but stars gave some light. Steele was not sure this was Allume Cove and I could not recognize it from where the boat stopped. However, we got in the rubber boat (this was the second time for me, and this was for keeps) about 1:45 A.M. and started off. When we had gotten between the points of the cove, I recognized it. The beach was another 300 yards or so at the innermost part of the cove. It was slow as hell in that rubber boat and I was tired after only 100 yards. However, we kept on until about 200 yards from the beach.

Then we saw a faint glimmer of light from a point about 50 to 60 feet up the cliff back of the small beach (which is about 20 yards wide and 5 yards deep). In another 15 yards we could see that there was a small fire in a cave up there. I told young Vierin we would pull over to the right side and then I looked to see if any watch were being kept. This might be our men — or it might be an Italian or German guard waiting for us. If it was our men, they should be watching particularly for us and give some sign. No sign of life was apparent. Therefore, we paddled in to the right side of the beach and put the rubber boat in the shadows, but near enough for a "quick" get-away. Still no sign of how many, if any, men were in the cave, or who they were. We stood there at the right side of the beach, in the shadow of the cliff, like Hamlet and Horatio looking for signs of the ghost. I decided we would have to approach it cautiously and it would take time to scale the rocks, so I flashed the signal to the PT to rendezvous at the appointed time — 4:30 A.M. We could not see or hear the PT from the beach.

I told Vierin what I planned. We would climb the rocks to the right to a point above the cave and then go over and down to the entrance. He was to take a position to the right of the entrance and out of sight of anyone within and I would go below a bit and about ten feet out (directly in front of the cave) and cover the entrance. He would then shout in Italian for those within to come out with their hands up. If it was his father and Joe, okay. If anyone else, we would start blazing away and get off the island in a hurry, trusting that we could survive drifting around in the rubber boat for the time necessary for the PT to return from its patrol (which was to continue after we were dropped).

We clambered up the steep cliff. It was pretty silent, I guess. Only one small stone was dislodged. This sounded loud to me, but I suppose the sound of the sea below would have covered it to anyone else. Well, it seems fantastic and unreal now — like a stage set. We go to the cave, took the appointed positions, and young Vierin called out in Italian. My gun, and his, was cocked and ready. There was an exclamation from within the cave.

The kid recognized his father's voice and rushed into the cave. This happened before I realized that it was our men. I went over to the cave then and Joe came crawling out. I did not recognize him, but said, "Who's that?" He said, stopping and still on his hands and knees, "Who the hell is talkin' English?" Almost hopeful, I asked, "Joe?" And he said, "Yeah, who's that?" He was crawling across a one-foot ledge just by the right side of the cave entrance. I was standing over him with a gun pointed at him. Well, we all wound up in the cave — and boy were they happy. So were we, Joe had very dark circles under his eyes and both looked a bit the worse for wear.

We found that we had gotten there just in the nick of time. The men had gotten on the island in swell shape and had to sleep on the beach the first night, not being able to climb the cliff in the dark. Then they had stayed at the doctor's hut, which they found when they climbed the mountain in the morning, the next night. They met a peasant (apparently the caretaker of the doctor's hut) and he brought them food. They could not make radio contact. They sent their messages blind. The last transmission, when the battery was getting low, was a frantic appeal to be picked up (this was on the sixth day). Then, having hid the radio on the cliff about forty feet up from the beach where they thought it was safe, one of the many storms came up and the sea washed the radio and battery away. The peasant had showed them the cave and they stayed there from the third day on. They were completely lost and desperate.

The only hope they clung to was pathetic. The night they landed,

I had said at the last moment as I shook hands with Vierin and he entered the rubber boat, "*Je veux vous voir dans deux semagnes.*" (This, in my poor French — he did not speak English — was said as a sort of bracer, and was not an arrangement for a pick-up). But this they repeated to themselves over and over again. By the time ten days has passed, they had convinced themselves that I had said, "I will be here to get you in two weeks." The two weeks passed — their food was gone after 12 days. Then went another week. And the afternoon of November 21 at 4:30 they were in the cave.

They heard a call from the mountaintop nearby and went to the entrance. The peasant was there, making warning signs — they could not understand what he said. They got the idea of danger, however, and rushed into the cave, put their things way in the back and Joe burned the signal plan. They then went out of the cave and started to climb the mountain to the left. After about twenty yards, they spotted one of the Carabinieri at the top of the hill to the right. They hid behind a rock just where they were. Seventeen soldiers appeared and began to advance on the cave. Most were Carabinieri, but about six or seven were Germans. They advanced down the mountainside toward the cave, alternately calling for our men to come out and firing at the cave entrance. Our men remained motionless behind the rock — they had not been seen by the soldiers, who thought they were still in the cave. Finally, the soldiers entered the cave. They found the stuff the boys had hidden there and took it away. They apparently departed because the mountains to the town could not be negotiated at night, and it was getting dark. Our men returned to the cave really desperate.

The peasant came down, asking them to burn any notes of information he had brought them. He cried, and said he was afraid of reprisals and that he overheard one of the Carabinieri remark that they and the Germans would be back in the morning to trap our men. He finally left them some food and went away. They built a small fire in the cave and tried to figure out what to do. Old Vierin thought of posing as a peasant, making his way to the mainland and attempting to get through to our Fifth Army lines, some 40 miles or so south of Rome.

This was possible (about a 1 in 200 chance) for him, but Joe was much younger and could not speak Italian like a native, though he spoke it well; his youth would make it almost certain that he would be picked up for military or labor service. They kept a sort of last, desperate, hopeless watch for us to come until a little after midnight. Then they gave up all hope. When we actually did arrive and they heard young Vierin call, they thought the soldiers had returned to capture them. They raised their hands, and Vierin's exclamation was one of surrender. Joe had been trying to crawl from the cave in a rather futile attempt to escape and hide when I practically stumbled over him. This all happened in a fast moment of confusion, despair and joy for them.

We were not out of it yet. It was still a couple of hours to rendezvous time. If the PT had met any ships or planes, it would have to do its job and run for home afterwards and we would be left stuck on the island with the certainty that the soldiers would come "hunting" in the morning. We decided to put out the fire and go down to the beach to wait. Standing on the beach, we smoked cigarettes cautiously by the rubber boat in the shadow of the cliff at the side. During this time I considered what could be done in the event something bad happened. I thought of trying to get to the Island of Monte Cristo — too far in a small rubber boat such as we had. Then I thought of Giannutri — an island fairly close, but uninhabited. This might be a possibility, but only in the most desperate of circumstances. All sorts of possibilities passed through my mind.

4 o'clock came. 4:05. 4:10. 4:15. We could not see the PT or hear any motors. I decided the important thing was to get off the Island, and rationalized that we would be that much nearer to the PT if it got there by 4:30. So I flashed the signal that we were coming out at 4:20, and said, "Let's go — *nous allons.*" I had my life jacket lying just behind me. I just turned around to pick it up — and, by God, those boys didn't have to have the order repeated — they were already in the boat about six or seven feet out. I splashed through the water and clambered aboard. I doubt if there was ever such a lousy launching. I took one paddle, old Vierin took the other. Young Vierin used the third as a helm, and Joe squatted in the bow. We proceeded about 50 yards. Still could see no sight of the PT. I gave Joe my flashlight and told him to give the sign again that we were coming out. This was at 4:28. When we got out about 300 yards from the beach we spotted the PT idling in. It was broadside to us, so for a moment I thought it might be going away, and told Joe to flash the signal low in the water and repeat it once. He did so. I was tired as hell and gave my oar to young Vierin who took over the helm. Old Vierin said he would stay as he was. We reached the PT and were helped aboard.

Old Vierin (who is emotional as hell before and after a job, but calm as hell while doing anything) practically kissed everyone, he was so happy. The PT started back. After an hour it developed motor trouble and had to slow down to about 15 knots. The accompanying PT slowed to stay with us.

Steele remarked that we would be on the open sea long after daylight, an easy target for planes or ships since we had no speed. The other PT stayed with us until about 9 in the morning when we were near Maddalena; then it shot ahead to port. We docked about 11 A.M. I reported to the commander of the PT's and thanked him. (By the way, I fired one of the starboard machine guns in test firing required before coming in — hit the designated rock too, by God!) I asked Barnes if he had a jeep to take us up to the Ilva. None was available — they were all out. I phoned Frank — both of our jeeps were out.

Then I noticed an old Victoria carriage, with one old nag and a sleepy Italian driver. It had driven a couple of the GI's to the PT base for a look around. When we asked if he was for hire, the driver said yes but that he already had two fares. I went over to the two GI's, my coat was dirty from mud, sand, water, and gray paint from the PT but I pulled the shirt collar out so the lieutenant's bars (Frank's old ones) that I was wearing now would show. I asked the two GI's if they would be there for a few minutes. They said doubtfully, "we don't know, sir." I replied, "I imagine you will." I was pretty tired — it has now been about 18 or 19 hours on the PT and the island, and I also was physically tired from the paddling and climbing. Thereupon, while the two GI's stood there helpless, I preempted the wagon and we rode to the Ilva. Turned out this was the same carriage the town's only brothel used to give their whores a daily airing. Some way to come back! But it added a nice piquant touch to the whole thing.

Frank sent a cable back to Palermo that mentioned I had planned and executed a "spectacular rescue." I didn't see this until a day or so after it was sent, or I would have shortened the adjective to "lucky."

Then on the 22rd Frank told me to get ready to go to Bastia for a few days and gave me carte blanche to set up a base and recruit and send men in if I saw fit. Boyohboyohboy!!

I am as near to being happy at this moment as I suppose I ever will be.

La Maddalena, Sardinia
26 November 1943

Now all packed for Corsica and waiting decent weather to go on a British Motor Launch (ML, something like our PT's).

The Italian high command has known for some time that the British submarines were going to make their base here on November 24. The British subs did not come on November 24. But at 7 o'clock that night, with low, heavy clouds 25 Gerry planes came. The raid lasted about an hour. 25 planes are not much in the scale of raids on big cities, but on a village like Maddalena, they ain't hay. An unexpected 20 mm. shell hit the wall of our place, just 20 feet from the window from which I was watching. A British gunboat was sunk in the harbor. A PT ran ashore, seeking to escape from the base. Two men trapped on the British boat. 7 planes were shot down. Developed that they were part of 50 that started out, but 25 went to Corsica and 25 came here. We can expect more of this now. The AA Colonel has advised us to move our hq — says we can hardly help getting hit where we are. Frank feels this base is not going to be much good anyway, but we may all move. In any event, if I can get to Bastia before Corvo gets back, Tom and I may be able to start something going there.

4

Corsica

Upon its liberation early in October 1943, Corsica was the northern-most Allied salient toward southern Europe, and became an important OSS advance base. It served as headquarters for the OG/Italy unit, as a dispatching station for SI operations into central and northern Italy and southern France, and as a forward field communications base.

OSS headquarters were established at Bastia, the northeast Corsican seaport, 35 miles from the Italian mainland, and approximately 90 miles from the strategic Ligurian coast. Administration and communications headquarters, as well as the OG training and staging area, were located at Ile Rousse, while a supply center was maintained at Ajaccio.

Corsica served primarily as a maritime rather than as an air base.*

Wayne Nelson was an SI Operations Officer in Corsica from November 1943 to July 1944, recruiting, training, and briefing agents for infiltration into Northern Italy and the Tyrrhenian Islands (including Elba); planning and preparing operations to infiltrate agents by sea into Southern France, Northern and Central Italy, and the Tyrrhenian Islands by sea; directing and/or executing more than 50 of such operations from Corsica and Sardinia (including landing in enemy territory on approximately 25 occasions).†

Bastia, Corsica
November 29, 1943

Boarded the ML Saturday at 4 P.M. and pulled out shortly thereafter. The two British officers were very nice — we had nothing to eat

*War Report of the OSS
†OSS Field Report, *22 May 1945*

but sausage and bread and cheese and it was all handled quite nicely and Tom and I enjoyed ourselves a lot. The evening on board we talked with the young lieutenant (only 21) about the future of the world and the commanding officer when he came down and spoke of his family in England. We were the leading boat for an LCT and came up the east coast of Corsica. This was a position that we had remarked several times when we went to Maddalena on the LST that would not be comfortable in mine-ridden waters. The trip was uneventful — the young officer laconically remarked at one point, "Well, if we hit a mine in this boat, there would not be a stick left as large as three feet. It would be rather uncomfortable, you know."

At Bastia we immediately contacted the PT boys who told us roughly where Pete (Karlow) and Dewitt (Clinton) lived. We walked over practically the entire city hunting for Pete and Dewitt's place and finally found them. The city was war-torn — the Gerries had been over the same night they hit Maddalena, November 24. And this raid was the big topic of conversation. They hit American Air Force HQ (which the Americans were just moving into), but fortunately everyone was out of the building. The rest of the damage had been done by Allied raids and earlier German raids and shells. It was somewhat nostalgic (I am beginning to understand why people get such a sentimental attitude toward Paris and France now). The first sight I had of Karlow was when I saw a car being pushed down a hill to start it and I said, "That must be one of our boys." It was Pete!

We went to the house and chewed the fat and found out what the situation was. Lt. Col. Russell Livermore had his headquarters at Ile Rousse, it developed. He was coming over to Bastia that afternoon to go out on an operation. We went down to the ML and got out things and brought them to the house. Here in Bastia you are really on top of the Germans. They have Elba that is only twenty-six miles away and can be seen as clearly as anything. So can the Island of Capraia, which the Germans have not occupied, but can have if they want it. We have an OP there secretly now. We saw Colonel Livermore briefly before he went and he said he would talk more in the morning.

Pete took Tom and I to the officers club here known as The Florida. The favorite drink at the small bar, I found, was the "Bastia, Avec, Avec" which has, among other ingredients, pastis, rum and cognac. It is potent.

The next morning we went to Ile Rousse. The Colonel asked me to drive with him. It is a two-hour drive and very beautiful. The craggy mountains of Corsica are tops. The road is narrow and winding. Some bridges are being repaired, having been blown up by us or the Germans. Colonel Livermore and I discussed the situation. I told him frankly that I thought it would be best to move the Maddalena base to Corsica and, as diplomatically as I could, tried to preserve some degree of autonomy.

At Ile Rousse our headquarters was in the Hotel Napoleon Bonaparte, a beautiful modern hotel with a magnificent view of the sea and a beach. I arrived a few hours before Tom, who came with Clinton and Karlow, and I took a room for the two of us. It was too good to believe after sleeping on floors etc.— real beds, sheets and pillowcases! We stayed there all day and drove back in the afternoon to Bastia—so didn't get a chance to use those fine beds after all.

The next day Russ Livermore came over and I had a letter to Frank prepared stating that he thought the situation was better in Bastia and culminating a proposal in three parts:

1. Frank to be designated by Scamp to set up Italian SI in Bastia;
2. We work from the same hq as Livermore;
3. Separate quarters to be taken for our agents etc. Russ agreed to this.

We interrogated eleven people who wandered into Corsica from the Island of Gorgona that morning and in the afternoon got together a plan to put an OP there.

That afternoon I got a message in our private code from Frank ordering Tom and myself back to Palermo and saying that the base at Maddalena was moving back. I showed this to Livermore, stating that it put us in an embarrassing position. He asked if I wanted to stay. I said Colonel Eddy had ordered me with Scamp at my and Scamp's request; that I went with Scamp because he was the only one of the old crowd left in the new Glavin setup; and that he had been the only desk with any action on. I continued that I felt a personal loyalty to him because it was under his general aegis that I got a chance on operations. Livermore said he would report to Glavin that the Maddalena base had been moved without this knowledge. I asked permission to send a message to Scamp through Algiers at the same time Livermore reported and I said in it. "Both Tom and I feel strongly excellent prospects Italian SI from Bastia with cooperation Livermore and his organization. Showing orders to return to Livermore and await instructions through Cadillac station here." The next day Livermore suggested it might be better if I went to Palermo and straightened the thing out with Scamp personally, so the following day I went to the airfield at Borge and waited around 'till a C-47 came in from Sicily. I had arranged with the Air Corps officers to eat with them — since they were just getting set up and only a few fighters up there, we ate out of mess kits on the ground. Here we were in full view of Elba.

Fourteen C-47s came into the small field in a bunch, nearly running into each other, as they buzzed around like hornets. They carried supplies for the air base — they were the first C-47s to come to Bastia. I was introduced to the pilot of the first one and he said he would take me to Sicily, and asked where I wanted to go. Not wishing to put him out any, I said, "Well, if I can get on the proper island, I can make my way to my destination." He repeated, Yea, but where?" I said "Palermo." He said his base was in the southeast part of Sicily, but if daylight held, "I'll drop you off in Palermo." He told base operations that his colonel had asked him to request fighter escort down the coast. The Operations Officer said he would see if any planes were available. The pilot finally said, "Aw, fuck the Goddamned Germans. Let's go!" So, the plane having been unloaded in a jiffy, I threw my bedroll and the musette bag and helmet and overcoat in, and climbed aboard. Up we went — no more than fifteen minutes after the plane hit the field. I am writing this in the plane somewhere around the southern coast of Corsica — we've come down in the shadow of the mountains no more than 300 feet off the water without escort.

If I can beat Glavin's message to Scamp as a result of Livermore's message and can possibly get to represent Scamp to Corsica it will be swell. Tom is perfectly willing to work under me and I know I can get something going. My general plan is to put OP's on Gorgona, Elba and Giannutri. (There is already one on Capraia.) They can be used as safe houses for people we would put in along the coast. Also the boats would be obligated to service them and these trips could be used to put others in. Then I would cable 110 (Allen Dulles) in Berne and ask for a couple of safe houses in North Italy or Switzerland near the Italian border. We can put people into North Italy with a rendezvous two weeks later. They could check with 110's men and return. 110 could report by radio what he got and we could get a full report on picking them up. I hope I can get Scamp's backing.

Incidentally, when we got to Bastia, two days after the raid, everyone was getting to the country. "Hitting the maquis" was the phrase for it. The Germans had announced over their radio that they would annihilate Bastia at the end of November, so for the four or five days I spent there, we were ready to duck every night. Must not forget the gesture — palm extended, face down, fingers like a talon. It is used for a silent description of woman. Means, "Fuck often, and for money." Other gestures are not as funny, there is a whole set of them.

Tunis
December 6, 1943

Flew Bastia to Palermo as noted elsewhere. Went to Vince's place there. Was not too cordially received by Vince and Max. They apparently did not think I had been entirely loyal to the Italian Section in going to Corsica, further Frank let me know they were sore because I had done a couple of operations from Sardinia. I talked Vince finally into setting up a section in Corsica. However, he said he would send a "real" member of the Italian SI to take charge, which may mean a screw-up of the whole thing.

One very interesting thing to the ego was being regarded as sort of a minor hero in connection with the Giglio job. The fellows came up with real appreciation. (I imagine the Vierins and Joe talked the incident up rather dramatically as Latins are prone to do.) Doesn't mean much, it did feel good as a counter to the cool way Vince and Max acted.

Had dinner in Palermo with Don MacKay and Sherman Kent, Fales and Sawyer at the Officer's Club. Saw a couple of short — and boring-documentaries after dinner. This war stinks from the aspect of writing and acting about it — the approach of American propaganda by its own people is rotten.

Passed several days in idleness in Palermo and then managed to get orders and on a plane for Tunis. This was en route to Bastia by way of Ajaccio. Another ride in a C-47. Had to lay over night in Tunis — got a room at one of the officers' hotels and that night went to the Sadsack Club (Officers' Club of the Second Area Service Command). They had a local orchestra and some fair imitation drinks. It's run by GI's of the outfit, and is a little like a rather gaudy New York bar.

The next morning I went out to the field to find my plane canceled and had to lay over another night. Sat around the field talking to some fellows for a while, then back to Tunis and lunch at a local hotel.

The lunch was interesting — it was a restaurant locally operated and not a mess. Seated at the table were two American naval officers, Coast Guard who had served during at least three major landings, two officers from an A/A outfit; and a young sergeant from a bombing crew. The latter had just finished his 31st mission — nineteen more and he could go home for a while. He had been shot down once and rescued and forced down several times. The interchange of views between this group, having such widely diverse jobs in the war, was most interesting.

Went to the Theatre du Chansons in Tunis the evening of December 6. A very small theatre off one of the arcades near the Boulevarde Jules Ferry. The performance was very low stock variety. A small theatre that could not have seated more than 150 and a small stage. However, it was interesting and I am now sitting in a room at the hotel writing this and just behind there is a bed — with a mattress! The way I have been sleeping recently — there was a spring but not a mattress at Palermo, and for the rest of the past six weeks I've slept on a mattress about five times — said mattress is most inviting and I'm going to hit it. Good night!

Bastia, Corsica
December 19, 1943

After some periods of doubt as to whether I would be "bumped" or not, got on a plane for Ajaccio due to my "2" priority. Stopped at Cagliari and Alghera in Sardinia on the way. Only a few minutes at each place. Met one of the men who had been with me in Maddalena in civilian clothes on the plane going from Cagliari to Alghera. We had loaned him to the CI boys in Sardinia. We passed a message or two without anyone on the C-47 knowing we were doing it. Got to Ajaccio, the birthplace of Napoleon. Not much effect of war there as can be observed in Bastia. Stayed overnight at our headquarters in Ajaccio — the Annex of the Hotel des Estrangeres — and was driven from Ajaccio to Bastia the next morning. A Major Gordon Grant, on his way to join the 63rd Fighter Wing in Bastia, came along. A sergeant drove us. He was one of the original thirty-four who had come in when the Germans were here and when our outfit lost a lieutenant and three men. One of the nights in Ajaccio I went to the American Bar. It's one of the most Americanized places I've seen since I've been overseas. Later that night went to the Canary Club — a dive sort of nightclub — with Colonel Mann and Lt. Crane.

The drive up to Bastia is one of the most beautiful anyone could imagine. Up the mountains, and around the mountains and through the mountains. Lowlands and highlands. Roads that, at the moment, I marvel that anyone could drive. We stopped for a few minutes en route and had some wine and C rations.

When I got to Bastia, I found that the Gorgona job that I had planned with Clinton and Tom had been set to go as an OG job. It was, however, arranged that Tom at least should be representing SI. I then managed to squeeze on. We took the Italian MAS boat (and what speed that boat has — it can go fifty knots). In the small cabin Tom, Colonel Livermore, Pete Karlow, Lt. Wood (of Amgot), myself and two GI's with an Italian sailor sat for the whole three or four hour trip. We left at six P.M. There were six GI's and a Lieutenant Manzani to remain on the Island. And we were there to get what we could for SI.

We reached the island about 9:30 and people were gathering along the mole. An unidentified plane flew overhead and caused some worry, but it did not change its speed or course, so we thought we were unobserved. As we idled in toward the port, two Italian sailors lay flat on the bow of the boat with automatic rifles trained in the direction of the shore. The British Lt. Commander and our Lt. Manzani got in a rubber boat to row ashore and look over the situation. If they gave the signal, we were to get out — fast — and leave them. Livermore had a walkie talkie on the bridge and I was standing behind him. All the rest were on deck. They gave the signal to come in and we entered the small port and moored stern to the mole. Behind the small port were the hills and the small village nestled on their sides.

The island is a small penal colony. The population was about one hundred, exclusive of sixty prisoners, forty guards, five regular soldiers, one Carabinieri — and seven Blackshirts who were being paid by the Germans from Livorno (the only ones on the Island receiving any money). After my experience with Giglio, the Blackshirts were the ones not to trust. Pete, Tom and I went immediately to the prison headquarters and cut the telephone lines on the Island by pulling out all fifty fuses. Then we went to the Post Office and seized documents and mail headed for Italy. Livermore came up with the men as they were inspecting the prison records and we decided to head for the Torre Vecchio (on the western side of the Island) where the Blackshirts were. We set out on foot.

It was a walk of about thirty-five minutes — all up hill. The old tower was beautiful — setting on the crest of the hill as we approached, beyond it a steep cliff dropping precipitously to the sea. It must have been several hundred years old. We knocked and finally aroused the head of the Blackshirts. We entered and put a guard on their arsenal of grenades and rifles and went up to the radio room. We seized the radio and I got the codebooks and messages. I took a small bayonet for a souvenir on the way out. After questioning the men, we came to the conclusion that it would be best to take the Blackshirts along. We left a guard and proceeded to the semaphore tower. This tower, about 300 yards to the south, was on the highest point of the Island. From it one can see the city of Livorno and the coast around Spezia on a clear day. Large fixed binoculars were already on the Island that would be used by our men to observe. After going through the semaphore and picking up things such as letters and railroad time tables that might be useful from an intelligence standpoint, we returned to the town. We stopped on the way at one of the prison cells and Tom and Wood talked to a couple of the prisoners to try to determine if any were political internees. They weren't. One of those they talked to was in for murder, the other for rape. The supposed murderer said he'd been framed. The rapist said he, too, was framed — besides he didn't get any satisfaction out of it.

The beauty of these mountainous islands is impossible to describe. It is most fantastic. The British Commander met us and said a strong northeast wind was coming up and we had better hurry. We returned to the boat, put the prisoners in the bow hold and set off. That is, we started to. The Italians in the crew — already nervous at being so close to Tedischi country — pulled up the anchor, only the anchor stayed on the bottom and only the dangling end of the rope came up. The boat started to drift toward the rocks, and we all thought of the prospects of being marooned on the damned island for a day or two. Finally, they maneuvered the boat out to open water and we really got under way (the anchor may still be there for all that I know).

We reached a point opposite Cap Corse about 4 A.M. but idled around until daylight because we were afraid our own guns might fire on us if we entered during darkness. We returned to the port right after daybreak, turned the prisoners over to the French for custody and returned home for breakfast: coffee, powdered eggs, and bread.

The next day we questioned the prisoners. It did not seem that they were giving us all the dope, so we got a couple of husky sergeants and told them to make threatening gestures and noises to the others while each was being questioned. This proved dangerous to our humane reputations, for the first one or two were forcibly shoved into the room, and the sergeants gave every evidence of being more than willing to put their hands, as well as their hearts, into the work. I got qualms of conscience about this and told the sergeant to be sure not to touch them, but to work on them psychologically. He did not appreciate this fine distinction. The Blackshirts turned out to be old militia for the most part, who lost their stomach for war. We got some information out of them, however.

The next day I started for Ajaccio with Clinton. He had been recalled to Algiers and was going to drive down and turn over to me contacts at Ajaccio with the Italian Communist Party and a certain forger. We started out in a driving rainstorm. Got a flat. A lug would not come off and he hopped a ride back to Bastia on a truck to send out help. Sitting there alone in the car in the black dark of a stormy night in Corsican mountains can play tricks on one's imagination. I more than once fingered my gun. After 3½ hours some men came out and changed the tire, however, and I drove back to Bastia in the storm.

The next day we started out at about 11 A.M.. We took along two bottles of Champagne and some corned beef and crackers for food. A beautiful trip and nice weather, all things considered. On this drive you see the bridges that have been blown up by the Germans and the effects of our bombing and artillery fire.

At Ajaccio I took over the above-mentioned contacts amid a lot of interesting movie type hocus pocus. Joe Bonfiglio was there with the radio operator for the Elba job. I said why not drive back with me. I was still inexperienced as a driver, but what the hell? We started out about two in the afternoon. They told us the roads were washed out, as were the bridges, above Corte, and that there were landslides. I said I was willing to start out if my passengers were, as I was most anxious to get back. So we did. We ran into fog in the mountains and one bridge that was wobbly. However, we managed to cross it and finally get back to Bastia about 7:30. This was a real drive and my nerves had been strained the whole time — I was surprised that nothing happened (for we had no spare, a slow leak and no patches). The car was a Peugeot with automatic shift (four speeds forward and four speeds in reverse), besides innumerable gadgets that we didn't know what to do with and a clutch for starting and stopping.

A couple of nights later two German destroyers shelled Bastia from a point off the coast. Everyone now is in fear of a commando raid. We have practically no troops up here, that is American or English, and the French have only a few Goums. We have a Fighter Wing, and the British have some MTB's and we have some PT's—that's all. There is no plan as far as I can find out as to what to do if the Germans raid us in force. So it might just have to work out. All of us have urged that a plan be evolved in the event of such a raid, but it is no go so far.

The taking over of the Communist contacts went like this: We had the name Peter (in Italian or French) who was to be the contact man. However, before we get to him, we had to look up another man. We found him living behind a bicycle repair shop on the third floor of an old building. We went in and gave as the password that we came "on the part of _____." He invited us to enter and we sat in a small kitchen with his wife and another man present. We say we're looking for Peter. He nods, and finally, after a glass of very bad wine and other amenities, while he sized us up, he gives us the address. We then go there. A little house on the outskirts of town. There are many people around. We inquire for Peter and a man comes forward. We stroll off a bit and tell him we had been recommended to him and he might know men willing to undertake missions in enemy territory. He says perhaps. He says he is going to Bastia soon and I say fine, he can see me there. He says he had difficulty getting about in Bastia last time, and I say he can get a pass saying he is in our employ allowing him to circulate freely. We then go. Clinton arranges with Lt. Crane to give the pass very secretly.

In Bastia we get on track of a guy who represents an Italian coalition party in the north. He is quite a fellow. We evolve a plan to get people in and for this group to give us several houses that are safe and other assistance inside. There is already underway a para-military plan, and I take precaution not to burn this and assure the chap we are interested only in intelligence and also political intelligence. In subsequent talks he shows that he is interested in the political backing of the United States. I tell him that our first consideration is one thing: The War. However, I continue that information we may secure may help to form our government's position. I do say that his principal inside North Italy can communicate with him through our channels when set up. I limit this, however, strictly to the fact that this can be used only to present the true picture of conditions in North Italy, and not as a channel for opinion.

Bastia, Corsica
January 5, 1944

Well, there is a fair amount now. We had the job across the way (Elba) set for New Years Eve, but a gale came up, so we couldn't do it. In the meantime a rather cryptic message arrived from Algiers that there were ten people to be picked up at the mouth of a little river on the west coast of Italy a little south of Giglio. It was given to me to take care of. A green light was to be flashed from shore and passwords were given. I went to the Special Ops commander here for a boat and it was laid on. Then I checked with intelligence and found there were four machine gun positions 500 yards north. Some fun! This was to be on January 2–3 between twelve and four in the morning. A PT was to carry it out. Our job on the island across the way was set for January 3–4 and I thought I would get two trips in two days. But at the last minute our job was put on for January 2–3 and I had to turn the pick-up over to Dewitt.

We set out at 11 P.M. The moon was to set at 12:30 and we were to idle in until we reached there at 2. We were in an Italian MAS boat. Two days before two ships were blown up just outside the harbor and no patrols were going out regularly. No commando raid has materialized as yet. No air raids for several weeks, though another LCT blew up inside the harbor a few days before and a gas dump blew up just yesterday.

Well, we had two American Italians in uniform to put on the Island. One Italian whom we put in an Italian uniform who knew the Island completed the team. Three containers, the radio and twelve blankets with three shelter halves. Two rubber boats were to go in. I would be in the bow of the first one with a .45 and a Marlin. Tom would row and one of the bodies and two containers would complete the load. The next boat would carry the rest, plus an Englishman loaned to us to row the boat. We went in. Dark cliffs greeted us, but a light was spotted on one of them nearby. We went in anyway. It was all rock. We could not spot the stream that was our landmark. But we knew this had to be the place. I got off and climbed on the rocks. I put the gun down and turned to take off the containers, knee deep in water and uncertain footing, and the waves coming it.

Cold as hell, though I didn't notice the temperature particularly at the time. I found the boat had backed off and was several rocks away to the south. I scrambled to it and got one container and placed it safely on the shore of rocks. Then I turned again. This time the boat was further down. I scrambled to it again, fell and sprained a finger and got to it in time to get the other container. That done, it was my job to make a reconnaissance. Then I couldn't find the gun. I said to hell with it for a moment and started up the steep pile of rocks. I gained a ridge about 100 feet up, and there, to the left, I could see clearly the stream that was our landmark. The mouth of the stream was covered by rocks and the water just trickled through — thus what was visible on the air photos as a stream was completely masked when looking at it from the sea. I scouted around up there a bit and then went back. I spotted several places the containers could be hidden in and joined the party once more. All was unloaded.

The Englishman got his boat off okay. But Tom and I had a hell of a time getting ours off. We did it finally, though. The MAS was not several hundred yards off behind a promontory. I could see the shadow of it dimly. We started for it. Tom had difficulty since the oarlocks had been greased and his hands slipped on the oars. The Englishman, a sailor and expert at this, came over to us and suggested I get in his boat to ease Tom's load. So I changed from one rubber boat to the other. (Was this me?) Tom still had difficulty, so we rowed over and I grabbed the painter from this boat. We returned to the MAS and clambered on board. The next morning we arrived back at 7 A.M.

We heard from the boys the next morning (a record short time!) They said they were okay so far and were going on up to Mount Capanne. That afternoon we heard from them again, this time they were still climbing but sent some intelligence. Again the next day a message containing good dope came in. Our first job conceived, planned and executed. If it continues to hold up, we're very lucky. Hope it will.

The other pick-up turned out to be an Italian general and a couple of Italian naval captains and other officers. They had a lot of good dope but some of it was so hot we had to send them back to Algiers by special plane.

Bastia, Corsica
January 6, 1944

This morning I made the run to Capraia with supplies. This means I've been to almost 100 percent of the islands around here from Elba up and on Giglio below. If I get to Pianosa and Monte Crisco, my record will be complete. It was cold as hell and the sea kicked up plenty of water, soaking me to the skin on the way over. A two-hour ride at about 35 knots. We passed Elba and could see the Italian mainland and Gorgona in the distance. The boat does a terrific speed — it was one of the MAS boats. We passed through the mine fields — the idea being that such a small boat with its speed would not crack a mine. One just stands on deck, behind the bridge in my case, and tries to turn one's head when the sea comes up over the head — in large quantities. The spray kicks up to about twenty feet or more and when the boat hits a wave it sort of skids like a horse putting both feet forward going down a steep hill and skidding along. Coming back, I was wise and sat in the wheelhouse. This has glass around it and is pretty swell. Once again I did not get seasick — I guess I can consider myself immune pretty soon.

Our Elba boys broke the record for quick contacts and so far have been sending excellent dope. Hope it keeps up.

It is interesting to note that here in Corsica we have only a long wave radio but we are not near enough for it to get any Allied station — all we can get is German and Italian Fascist stations. The music is good, though.

We finally have some A/A here. Some 90's and 75's. This will probably discourage the Germans from raiding here for the radar equipment is installed. There are always phone calls asking if our outfit is running anything on the west coast, etc. because firing has been spotted or some ship nearing the coast.

Mines are pretty bad still — and the harbor is not safe for shipping generally, which has complicated the supply system. The Germans still have a couple of destroyers around these waters — much heavier than anything we have.

It is funny to think that all I put down as interesting in the first six or seven months would be more than prosaic compared to any moment in the past three or four months. Yet I can't seem to think of anything to put down. It just happens — and that is that.

There is a theory, I suppose, that commissions to people under thirty-eight from civilian life will just keep them at desks. So the War Department turned down my commission and this has been the first thing to make me a bit bitter. I am not exactly doing a pantywaist job here and yet I can't be commissioned because of this damned rule. I don't really give a damn, though, as long as I am doing a job that I feel to be a real job.

I am too tired to appreciate and get a kick out of it all now, though. If I had gotten into this sort of thing a half-year ago, I would have been getting a tremendous kick out of it. But those first eight or nine months took almost all capacity for enthusiasm out of me.

The frustrating work at Algiers and the disillusionment of seeing good men kicked around and high policy in all its expedient cynicism takes a lot out of a guy. When the heat is on, I think I have proven that I can take it — at least so far — but my moments of enthusiasm are short. I'm tired. And it is a damned shame, too. For I think I have as much capacity normally as anyone for getting a kick out of things. I'm tired as hell. I'm debating within myself right now as to whether to ask for a leave when my year is up. The only deterrent is that now I'm doing a job I've wanted to do. There is a chance that it will get over — and I'll certainly be to a large extent responsible if the plans we have evolved for North Italy's infiltration go through. I would also have a major operational share in those plans. Yet I'm too tired to put up a fight for personal recognition (which I don't care about, except that everyone else seems to thrive on the use of the first personal singular). Whether I'm too tired to do a good job, I don't know. I'm afraid that a tough spot might come up and my reaction would be to say, "Aw, to hell with it," instead of fighting to the last ditch. From all that, I should try to get leave. Yet if I try to get leave — and get it — I may be leaving just when the ball is going over the goal line, which might be throwing away all the work I've done. I guess I'll stick, but I don't know if I'm right or not.

Bastia, Corsica
January 7, 1944

Sitting here in Bastia by the fire on a cold-as-hell day. I was at the Florida last night, one of the two officers clubs in town. It's referred to as an "Allied Officers' Club." There were three British naval officers at the end of the bar being very quiet. I know that they are assigned to minesweeping that means dragging for mines, bringing them in or exploding them. Occasionally, of course, as happened to one minesweeper last week, the mine explodes the sweeper. They sip their drinks quietly, occasionally dancing with one of the girls around the place.

Further up the bar are two British naval officers and one army officer.

They are engaged in our type of work. Every other night or so they are at the enemy coast on special missions. Putting "bodies" ashore, etc. One of them was repulsed by enemy shore batteries the other night and is a bit low because the mission failed. These guys are hard drinkers and boisterous.

Down the bar are two French officers who are with one of the Moroccan (Goum) regiments. They are quiet, but lend of a touch of loud color with their repies and fawn-colored trousers. Then there is Vinnie Russo, one of the original thirty-four in Corsica who saw action against the Germans here, hurt his leg in trial parachuting and is relegated to being our Administrative officer in Bastia.

Over at a table near the piano there is a young blond girl who is lovely and has legs that are not thin (as most are around here) and breasts that are the focus of all male eyes in the place-and that's an understatement! Her face is sweet and pretty from across the room. Standing next to the piano and watching her dance, however, one notices that while she is young and pretty, the sweetness has been tempered by a bit of something or other.

At another table there are four fighter pilots and three American nurses. They look tired and work too hard in that cold barn of a field hospital up the mountain. It is the damndest place I ever saw. To get there, you wind around and around, and up and up, to the top of the mountain. And there, in a barren, bleak, cold building you find what they call a "hospital." The pilots are Air Corps boys and all young, even the major. They are boisterous and ready to raise hell. They are conscious that they face death often and glamorously and they want the world at large to realize it.

At another table is a young PT officer, just a kid, having a drink with one of the local "floosies" who hang around the Florida. His father is a director of a large company who was a defendant in a case in which I once worked for months. He got his first taste of action the other day so I'd guess that at the moment he feels a bit grown-up, if self consciously so. The girl he is with is probably "sympathique"—of course, older than he, and vastly more experienced in many ways of the world.

At another table there are three French officers from the French commando unit at St. Florent with two local floosies. The two girls are like so many of them around the Florida—sleepy-eyed, brunette or bleached with rather square shoulders and thin legs.

Over at the piano, playing, is an A/A captain. The guy used to play sax in an orchestra but can also do himself proud (at least up here) on the piano. Sitting in a corner near him is the regular Florida pianist. He's an older man with gray hair, a limp and a cane. He can't compete with this new stuff from America, nor can he understand it. The extent of his repertoire is a jumpy version of Strauss waltzes, and a mechanical and prosaic version of European popular music and a few songs imported from America many years ago.

A couple of well-groomed, clean-cut RAF officers in blue-gray battle dress are standing near the piano. Whereas all the Americans and other British are dressed in field jackets and some faces and clothes are not clean, these two could fit into a London bar at the moment.

Hanging around, drunk as hell, are three PT officers. I've been out with all of them. Each has seen much action, and when they go out they must be alert every second. In the dark of night, on a mine-infested sea, also infested with E boats and destroyers, with the ever-present danger of enemy planes, radar and shore batteries all over the place, they patrol the enemy coasts and take our missions — often to within a few hundred yards of the shore. A swell bunch of fellows.

I'm an observer of all of this in some respects since I have no commission, but I am also part of it. With our British opposite numbers and the PT boys, I am a kindred soul. But at least I'm off the bench and on the field, in contra-distinction to last February and March when a lot of other guys were going up to Tunisia and I had my pants glued to a chair in Algiers.

Oh, yes, behind the bar is Rini. She is a plump woman with brown hair. She is pleasant and good-natured looking and has vast good humor. She is a prize; she knows how to handle the guys when they get drunk, and does so in excellent humor. Anybody who serves in Bastia during this "pioneer" period will probably remember Rini.

Further, there is the proprietor. He is tall and thin and wears dark, tortoise shell glasses. He has a high forehead and hairline and looks a good deal like Lanza di Trabia. He hovers around the edges of the room with an eye on everything that goes on and everyone who comes in. Occasionally he sits and talks quietly with some of the French officers or local citizens. When the joint closes, he will be behind the bar with Rini, going over the day's accounts.

This is the Florida at Bastia. In a city that might easily be called the furthest outpost of our forces in the theater. Geographically, anyway — the Fifth Army is still well below Rome.

Bastia, Corsica
January 8, 1944

Well, we went on a boar hunt today. Tom had had this in mind for some time and, as it came off, Tom, Croft, Johnson (Wing Commander "Johnnie"), Buist, Commandant Giusti and myself were the personnel, with the Mayor of the Village of Casta ("O'Cass") and one Columbanni as hosts and hunt-masters.

Giusti, the mayor and I left Bastia at 2 P.M. We took 2¾ hours to reach Casta (normally a one-hour drive). This was because Giusti or the mayor knew everyone in Corsica (and I do mean everyone) and we had to stop all along the way. In St. Florent we met the mayor on the street — a Barry Fitzgerald character-and others. I believe there are no more picturesque characters in this world than the Corsicans — the men, in particular, with their mustaches, shotguns, corduroy suits, leather boots, dark piercing eyes under slouch felt hats or caps.

Of course, at every place we had to stop and sit and have a glass (or two) of wine. We finally reached this old, broken-down stone house near Casta, where we were to stay the night.

We sat before a fire in the huge stone fireplace and talked before dinner. Some remarks were made about leaving Bastia this night, when a convoy came in and there might be a raid. Conversations then turned for a moment to theatre, then to hunting. Then Arctic exploration (Croft had been an explorer, and Tom had had some experience in that line). Much joking about joining the "garlic circuit" — as odors or garlic emanated from the kitchen.

Dinner commenced with soup. Then some sort of croquettes with Port and garlic (much of the later). A nice local rose wine. Then some cold meat with olives and mushrooms. Bread. Goat cheese and large oranges. Then we sat around the fire and drank coffee, American, which we had brought.

(I must remark that in meeting the commandant's friends en route here today, I have probably shaken the hand of more Corsicans than any living American.)

Then, about 9, we retire to our various rooms. I'm writing this now by the light of a taper in a pitcher. The room is small. There are several religious pictures on the wall. One iron-frame bed. A small table with a water pitcher and wash-bowl. One straight chair. And a pot under the bed.

The houses are unbelievably poor in external appearance. Stone, showing much age. The people are war-beaten. But if the men, at least, are beaten in spirit they do not show it. They are born actors, the Corsicans. The women all look like character women in a hillbilly play. All except the youngsters, and, if they have any chance at all, Corsican girls are good-looking. After the age of about 26 though they age suddenly. All work and no trimmings. Too bad. We are in the heart of the path the Germans cut across Corsica. Everywhere are the signs of war (it is only a couple of months since the Germans left). A wall may be broken here, or a part of a house out there due to artillery fire. Practically all the bridges around here are blown. Shell craters dot the roads.

And tomorrow we "hunt the 'wild boar'." The title of this piece should be "The Boar Hunt, or War is Hell, Ain't It?"

Bastia, Corsica
January 9, 1944

Still in Casa. The room where the rats woke me up at 6 A.M. this morning when it was still dark. I thought that if it were time to wake up, the lady of the house would wake me, as promised. So I waited to be summoned to get up. Some time later, Pete came rushing in and said everyone else was ready to go (it was 7 o'clock).

After sitting by the fire a while, we got breakfast: One fried egg (a great treat for us), café au lait (that is 60 percent or 70 percent boiled milk) and local sausage (which I did not have, but which the others enjoyed immensely).

The boar hunt started by getting into an English truck, an Italian jeep and a French car. Then a long climb up a hill — of mountainous proportions. When anyone was about to give out we would stop for a while — this happens twice. Everyone gets a position, about fifty yards apart in a line along the side of the hill. The dogs are across the valley. Pete is the only one who sees a boar, but it comes from an unexpected side, and his shots miss the boar, and — fortunately — the rest of us. No boar is shot. We return to Casta about sundown.

After a long and excellent dinner, all the others retire except Buist and myself. And the Corsicans of course. We start singing French songs.

Then an old toothless Corsican bandit gets up and sings some of the old monotone, minor key folk songs of Corsica. This was a Hemingway scene. Buist and I order several bottles of wine for the crowd as the evening goes on. We apparently are accepted as okay when they produce Cognac. A second unsuccessful hunt the next day and back to Bastia. Vacation in war!

5

Operations from Bastia

American PT's of Squadron 15 and a flotilla of British motor gun-boats and motor launches of the African Coastal Forces moved up from Sardinia and had begun to operate out of Bastia by the end of October, both for naval sorties and for clandestine operations. In addition, a flotilla of five Italian MAS boats, manned by volunteer Italian crews from Maddalena, was also made available for the latter. Although the Italian boats had the advantages of low silhouette, high speed (up to fifty knots) and special auxiliary engines to permit silent maneuvering off pinpoints, the American PT's were used for the majority of operations. The radar of the American boats was important for defense and navigation, and their range made it possible to reach as far west as Toulon and as far south as the Tiber River.*

En Route From Corsica to Sardinia
13 January 1944

This is written on a C-47 going from Ajaccio (Corsica) to Alghera (Sardinia) on a recruiting trip. It is exactly one year since I left the States. By a curious coincidence, there is on this plane a captain who was on the boat with me and who I have not seen since we landed at Oran.

I left Bastia the day before yesterday and drove to Corte with Joe and a native Italian. We stopped there and recruited a couple of Italian soldier radio operators. They will be detached to our service. Joe then took them back to Bastia.

I came on to Ajaccio with Commandant Giusti in a civilian car.

Giusti and I had some interesting talks about songs, and took turns singing French and American and (he) Corsican songs.

*War Report of the OSS

Giusti, an American lieutenant, Weeks (who was flying a plane to meet the General in Algiers) and I went to the local hot spot, the Cavot Parisienne (formerly the Canary Club) after dinner. We drank Courvoisier. I expressed a question that still puzzled me about Corsica — why a man could cross the room and ask a girl he did not know, and who might be with another man, to dance. Giusti explained that this did not mean the girls were prostitutes or "on the loose." Rather, that it was an old custom that at any public party (a night club being so considered) it is an insult if a girl does not dance with a man who asks her to, whether accompanied by another or not.

At the table behind me were a couple of very drunk American lieutenants trying to talk to a tall, sullen faced, big lipped and high hipped blond. They could not make themselves understood, so I was called on to translate. One guy was trying, I thought, to say something about "couchere." I thought the girl was trying to remonstrate with them, for she said, "He wants to spend the night with me. That is not possible." I started to patiently explain to the drunken lieutenants what Giusti had told me, that girls in a Corsican night club would dance when asked but that did not mean that they were whores. The girl supposedly guessed what I was saying, for she interrupted me in French and said, "He wants to spend the night with me. That is impossible. But if he wants to spend 15 or 20 minutes —?" I said (mentally laughing at myself). "I see." So I translated this. And she interrupted to say that both of them could come along. And they said fine. And she said 500 francs each. And they hiccupped fine. And they went to her house — she leaving a few minutes before them and meeting them outside — discretion, you know. And while they were waiting in this "discreet" interim they asked me to have a drink with them, and I laughed and said "Thanks, no. I'd feel too much like a pimp." I returned to Giusti and Weeks and told them the tale, and we all laughed like hell, and agreed that the guys were suckers to pay that price, and we later went back to the Hotel des Estrangeres Annex, our HQ in Ajaccio.

The following day I went around with Giusti, meeting a lot of French people whom I will never remember, but improving my few words of French, however slightly. We stopped at a sidewalk café and had good eau de vie and bad coffee, then to a Cercle Privee and had Pernod before dinner. Then to dinner, and I turned in early, for I had to get the plane I am now on at 7:30 A.M.

So I'm in this C-47 flying over the Mediterranean between the southwest part of Corsica and the northwest part of Sardinia. Voila!

Bastia, Corsica
14 January 1944

I don't know whether I have mentioned that I don't like the bombing of civilians, whether they are our enemies or not and have had arguments with others, our people and military officers, about this subject.

Sassari, Sardinia
14 January 1944

This morning I woke (tired and early) at about 9, but did not get up until 11. Went to a local barber for a shave. Noticed the kids here all cry for "piccola-piccola." This means cigarette butts. They'll follow someone who is smoking for blocks, waiting for him to throw the cigarette away. You feel guilty if you step on the butt after you drop it; you feel guilty if you don't. Finally found the HQ of the Allied Commission. Found that the HQ of the two Italian regiments (a person in each of which I particularly wished to see) had not yet been definitely placed. However, it was thought that one of them (at least) was in a small town named Macomer, about 45 km. from Sassari. Tried to get transportation, but could not. Went to lunch with the Allied Commission officers here.

There had been a riot in progress when I arrived yesterday, a foot riot. The crowd in front of the Allied Commission HQ building, yelling and pounding on the huge barred doors, had not seemed hostile. Rather their shouts were for the Americans and British to take over the Island and (this seemed to be their particular gripe) they wanted the prefect to be put out of office, calling at the same time for the removal of all Fascists.

I have finally (and I write this hesitantly) been so immersed in some form of action, that my own recollection of— hating, and I do mean "hating" this type of our action when something is "almost" won does not seem quite so near. But it seems "near" enough to trouble me. And perhaps to handicap my doing something worthwhile. It's like this: I finally went to lunch with Captain Parrott (Public Security Officer of the Allied Advisory Commission; British). We went to the combined British and American officers mess. Everyone is, of course, charming. Everyone is a gentleman (whether inherently or not). Parrott's idea was that his predecessor (Captain Fields, an old Scotland Yard man, whom I met at Maddalena and thought a good fellow) had taken things too seriously. He (Parrott) thought that it would be well if the people did starve for a while and be maltreated because the Fascists were still in office. I didn't say anything at the moment, but turned the conversation to the theatre and sports. (Fortunately there was a British major at lunch who had always been interested in the stage — he was a good stooge), but I felt the implication of Parrott's remarks. I had, it is true, before I became polite and a good guest and turned the conversation, made some rather caustic cracks about what sort of ideals we were fighting for, etc., but I didn't follow it up.

Finally, after a bit of wrangling during the afternoon, I got a car to take me to Macomer. Tony (Cambino) and I went. Finally, after trying several places, we found out where Winspere (Italian medical doctor) was. We went up to his little room and had coffee as we talked. I explained to him that I was a friend of Al's and he brightened visibly. I got from him a number of safe houses around Livorno. As I was about to bring up the subject, he reiterated what he had told Al — that he would be glad to go on a mission himself. "A vostro disposito," were his words. I more or less recruited him, subject to obtaining an appropriate covered release from the Italian army. And from my impression of him, this was a successful conclusion (if it were a conclusion) of my trip.

(I forgot to mention that this morning when I got up, there had been another riot and a few people shot. All the officers at the mess at lunch were talking about the "revolution" and joking about "how many were shot and killed." I don't know whether I can express here the feeling of semi-revulsion that they should in a sense seek to justify their own "cushy" existence here in wartime by taking a small threat of danger so seriously, or semi-revulsion that they should not take more seriously the plight of the people, who should be their responsibility (even if Italy is termed a "co-belligerent"). At any rate I hope I'm trying (all one can try to do is "try") to keep something of an even balance in my outlook on this war. I know that my balance in action is not complete — that from a standpoint of security I should not be doing a lot of the things that I have done. And yet I know that I would quit if I were not allowed to. I've gotten a lot of breaks; but a lot have been "breaks" I helped to make.

At any rate, I got back to town this evening and went to the officers mess. No one was there. So I hunted up the restaurant where Tony and Vince Pavia would be. They finally showed up, and we had dinner. The proprietor liked to sing opera. I led the applause. He sang snatches of many arias. We went from the restaurant to a club (a private club); there had been an 8 o'clock curfew installed tonight in the city due to the riots and demonstrations yesterday and today, and played at an Italian type of billiards. I had hoped to meet a certain Italian doctor there who might be recruited, but apparently he had gone back to Maddalena (he is the same doctor who gave us a great deal of dope on the Giglio job).

Then we went to an Italian apartment to eat "fratelli," a type of doughnut. We ate fratelli and drank wine. And I returned to the hotel.

I stood for about 15 minutes looking out of the window. The street is half-lit by a couple of dim lamps. There is a half-demolished building across the street. An air-raid shelter is, rather tardily, under construction. It will probably never be finished. (There is no reason why it should be finished for this war.) And I began to realize, as one often realizes here or anywhere "back" here, how we do not sometimes really consider how much we are in the "front lines" up in Bastia. Or, come to think of it, how much more "at the front" are others on the mainland.

Ajaccio, Corsica
16 January 1944

Just got back to Ajaccio from Sassari. Went yesterday to hunt up the other of the two Italian officers — this one a lieutenant in the artillery — younger, but expressing himself as willing, one Piero Maggini. He is, I am sure, a good guy. The only impediment to using him is getting him released from the Italian army with security (for many of their higher officers do not really want us to win) and the fact that he is young, about 32, which makes him squarely of military age and subject to military or labor conscription by the Germans on the continent.

To find him I had to take the jeep from Sassari down to Macomer, over to Sindia (a little group of hovels where this chap was stationed and where we talked to him in a dirty little room), then around through winding roads, up and down mountains, to Alghero Airport. There I made arrangements to get a plane to Ajaccio.

When we got ready to go, the plane was piloted by two young second lieutenants. The passengers were five enlisted men, a warrant officer, a British Lt. Colonel, two American majors, a Signal Corps 2nd Lt. and myself. Just as they were revving up the motors preparatory to take-off, something in their sound was noticed by the crew. They found time that would be necessary for repairs, so we had to lay over for the night. We went to the officers mess, where they had a bar and slept on the couches there. The British colonel (name of Stewart) and I had a good conversation — politics, poetry, philosophy, etc. His name was Charles Stewart, about 36 or 37, a good egg and I hope to see more of him.

The plane was fixed by 11 A.M., so we took off immediately after lunch and got here about 1 hour later.

(It may be noted that when the plane took off this morning even the cocky little warrant officer fastened his safety belt.)

Found that Pete had not waited for me, but had gone on up to Bastia, and am now wondering what sort of transportation I can get.

Ajaccio, Corsica
16 January 1944

I am sitting in the headquarters room of the Hotel des Etrangeres Annex, our place in Ajaccio. The radio is on — a German station. A violin is playing a sloppy version of the Meditation from Thais. And this brings to mind the curious phenomenon of war that men in war will go immediately from sloppy sentiment to raucous bawdry in choosing music. There must, I suppose, be extremes in a world of war where life, death and suffering follow upon each other so suddenly. For instance, the way air raids come up. You are doing something or other — eating, sleeping, working, drinking, playing cards — and a siren sounds. It is followed, at any interval from 10 seconds to 20 minutes, by the sound of guns and bombs, quite often, if they are diving, by the hornet-buzz of planes. Fear is not generally shown, but quite often it is felt; and the result is that a lot of guys play or eat or drink or do whatever they are doing just a bit harder afterwards.

Or take one of those occasions when Bastia was shelled by destroyers. I was at the Florida. It was about 1 A.M. We heard the firing without warning, and the explosions of hitting shells. People stopped drinking for a moment. What the hell is it? Doesn't sound like bombs? The women show a bit of fear and so do some others. Some show their fear by exaggerated fear or jest.

Or on a PT at night. You go along just sitting there in the small charthouse below the bridge. The hatch is open and you can see the legs of the officer on the bridge, practically beside your nose. You have a cigarette cupped in your hand. You watch the ever-whirling radar circle across the cabin casually. An island 20 miles away whirls lazily toward the outer edge of the circle. Half the crew is asleep below. The other half are above, relaxed but ever alert. Suddenly the officer on the bridge throttles down the engines and calls tensely through the hatch, "Action stations." The motors idle softly and the silence is terrific. The rest of the crew come up, buttoning helmets and storm jackets. The officer calls for a bearing — everything is ready for action. The result may be a battle, or it may be one of the many false alarms. But you soon learn that if you accept the old tale of "Wolf" too often, you're courting Davey Jones.

*   *   *

This is written after arriving home and having cocoa and fruit juice, about 6:30 A.M.

The climax to the above was going to sleep curled up on a corner of the bunk. In a few minutes we hit the rough water out of the lea of the shore and opened up speed. We had to stay out till after 5 A.M. because other boats were out (Allied), but might fire on us; in addition, the Goums manning the shore batteries have itchy trigger fingers. Therefore, we had to spend a couple of hours extra on the sea with the possibility of E boats, German planes and mines. So, as I was saying, just as I got to sleep we picked up speed and hit rough water. The waves bounced the boat so much that I went up in the air two or three feet and came down with a thud. This nearly knocked me out, and if it did not, the ensuing bouncing around damned near did.

We were challenged a couple of times from shore stations on Corsica, and fired Very pistols with recognition flares.

Then when we got to the dock, we found that the soldier who was to have waited for us in a car did not do so. He had waited about 20 minutes and then gave up. So we had to walk all the way up to the Villa Mimosa at 5:15 A.M. I was carrying my wet pants and leggings — it was cold as hell — and had my overcoat on over my OD shirt and Tom's overlarge long drawers. Some sight!

This was the second straight night I was out. The day before this, I arrived from Ajaccio at 3:30 P.M. to find Richmond No. 2 prepared and being held for me if I got here in time. This operation involved putting six bodies ashore (including one woman) at a pinpoint at Fossa del

Tafone (just below Giannutri). Merely a conducting officer job, as I was not allowed to land (Winney had known the pinpoint before and was free). The job kept me out till 6:30 A.M., however; and yesterday had to be used in final preparations for last night's job. No particular incident, though no one really knows yet just how well the coast around there is fortified. We did run across an F lighter and an E boat escort, but no fight. They were hugging the shore. Lost the covering PT en route and let her go.

On Richmond 2, an interesting sidelight is that one of the PT sailors said to me, "Don't see how you fellows get along without a complete change of personnel every week or so — I'd think your nerves would be shattered to hell in no time, doing this sort of thing. Just standing off the coast waiting for you guys gives me the willies." A PT guy, too! Well, they think we're screwy — and we think they're screwy in some of the things they do. Maybe we're both right! Maybe the whole world is screwy!

Bastia, Corsica
21 January 1944

The night before last I played bridge, night before that I was on Elba, night before that on Richmond 2; last night I went down to Fossa del Tafone on Richmond 3.

This was a job to put in 8 agents (brought up from the Fifth Army sector; including a woman) and take out agents and any P/W's that could make the rendezvous.

It developed that only one P/W came out. He was a young corporal in a British artillery regiment who had been captured in Libya 18 months ago. He had escaped 3 times and been recaptured twice. The last time he was put on a train to be taken to Germany, but managed to get out of a window. He found a girl who fell in love with him. He spent the last couple of months hiding in the fields and forest by day and eating and sleeping at night at her family's house. He said, "I'll tell you, sir, if you are captured, sir, have some girl fall in love with you, sir. And you'll be all right." This was on the MAS boat. All we had to offer him in Bastia were C rations and a cot and blanket.

Two MAS boats did the job; we communicated by handy-talkie — about 100 yards apart till 2 miles off the coast, where the second boat stayed to observe and cover, while we went in.

Observed many flashes on the Italian coast on the way down; probably Allied air raids.

Of course we know that "Shingle" Operation (Anzio)—the invasion of the coast which is to take Rome—is coming off in a day or two, and one of the people we put in last night was an American en route to set up a sending station in Rome. (Pete Tompkins.)

I concocted a line for Winney's technique in receiving a woman in a rubber boat: "He fastens his arms firmly around her buttocks, sticks his nose in her navel, and lets her slide gently until her breasts are parallel with his eyes—whereupon he lets her drop!"

We left at 5:45 P.M. Idled out of the channel through the minefields. Then hit 30 knots until just west of Giannutri, where we turned southeast. Just south of Giannutri we went on auxiliary motors and idled in at about 6 knots. The other boat followed at about 100–150 yards.

Tom Stoneborough, Colonel Russell Livermore, "Bo" Wentworth and Wayne Nelson, Bastia, Corsica, January 1944.

Sample conversation over handy-talkie: "Follow us in. Can you made 6 knots on your auxiliaries? Over." "We will try. Over." "Stay not more than 150 yards from us and keep a sharp lookout. Over." (There was a code station spouting morse on the same frequency, making it difficult to understand.) Please repeat. Could not get your last message. Over." "I said—follow us at not more than 150 yards. Keep a sharp lookout. Keep a sharp lookout and cover us. Come in if you see anything. Come in if you see anything. Over." "Check. Will do."

So we idle in, looking for the signal from shore. I am at the left of the bridge with the handy-talkie. Next to me, on the bridge, is Winney. Next to him is Ginger Cosalitch, the Italian skipper. His words can be heard occasionally over the drone of the motors as he gives instructions down to the wheelhouse: "Via destia." "Via sinistra." "Via diretto."

The shoreline looms as a dim silhouette ahead of us. There is a flash to our port. But it is far away. And another flash off in the darkness. Probably an air raid. Eyes, apart from those on the bridge, are scanning the horizon to port, starboard and astern — for there is no radar on these MAS boats.

The signal is to be a green light flashing steadily for 10 seconds every 10 minutes. We started to idle in at 8:45. At 11:15 we spot the light. Over the handy-talkie: "Are you there? Are you there? Over." "Yes. Do you have a message for us? Over." "Yes. Stand out here and wait. We are going in. Cover us, and let us know if you see anything. Over." "Check. Good luck."

At 11:40 we are 150 yards off the shore, the rubber boats are loaded and go in. At 12:15 the bodies are landed, and those to be brought out are on board. We follow the same course out and pick up the covering MAS on the way. It follows us back to Bastia, where we arrive at 5:15 A.M. Two cars are at the dock. They take us to Mimosa, where we have cereal, fruit juice, coffee, crackers and apple butter.

That makes my 9th or 10th operation, and 3 out of the last 4 days. Some fun, eh, kid?

Bastia, Corsica
24 January 1944

Well, I did Richmond 2 and 3 and Arctic 2 last week in four days. The Richmond ops were intimately connected with Operation "Shingle" (Anzio).

Then, the following day I met Bill Doyle in our villa and he mentioned that the PT's and MGB's were to do a diversion that night north of the place actually intended for the landings. I began to immediately think how I could get on one of them. I was in the crapper when Tom and Pete came down the hall. I called out that there was something going on and why didn't we try to get on one of the boats? Before I got out of the can, Tom had rushed over to HQ to see Buist and when he came back he had managed to get a spot for one person on an MGB. This made it a question of which of us was to go.

They went in to Livermore and he said that one of us could go, but only one. We could draw cards. Tom claimed I couldn't draw, since I'd been out 3 out of 4 nights and was having all the fun. Well, all my jobs had been in silence — if anything did pop, it would mean the job failed. I wanted, just for once, to go on a job where the object was to do some shooting. The plan was that the PT's and MGB's would go north of the place actually intended for the landings. A British cruiser and two French destroyers would stand off and pile heavy fire in. Then the PT's and MGB's would rush in and close the shore and let loose with everything they had, including rockets, in an effort to rouse anything around there, draw fire, and see just what there was in the way of defense.

Well, if Tom had appealed to my sense of decency by saying I had been out a lot recently and someone else deserved a chance, I believe I would have been honest enough to admit he was right. As it was, he was so goddamned obstreperous about it that I mentally resolved, "Okay. You guys go on and draw cards, and I'm going to get on this show anyway." Pete, Tom and Al drew cards and Pete won. Thompson, Tom and Pete went down to the MGB's, Tom intending to hitch a ride somehow.

I went down to see Paddy Davies and asked him if he could get me on something. He called Sois and said who I was. Sois asked how the hell I knew about the operation. Paddy replied that I had handled some special operations in preparation. So Sois said, "He's an American; let him talk to the PT's." So Paddy called Muddy and said Sois wanted them to take me along. Muddy said okay, tell him to come down at 7 P.M.

I went back to the house and told a couple of the guys I was going out to dinner and maybe to the Florida later. Then I walked downtown about 6 o'clock and over to the PT base.

The PT officers were all controlling nerves. They thought this a ticklish operation. I felt like a heel for a minute or two sticking my nose in, but resolved that I was going to see this show whether it was job of mine or not.

I was on the 211 boat. We left the port after dark, 4 dark shapes gliding along, each merely a shadowy silhouette to the other, and the white wake behind. We were to rendezvous with the MGB's about 11:30.

The big ships would start hitting the coast between 1:45 and 2:15. Between 2:15 and 2:45 we were to dart in and raise hell. I went below, and came up at 11:15. We met the MGB's just south of Giglio (my old territory). We proceeded between Giglio and Giannutri and started south along the coast. We were going through some sort of maneuvers and could hear firing off to starboard and astern, where the MGB's were. I was standing just behind the bridge and Muddy's voice from the lead boat could be heard calling the MGB's: "This is Muddy calling Seabreeze. Can I help? Can I help?" This went on several times (we could not hear the responses on our boat).

Then there was a tremendous explosion about ¾ of a mile off our starboard stern. Various colored lights flew up in diffusion and confusion. Some PT sailor remarked, "Hope it's not one of the British boats." I thought, "Christ, I hope it's not the MGB Tom and Pete are on." Shortly afterward the skipper of the 211 said, "Might as well go below. No show tonight." I asked why, and found that the battle the MGB's had had, had taken so long that the time schedule had been thrown out and anyway the scrap and the cruiser bombardment had raised enough hell to accomplish the purpose of the diversion. So we turned back toward Bastia. I went below about 3 A.M. and got a couple of hours sleep. We docked at 6:30. The MGB's were slower than we and were not expected back till 10 or 10:30. None of the PT boys knew whether or not it had been an MGB that blew. I sneaked into our villa about 7 and went to my room.

I came up for breakfast around 7:45; Livermore never knew where I'd been. After breakfast he asked for the operation report on Arctic 2 that Tom had been doing. I said I would go downstairs and ask Tom if he'd finished it. I returned immediately and told Livermore it would be finished in 20 minutes, and then rushed down to do it myself to cover Tom. He came in about 10 and the report was finished together.

It turned out that Tom and Pete had been on the MGB that hit an E boat and sank an F lighter loaded with ammunition and had a glorious time. In the middle of the scrap, when I had been worrying about them, they laughed (thinking I was home) and said. "Ha-ha to Nelson. He missed it." My pals! This was in good humor though, and I know they really wished I'd been on the same boat with them. Well, I was somewhere around anyway, and if that damned F lighter and E boat had not happened along at that time, I'd have had more fun than they had. Oh, well. C'est la guerre!

The general (Donovan) came in yesterday. Of course, he'd been
with the Shingle landings at Anzio. He has a special PT assigned to run
him around. He is in good shape; but I hope he can leave our set-up
here alone. For we're doing all right and will continue to do all right if
they don't try to load us up with dead weight and brass.

Bastia, Corsica
1 February 1944

Last night went up to Genoa. Our big job was to get our first team
in to contact the committee up there and set up machinery for others.
(Youngstown operation). We had a safe house indicated at one point
near Carnogli, but the English had a reception committee for the Comi-
tato's representative whom they intended to put back in. PT transport
was cramped. So we decided to put our two boys in on the British reception. Our boys, Alfredo (radio) and Gianni (an ex–Italian officer) are
wonderful guys.

The pinpoint was the dock at Voltri, a suburb of Genoa. We started
out with 2 PT's. Then, about 2 or 3 hours out, in the middle of the
Gulf of Genoa, the leading PT had a motor conk out. So everyone, and
equipment, had to be transferred in the absolute darkness to the other
PT which carried on alone. Then, about 3 or 4 miles off shore, the radar
stopped working. We got there about 2 A.M.

No reception signal was seen, so Croft put down two boats and went
in to investigate. Our men could not be landed at this pinpoint unless
the reception committee showed up, so we waited in the readiness on
the PT for Croft's signal in case he found the committee there.

There were plenty of lights around. An electric train runs near the
shore there, and there were intermittent flashes from the wires that took
us a while to figure out. Flares were seen two or three miles to the east.
They would go up as one light, hang high in the air for a moment, then
fall in three or four pieces. We spotted two E boats to the east through
glasses, and hoped they had not spotted us.

Croft was ashore for about an hour and a half. We were plenty worried before he got back. Cars could be seen driving along the coast. There
was a searchlight behind a hill east of us and a radio boom making an
arc further down the coast. Road lights could be seen to starboard. Interesting as hell.

We stood in about 300 yards from shore for about 2 hours. Croft came back. He had tried to find the reception committee, particularly since they were to have sent out some escaped Allied prisoners. But he could find no one. He had one interesting note: He was near one house, and an old woman with a lamp came out of the door, set the lamp down on the stoop, looked at it for about a minute and a half, and went back into the house. Croft went up to the house and called the reception password, but there was no response.

The morale of our boys was magnificent. I'd give my right mit for 5 teams like these two fellows.

It was too late to go to Carnogli, so we had to come back with our first failure. We haven't had many tries, but we are sick at having this one fail. Well, perhaps we can have better luck the next dark moon period.

Then, too, the last couple of days the boys on "3" (Elba) have reported that Germans know they are there and are searching for them. So we'll have to try to pick them off. I'm to try this tonight (perhaps this will get to be a specialty, after the Giglio experience). I'm now awaiting a message from them confirming pinpoint and signal arrangements. They have not come through today so far (it's about 3:30 P.M.) I certainly hope they're all right.

Bastia
4 February

(Just learned that the night we went to Genoa, a dark object floating past us in the water about 10 yards from us as we closed the shore (which I thought was a buoy) was actually a man rowing a boat, who probably mistook us for Germans. Looking back, it was rather eerie — a PT idling by this guy in a rowboat at about 4 knots, in the dark of night, with the lights of the north Italian coast only a few hundred yards away. Quite a war!)

Well, the whole of the day of February 1 we waited for radio contact with the boys on "3." No go. I had already talked to Mario and knew he would go anyway, but it promised to be ticklish if we did not hear from them. They had already received and sent messages mentioning the pinpoint and we knew the Germans had been chasing them from their previous messages, and that the situation for them over there was very hot.

I must admit to feeling qualms at this point on several scores: (1)

the safety of the boys themselves; (2) going in, if we did not hear from them, with the evident possibility of a German reception committee, etc. One of the PT officers came to dinner, however, and we settled down in a game of bridge. (The MAS boat was to leave at 12:30 A.M.) About 8:30 I got word from the radio room that our message with plans for the pick-up had been received by the boys on the Island and confirmed. This, of course, made it seem like a comparatively simple job. I still did not feel entirely easy in my mind because in work where so many things can go wrong, with disastrous results attendant on the most minor slip, the "easy" jobs can become most difficult in a fraction of a second. The PT officer never knew I was going out that night until he was ready to leave and I drove him down to the docks. First, the car would not work (someone had used it and run the batteries down). Therefore, Pete drove us down in his Italian jeep, picking up Mario at the apartment on the way. Joe, Mario and I were going to do the job. (Mario had had experience rowing wooden boats, but had never been in a rubber boat before. I knew this, but did not tell the others, since I wanted to give Mario a chance and we had recently had the arrival of two Marine sergeant experts on rubber boats. Mario had certainly earned the right to go on an operation, however, and I wanted to see if I was right in my judgment of him (which was pretty high).

The plan was that Mario would row the boat, I would be in the bow with a Marlin, and Joe would stay on the MAS. We got down to the MAS early. Just behind here were the dark silhouettes of 2 MGB's. Off to the left, about 150 yards, was the breakwater of the new port at Bastia. Several gaping holes testified to the effects of war. On the docks to the left were sheds — torn, twisted, scorched by bombs and shells. Behind the sheds was a pile of junk (guns, jeeps, trucks, tanks), which the Germans had destroyed before leaving. About 100 yards to the left was the twisted hulk of a freighter that had been sunk in the harbor when hit by bombs. Just behind that, a part of the LCT that had hit a mine in the harbor as late as December 26 thrust directly above the water. On the deck of the gunboat, above and behind us, could be seen the glow of a cigarette which the watch was smoking. We were the first ones there.

We sat around the MAS for about 15 minutes. I told Mario the procedure: "You will get in the boat first. I will pass the oars and Marlin down to you. Then I will get into the bow, you pass the Marlin to me, fix the oars, and shove off. Joe on the MAS will cover for us — try to keep it around as long as possible if anything happens." We sit there in the dark, smoking.

Pretty soon we hear the singing of Italian songs over near the sheds — the Italian crew is coming. They have been drinking wine — the singing is to cover their nervousness. They clamber all over the boat; the two Italian officers get out of their bunks in the small cabin, and Joe, Mario and I descend. A small truck comes down to the docks with Maxted (the British officer) and his rubber boat that he is lending us. I go over to the dock with him and discuss final details. We go over the signals and the course and the probable time we will arrive and how much time I estimate that we will want on shore. He repeats the old stuff we hear every time: "If there is any firing while you are on shore, we will lay off as long as it is nothing heavier than machine-gun fire. If it is anything heavier, or if we are in danger of attack from the sea, we will leave and try to return in an hour: if we can't, we will try to return for you tomorrow night, same time. If we should get chased by an E boat, we will try to shake it and return in an hour; if not, tomorrow night if possible. If something goes wrong on shore and you can't come out, flash "M" repeated, and we will try to get you tomorrow night. Try to get back to the MAS as quickly as possible, for we haven't too many hours to daylight." "Okay." "Righto."

I then go below and doze off on half of one of the bunks. (Having been out the previous night to Genoa, and only having had the brief and intermittent sleep one can get on about 2½ feet of a PT bunk in a few hours of bumpy and rolling ride the night before (I didn't sleep during the day), I was a bit tired. (I am amazed at myself these days — only four or five months ago, I would have sold my soul for anything even as close to an adventure as this. Yet now I sleep through most of the ride and take it more or less casually — though underneath I suppose I realize that it is an interesting job.)

I was awakened by Maxie, coming down to check on the signal at about 2:45 A.M. I repeated the signal to him, and he said we would be off the pinpoint about 3, but would not have idled in fully till about 3:30. The signal: light 5 seconds, darkness 5 seconds, light 5 seconds (this to be done once every quarter hour) was to start at 3:15. I repeated this to Maxie and said I would be up soon. I smoked a cigarette, in the darkness of the cabin (Joe and Mario were there, but you can't see even a foot from you in the cabin's darkness).

I went up at 3 o'clock. I was standing next to the bridge, on which were Max and the Italian skipper. Elba was a dark blob ahead of us. The night was dark and misty. No light was seen. Max is leaning over, with large night binoculars, scanning the coast. At the stern of the boat an Italian mans a machine gun on which to prevent a surprise attack from the sea. Other Italians constantly peer into the darkness to port and starboard for unwelcome floating visitors. We anxiously watch the coast for the signal. I glance at my watch frequently until 3:15, then watch the coast ahead intently. There is no signal.

Max hands me the glasses and says, "There's Pulveraja Lighthouse over there — see it?" "Where?" (Taking the glasses.) "Just above the point there. (Indicating.) It looks like a white house with a tower." "Oh — yeah. I can see it." We idle in about 300 yards of shore and still there is no signal. We wait until 3:45 and still have seen no light. Something has gone wrong. But what? The "easy" job is now the uncertainty of a thousand things that could have happened, masked by the darkness of the night and the enigmatic silhouette of an unfriendly shore.

I say to Max, "I think we'll go in and have a look around, okay?" "Right you are." I go back and get Mario, "There's no signal, but we'll go in and have a look around anyway." "Check." "Tell the Italians to lower the rubber boat, will you?" "Right." All this is in a whisper. The boat is lowered. Mario gets in and I follow, after handing down the oars and the Marlin. I cock the Marlin, and put it on single-shot. "Let's go."

We shove off. I tap Mario on the right or left shoulder to indicate direction and he plies the oars. It is a rocky coast, but a calm sea. We don't see any light as we get closer to the shore. We poke around a cove to the left of the point on which stands the lighthouse, but there is no one there. I whisper to Mario, "I think we'll go in and try to climb up to the lighthouse." We finally get in to a rock below the lighthouse, which is on a cliff about 50 feet up. I get out on the rock and hold the boat close while Mario gets out. He starts to climb up and slips and falls into the water between the rocks — he clambers out, wet to the waist.

We crawl — and I do mean "crawl" — up the rocks in the dark. The boys are not there. We crawl down, get the boat and go into a cove to the right. I get out on a small gravel beach, telling Mario to stay with the boat. It is so dark that I do not see a small group of houses there until I am about 15 feet from the first one. I whistle softly, and call in a stage whisper "Bob. Bob." No answer. We finally go back to the MAS.

Max agrees to go a mile up the coast. But we are sick at heart. We had certainly found the pinpoint, and just as certainly the boys were not there. I stand next to Maxie on the bridge. I say morosely, "Aside from the safety of the boys, this is the second flop running." He says, "This is the fourth consecutive failure for me." We do not look at each other when we speak; we are eyeing the shore hopelessly. No light. Finally we turn back toward Corsica.

Suddenly, when we are about 2 miles off the coast, we see a light. It is a couple of miles north of the pinpoint. We turn back — anxiously, but still idling at about 5 knots, so as not to give away our position or alert the enemy. The light flashes crazily, here and there, up and down; once it seems to slide along the mountain, almost like one of those little white balls that used to hop over the words in a cartoon song in the movies. We mutter, all of us, "All right. All right. We see it. We're coming as fast as we can. But for Christ's sake cut out that God damned light. Do you want to give us all away? We're coming!" Max says, "Are they crazy?" I mutter, "I don't know." We go back, prepare the boat, and Mario and I go in. Max's last reminder, "Make it fast."

There's not much darkness left. We lose sight of the light as we come under the shadow of the hills, but find a large flat rock on the coast just under where I believe we last sighted the light. Not knowing what the situation is, with the crazy antics of the light, but figuring that the boys have been running, I tell Mario to stay at the oars, and I get out on the rock, holding the boat closer by the painter — ready to shove off as quickly as possible. I did not bring the Marlin this time, but have my .45 out and cocked, as does Mario. We are under a 15-foot rocky hill and can't see the light for a few minutes. Then we see it once more, through a crevice in the rocks above us. We hear Bob's voice, hushed but excited. I see a figure stumble and fall on the rocks and lay quiet for a moment. I can't go up to help and still hold the boat ready for an emergency getaway in a hurry. They finally get down to us. Carl had stumbled and fallen over some wire entanglements put up in the last few days, but not as yet — fortunately — mined. The boys, I note hastily in the dark, have beards, torn and ragged clothes. They get in the boat and I hand in the two bedrolls and radio. I shove off, perch precariously on the stern, and we start back. About all the boys can say is, "Jeez, am I glad to see you. Thought we were goners. Jeez are we glad to see you!" This they repeat over and over.

It seems the Germans had discovered their presence on the island. They had been living on nuts and berries for 5 days, dodging German search patrols and dogs which were looking for them. The Gerries had almost got them the day before. On the day we arrived, they had at one time hidden among some rocks just 30 feet from where 4 Gerries, heavily armed, were scanning the countryside with binoculars for them. In dodging the Germans they had gotten lost and could not find the pinpoint. It was just sheer luck that we got them.

Thinking about it later, I realize how it was just lucky that we saw that light. If we had not gotten them, I would have been kicking myself from hell to breakfast for deciding not to spend more time searching around the actual pinpoint. There would have been no reason to kick myself in any case since they were not there, but just not knowing, along with the realization of failure egged on by the boys' fate —. Well, you make a decision as you see it at the moment. If it works out, okay. If it does not, if you have done your best — What the hell. Sure was happy to get those guys, though.

Bastia
7 February

Donovan was up here a week ago. He was quite nice to me. I told him about our plan for North Italy, and he approved. He said the Admiral commanding Allied Naval Forces in the Mediterranean (Cunningham) had praised the reports of our boys on Elba. He said he was proud of me, etc.

After he left Livermore said he had inquired about my commission. Livermore had not known what happened and asked for a memorandum. I gave him one and he said he would recommend a captaincy. I suppose they will offer me a first lieutenancy, and at the moment I don't know whether I will take it or not. There is a feeling in the back of my mind that I could not do as good as job with a rank as I can without it. We'll see.

*   *   *

Found a place the other day, way out on the Cape, where one can have dinner served if a day or two's notice is given. Took our two bodies out there for dinner and it was splendid: An omelette, noodles with sauce, two kinds of lamb; a dessert made of egg custard with oranges and peels, and meringue with jam on top; Corsican cheese that you eat with sugar, oranges and coffee. Four bottles of wine, and three of Cap Corse. The two bodies, Mario, Pete and I comprised the party. On the way back, at 11 P.M., we got a flat tire and had no spare or pump. Had to sit in the car on the road all night.

*   *   *

One afternoon we were in a little town just north of Bastia: Bo, Vince Russo, Pete and I. We had two or three pastiches. A lot of kids outside began asking for "chew'm gum." We finally told them that if they said "Daddy" in English to Vinnie that he would give them chewing gum. Vince had to walk about two or three blocks to the car with about 20 kids running after him, all yelling, "Daddy."

Bastia
19 February
Well, last night we tried to repeat on the Youngstown job, which is the team going to Genoa which we tried on January 31 and which we failed to land successfully.

After a lot of haggling with the British services, we finally agreed to land two men for them at the same time ours were landed. They supplied their own oarsmen and were to follow Tom and myself in. We got on a MAS with Maxted doing the navigating for the British Naval Forces. The Italian crew was just as all Italian crews. Our party was the two boys, Tom, Henry Leger (observing), Mario and I. It was fairly rough after we cleared Cap Corse. Mario got very sick. All of the others of us were all right, however. When about 5 miles from the promontory at Portofino, I noticed a light on shore, which had been on our right, on our left. I said to Tom, "There's another light." He said, "No, it's the same one." I said, "What's it doing over there on the left." He said, "We've turned." "Why?" was a logical question and we soon found out: The rudder had broken. This was nice, for German convoys and patrols along the coast had increased since the Anzio affair, and we were right in the path of anything that might come along and MAS boats have no radar. Finally, a hand rudder in the back of the boat was gotten into service. This meant that, whereas ordinarily orders are given from the bridge just down through a door to the wheelhouse, they now had to go through

"channels" all the way to the stern of the boat. This was very amusing —
with overtones of things more serious — due to our position.

We were already late, and it was about 12:45 A.M. The moon was
due to come up at 2:30 and Max had orders to leave at that time. Then
one of the auxiliary motors conked out. This meant we could not reach
the pinpoint before about 2:30. Maxie finally agreed to take us in later
than 2:30, as the moon was hidden behind the promontory for a while.
We lowered the boats about 3:25. Tom and I got in, the radio and batteries were passed to us. Then the oars. Then the Marlin to me in the
bow. Then the bodies got in. (In case the boat was chased away while
we were on shore, or something else happened, I had a handy-talkie
strapped to my shoulder.)

We started out to about 25 or 30 yards of the MAS, which was about
300 yards off shore. There was a strong wind from the northwest. Then we
waited for the English rubber boat to start behind us. You could easily see
the houses on the shore. And up north, about a mile or two away, a fac-
tory was working at Recco. When we got in to shore we almost hit a rock
and I (mocking the Italian MAS boat skipper) whispered to Tom, "Via sinistra, tutti sinistra." He started to laugh silently and we damned near hit
the thing. We found nothing there but a straight wall of rock surmounted
by some houses — no place for the boys to get up. The question was whether
to try further south or north. We finally found a little inlet under a house.

We got in and I got out, holding the painter of the boat. The boys
got out, and Tom passed the equipment to me. I gave it to the boys and
warned them not to make any contact until they were sure they were
secure. They started off up the rock, which was smooth and led to a stone
path along the coast between Camogli and Punta. About 25 feet above
us, on this path, was a house. No one was stirring. We knew that there
was a machine gun position somewhere up the hill, probably 400 or less
yards away. I called the boys back and, seeking words in Italian which I
didn't know, said "Esperiamo cosi grandi de tutti due voi." The older
chap, Gianni, gripped my arm and the younger, Alfredo, hugged me.
(He was scared, but he would not show it if you killed him I'm sure.) I
got a very great kick out of the fact that these boys seemed to like me.
I don't know their language, except for a few words here and there, but
I had handled their training and had taken them out for rides and once
to dinner, and we had sung songs and been regular guys together, which
they seemed to appreciate.

We stayed at the rock, I standing there holding the painter of the boat, while the boys walked up the hill. My last sight of them was the two of them, reaching the path, radio-suitcase and battery in their hands, looking up at the house and the forest beyond. Then I pushed the rubber boat off, hopped on, and we started back to the MAS.

I sat in the stern and kidded Tom by giving him directions in Italian, imitating the MAS boat skipper's commands. We got back to the MAS about 4, just two minutes after the English boat. We climbed on board and started back.

Just as we rounded the point, we saw the moon clearing the top of the promontory. Just in time (4 hours late)!

Then we hit bad water. The boat bounces, and I do mean bounce! So hard that the settee along under the bunks was broken completely by the impact of assorted derrieres. Mario was really wretched, puking bile. Henry, who has done a hell of a lot of ocean traveling and never been ill, was nearly so. Two-thirds of the crew were seasick. I was not, which is something of a miracle but makes me feel I never will be. The boat was bouncing around in the middle of the Gulf of Genoa, trying to steer from the rudder in the stern. You couldn't go topsides without being absolutely drenched as the waves engulfed the boat. Henry had to stand up on deck to keep from being seasick. At daybreak, we had no stars to steer by, and still had not sighted land. This made the situation worse, because we had only a couple of .30 machine guns and in case of enemy planes we would be easy prey.

Eventually we sighted Capraia and then Cap Corse. But we were to the right of the Cape and the sea was so heavy the wheel would not pull the boat around. Mario was so sick that Tom suggested we try to put into Ile Rousse or San Florent and send him on by car. Mario got momentary relief by going up and getting soaked, whereupon he shivered like hell, but his stomach would stop retching for the moment.

6

Interlude

In between his duties as an SI Operations Officer, recruiting, training and briefing agents for infiltration into Northern Italy and the Tyrrhenian Islands from Corsica, Wayne Nelson went on a brief home leave to the United States flying via Algiers (where this portion of his diaries begins), Casablanca and the Azores Islands.

Algiers
March 6, 1944

Tom and I hopped a C-47 on March 2 and headed for Algiers. We felt exactly like a couple of hicks coming to the big city. We wondered how we would react, or how it would react to us. When we got to Maison Blanche, the airport, it was raining and cold — about 6:45 P.M. We phoned Dewitt and he said there was a new rule that no cars went to the airport — for anyone under a full colonel. We finally hitched a ride on an English truck. Dewitt had given me the dope over the phone as to calling Freedom, then asking for Forecast, then asking for anybody at Sinety by name. Hell — there wasn't anything but Freedom and the local French line when I was last here. I knew only one or two of the names he reeled off familiarly. And I was one of the first out here and knew every one but a few months ago. Finally we got a station wagon to take us up to Sinety. We were feeling pretty miserable generally, with the cold and rain and all this damned nonsense to get anywhere. But I, particularly, felt strange. Here, I'd been telling Tom, "Just wait till we hit Algiers — that's my old stamping ground, I know everyone there, we'll be treated like visiting royalty." Huh!

Dewitt had mentioned that Colonel Eddy was back in town, passing through. Tom and I had on our dirty coats, field jackets and dust-stained green trousers. When we reached Sinety, I saw a bunch of strange officers eating in the front room, and many changes in the place itself. I didn't know one of the whole damned bunch in that room of perhaps 20. We pushed through before anyone could stop us, after tossing our barracks bags in a corner. A few of the officers looked up, a sort of "Who the hell are those two hoboes?" expression; I guess they would have stopped us, but I was grimly mad now, and determined that somewhere in this Warner Brothers rambling villa there must be someone of the old crowd that I knew. We went into the inner room where the mess used to be. The room was jammed. Obviously here was the inner sanctum mess for some visiting guest of honor. I stood in the doorway for a moment, accustoming my eyes to the light. No one near the foot of the tables near the door was familiar — and the hum of conversation was dying down as people looked up resentfully at strangers intruding. Finally, way up at the head of the table at the other end of the room, I spied the guest of honor — it was Colonel Eddy! Around him were a few of the old faces — Crosby, Dot Taylor, Warwick Potter....

Eddy called out, "Wayne!" and I yelled, "Well, Colonel!" He pushed his big bulk toward me, and I pushed toward him, practically pushing peoples faces into their soup. If I had been feeling depressed a few minutes before — this suddenly became one of the high spots of my time out here. The old crowd seemed as genuinely glad to see me, as I was to see them, and having Eddy chance to be there at the moment made it perfect. We sat down and ate, and I introduced Tom around, and it was fun. The new faces? The hell with them.

Eddy asked if we would come down to Potter's place afterwards for a few drinks and we did. Henry Hyde said to come on with him to stay at his place — he had Ken Pendar's old villa with Lord Duncannon and a couple of other English officers. We went around to Sinety quite late to get blankets, and had to wake up the enlisted clerk. The supply captain came out and we had a brief tussle in which we expressed our disregard for the reorganization and military regulations. Tom was quite brusque — I think he should have toned down a bit and left it to Henry and myself, who were, at least real old-timers. Henry was one of the old stalwarts fighting military encroachments and has been able to keep it up in this den of would-be military propriety because he is producing fine results with the French desk.

The next day we went to Magnol, and the place was completely changed, with people sitting in every corner of halls, bathrooms for officers, etc. I gave one big horselaugh at all this, and I don't think I'll ever be forgiven. However, Tom and I managed to swim all right, and people were somewhat impressed with what we had to offer. Glavin (Colonel Edward J.) was ill so we couldn't see him.

After one day, however, wherein everyone who had gotten there even a day before I left to go forward cried on my shoulder and joined, privately, in deploring the changes, Tom and I became a bit depressed. There was literally no place to sit down. One felt unwanted and in the way. You couldn't get a car to do anything. Just hell. Old friends, like Dewitt, were fine, but the French desk works at high pressure and it was a busy period.

Sunday afternoon, Tom and I did get downtown and saw "L'Ecole des Femmes." It was a nice performance and we enjoyed it very much, but it was an empty enjoyment, because there just wasn't the old spirit. We convinced ourselves that we enjoyed it because it was like old times when one could go to the theatre, perhaps Tom enjoyed it more than I, because he had not known Algiers of last year and saw it only slightly in its heyday when he was through four or five months ago. It was fun to go to the theatre, however.

Today we saw Glavin at his apartment. He gave us the dope on commissions and said it was a crying shame we had not been commissioned before, but that it was practically impossible now. Navy was mentioned and my work, except that Tom was born in Berlin and I have no college education. Tom and I in this interview played some good teamwork and tossed the ball back and forth. When it was brought up that I should go home for a while, Tom agreed to shoulder the burden while I was away (if it was not too long) and backed it up with the opinion he had stated before to Livermore and others that I was living on nerves alone. Glavin agreed, and said, "You'll have your travel orders tomorrow, but we don't want to lose you and return orders will be included." I said swell.

So here I am (by the way we just went to the PX and they now allow two bottles of Coca-Cola a week here in Algiers — what a world capital this has become!) I had my first Coca-Cola in 14 months!

Hope to be on my way back in a few days — as Pete said when I saw him in the ambulance at the dock —"What a sensation!"

Algiers
March 7, 1944

Today was a big day! Received a cable from Corsica subsequent to
the previous one about Youngstown which said it had been heard, to the
effect that it had been heard on Monday, March 7. We tried the big
league stuff, had more luck than possible to conceive, and made it — so
far. Then a naval lieutenant from our London outfit came down here.
He was to learn about sea operations, and they referred him to us! Eventually we may turn out to be the old maestros! I say all this at the moment
because Tom and I naturally feel completely exalted (if there is such a
word, perhaps I mean elated). Underneath, we are perfectly conscious
of the hazards we run and how little it would take to collapse our house
of cards. But we might as well feel happy for the moment; the headaches,
and heartaches, are sure to come, as we had them in the past. I think we
have earned a bit of feeling good, no one in the organization in a comparative spot has run the risks we have run (I said in comparative spot),
and no one has been as lucky as us so far.

Algiers
March 8, 1944

Saw Tom Beale, one of the old timers in Washington, who's doing
a visiting fireman act, today. It was rather pleasant personally to hear
that he had been hearing of me. Apparently, around certain circles in the
outfit, our "exploits" are becoming known. This is quite a feeling for
me — for it satisfies the old ego that was what always (possibly) made me
want to be on the stage as an actor.

Algiers
March 9, 1944

My plan for a trip to the United States got balled up. Glavin had
agreed to it and said it was all set. Then, the next day, there was a hitch
on travel orders and the air priority. You see, if I can get out in a hurry
and get back by the middle of April I'll only miss one moon period
(March); if I can't get back by the middle of April, I just can't make the
trip because I couldn't do it with any sense of responsibility to our own
agents and to Tom, who will have to bear the extra load. It seems that
G-3 questioned the whole business. I drew up a memorandum of the
reasons for the trip (the Swiss courier plan) which was most secret and

then told several of the commanding officers here that the memo had the reasons for the trip but that I did not agree with having them spread over AFHQ. I said I thought it was a bad precedent in the first place; secondly, that if it had to be done, perhaps the best thing to do would be to change it to read a request for any type of priority or sea travel, the reason being, not a business mission, but that Mr. Nelson had resigned and was going back to the States.

Last evening at a buffet dinner at Sinety I saw Glavin. He said I was all set, he had talked to General Coffee about it, and it was all set. That sounded good. So I saw Tom off to Corsica on a B-25 this morning and came back to Magnol to see what was up. Some of the pricks around said they thought I could not go — G-3 wouldn't permit it. I turned the memo, with some verbal explanations, over to Colonel Rodrigo, and I added that still more questions could be asked but that if that were carried out to its full conclusion, you could ask "Why this outfit at all?" Right now, I'm sitting in this madhouse of Magnol and trying to figure whether to (1) quit, (2) go back to Corsica in disgust, or (3) wait around here and hear that I can go when it's too late to go and get back by the April dark period, in which event I won't go at all. Don't know which course I'll take as yet.

Casablanca
March 12, 1944

Yesterday at 4:30 P.M. I was told it was all set and that I was to go today, that I had a 2 priority. I said goodbyes and got out to the airport, Maison Blanche, at 11:15 — the plane was to go at 12:30. The plane left at 1; a C-47; flew to Casablanca. It was cold. Nothing particularly interesting, except the feeling inside me that in perhaps a couple of days I'll see home and.... In those bucket seats we had a blanket apiece. When it got cold, you wanted them around your feet and legs; then you wanted them to keep your seat from being put out of commission by the metal seat. You pays your money and takes your choice!

What is an average crowd on one of these rides like? Well, there are two nurses going to Casa. There is an English major with a bandaged head who was wounded at Anzio and is on his way back to Great Britain. There is a sergeant, on his way home for a two weeks leave. There are three American majors. There is an English naval captain. There is a Polish flight lieutenant. There is an English flight lieutenant. There are three enlisted men. There are two French couriers — and very secret parcels. (Hm!)

On arriving at Casa (we left Algiers at 1; arrived Oran at 2:30; left Oran at 3; arrived Casa at 6:30), we were told there was a bus leaving every half-hour for town. I was told I should call back the airport between 11 and 11:30, but that it would be wise to get a billet. So I got a room, thru the billeting officer, at the Hotel Excelsior. I got in too late for mess and went to a local restaurant. I stood in line at the door for 20 minutes and then got a place. The meal was wine, soup, spaghetti (gray) and ravioli (gray-brown); three dates for dessert (this was one of the better restaurants in the city). The price was 40 francs — 80 cents.

So I wandered back to the hotel at 9:20. Finally went to a movie and saw the last half of an Andrews Sisters piece at the local Red Cross Theatre. (Free to anyone in Allied uniform.)

Casa is a whiter looking city than either Algiers or Oran, though it is closer in appearance to the latter. You cannot see very much of the effects of war here; there have been no bombings; the buildings are intact. You see a lot of American officers, mostly Air Corps, and many, many American naval officers (many, many Shore Patrols, aussi!)

If Casa is the international place the pictures claim it to be, it is not apparent at a quick glance. I've no doubt the proper spots, if one could spend a few days here and get to know them, would show a great deal of interest, but just passing through, and alone, you don't see much.

This is the life, though, of a traveler in wartime: From Algiers to Casa in 5½ hours; thence to a hotel, where accommodations are a dirty looking bed, a sink, a clothes cabinet, a chair, and, of course, a bidet. Thence, since the mess is closed, to a local restaurant for the meal described above. Thence back, but seeing nothing of undue interest. Thence to a movie. Thence to the hotel and writing this, which has consumed enough time to make it five of 11 and time to call the airport, and which — to bed. But soon, cross my fingers, America!

In an ATC C-54
(Somewhere between Casa and the Azores)
March 13, 1944

So you get to bed at 11:45 and leave a call for 7. They have told you to call the airport at 8. You waken at 8 and call the airport before you are dressed. They tell you to be out there at 8:45, so you skip breakfast, shave hurriedly and catch the bus out. This scares the hell out of you, for the bus leaves at 8:15, and with their insisting on 8:45 promptly, and a trip home at stake, your heart pumps like hell in trying to make it.

Then you stand around for hours, and finally you are told to board a C-54. You do, and with great attempt at appearing calm on the surface, while your heart is pumping along so fast and hard it seems it will bust right out of your chest. A lot of Ferry Command pilots and a couple of English flight officers are the other passengers. So here you are in this plane, nothing to look at but sea, sky and clouds — inside a beautiful dream of home, and under you a hard bucket seat!

So everyone looks for a space on the floor to sleep, or lounges around awkwardly on the bucket seats, and after 5 hours someone says we are coming down. So you look out and, sure enough, you are descending slowly. Still above the clouds. You can see the plane's shadow below you on top of a cloud, and there is a perfect rainbow around it. This, you learn, is a "Pilot's Cross" and is considered to be an omen of good luck when seen.

Bastia, Corsica
April 25, 1944

Left the U.S the night of April 13 at 1:15 A.M. The only other civilian on the plane was a chap named Dewing, a former INS man now with CIC. It was a C-54, but, instead of the bucket seats I had on the way to America, it had regular bus seats. Wonderful! We reached Bermuda about 7 in the morning. Dewing knew a colonel there (the G-2) and got us a car for the day, since we were not to leave until that evening. We went all over Bermuda, stopped in the town of Hamilton and had a Scotch and soda or two. Then we went to a little cottage in the country where we had a fine lunch of turkey and vegetables, soup, and a good custard dessert. We heard from the sergeant who was driving us all the local gossip — that the officers all played golf, tennis, etc., that officers assigned there could bring their wives down if they got them a job there (which many of them had done), and that there were no women on the island for the enlisted men, and that there was one known as "Black Mary" who "did it" for most of the enlisted men as part of her contribution to the war effort. We dropped by the large country clubs (like the Mid-Ocean) that had been converted to officers clubs. It was very nice country, and easy to understand why Bermuda is such a popular vacation resort.

We took off at about 8:30 that night and got to the Azores the following morning. We were assigned to tents (that is, a cot in a tent). We went up to a tent that was the officers club tent and played some poker. I went to bed afterwards, at about 12:30. Then I felt hungry, so got up and just made the mess (lunch) before it closed. Then I went back to bed and woke about 5. We went up to the "officers club" tent and had two bottles of beer and then to the mess tent for dinner. No one could get into the Portuguese town on Terceira unless he had had bubonic plague shots, so we all stayed "on the reservation." We found that we had not taken off during the day because there had recently been attacks by air on American convoys off Casablanca, so we had to fly at night. We took off about 8 P.M. and got to Casa at 2 A.M. We were put in transient barracks that night. The following morning I phoned Dave King and he sent a car for me. I got to the office and chatted with him for a while. I was in wool greens uniform. He said the new rule was that you could not use "U.S." insignia and he called to verify it. We found that it was all right for me since I was a transient, but that he himself was out of uniform because everyone permanently assigned there was to have gone into khaki that day (April 15). I went to a local restaurant for lunch, rather than to a mess, and had, soup, sardines and beets, and then a fish that was accompanied by a damned good lemon sauce, a bottle of wine, and the inevitable few dates for dessert.

I managed to get billeted at the Hotel Excelsior and had the amazing experience of seeing a fire in Casa. The firemen with their ornate equipment and brass helmets were quite something — to look at! National pride forces me to state, however, that the GIs did most of the actual work of putting the fire out. That evening I met Michel (Pinkeye) at the American bar in the Excelsior and we went downstairs, where they have a local orchestra. We drank a few local, bad, brandies and watched the crowd and talked.

The following morning I got a plane for Algiers and reached there about 3:30 in the afternoon. I got into the JICA office with a Colonel Goodwin and phoned for a car from Sinety. I got there about 4:30 and was billeted on a cot in a room upstairs. The ensuing few days were horrible, waiting for transportation. I could not get an operational plane and had to wait for orders, etc.! Finally, I got out with a 2 priority for Ajaccio. This was, I believe, on April 20. (It took longer to get out of Algiers than to get from New York to Algiers!)

The dark moon period started about April 17 or 18, and I was naturally wild to get back to Bastia. I reached Ajaccio on April 20. Went to a movie in the open air that night that NORBS was throwing. Went with Sergeant Markajani, Livermore's driver, OG. The picture was one of the latest, "Going My Way" with Bing Crosby. Before the picture there was a program of songs by a GI orchestra, and five or six folk songs by a choir of Jugolslav prisoners. Interesting and, particularly the Jugoslavs, very good. The following morning I got a jeep and drove up to Bastia alone, reaching there about 3:30.

I found there was a job on that night. This was to put two men on OP No. 2 and two men on OP No. 3 (Capraia and Elba). We boarded the PT, with the usual spare covering, at about 8 P.M. I was to be lead man in the one boat, with a Lieutenant Walter Taylor (Marine) rowing; Joe and Mario were to be in the second boat, this for Capraia. Little was known about the pinpoint, so it was a question of finding the general area and then trying to find a place to land the men where they could climb up later, on a steep, rocky, almost perpendicular coast. There were a lot of supplies.

Walt and I got in the rubber boat; the supplies were handed down; one of the bodies got in. Apparently this job had not been "dry" rehearsed, as it should have been, for there were too many supplies. An improvement was that the PT had a scramble net down the side that made getting in the rubber boat easier than it used to be. The second body was just getting in the boat when a flare was dropped from an enemy plane to the stern of the boat. There was a moment of "freezing," everyone becoming motionless. or as motionless as possible on a moving sea. Then we were ordered back to the PT. After a wait of a few minutes we descended into the rubber boat again, as flares continued to be seen further to the north and further to the south. We pulled off and waited for the other boat about 25 yards away. Then we started in. About 200 or 300 yards off shore we spied a vague object just off the coast of the island about half a mile south of us. It looked like a patrol boat.

We stopped for a moment and decided our best bet was to make for shore. (My thought had been that perhaps an enemy boat was creeping up the coast to intercept us, too close to shore to be spotted by the PT radar — learned later that they had spotted it after we left and had the Beaufors 40 mm. and other guns trained on it — it was just a large uncharted rock!) The other boat lost us. Finally, we found the other boat, and Joe managed to keep up with us for a while, but lost us again. We found a cove to land where we thought the bodies could get up. The other boat finally came along and the people and equipment were landed. I had difficulty getting Tom on the handy-talkie, but finally I did. We could not see the PT, so I wanted to know if it was all right to come out. Tom said come on, and finally we got back to the PT. It was then too late to do the other job, so we came back to Bastia.

(Later learned that Joe, when he got separated from us the second time, had fallen "in the drink" twice, pulled out by Mario. When he approached us he had his .45 cocked and aimed at me at a distance of about 6 feet, shaking like a drowned rat. He'll stay on the big boat on any further jobs. He's full of spirit and desire to do landings, but he's not temperamentally fit.)

Two nights later we did the Elba job. Here, Tom and Walter went in on the first boat and I followed in the second with an English sailor rowing. (The latter was a young sailor no more than 19, and we had to use him because Mario had hurt his leg falling on the rocks on OP No. 2.) We were set down about 800 yards off the shore and started in. We finally got to shore in a little cove. On this operation there were three PT's: One for us, one to guard, and one to take a French team in somewhere north of us. We were unloading the boats when Tom suddenly said, "Look!" and handed me a Marlin—Walt and I were at the edge of the water, handing cases back to Tom and Bob. There was a shadowy silhouette, obviously a boat, coming down the coast, just off the cove. We "froze," and Walt and I got the Marlins ready. As the boat passed the mouth of the cove, I whispered to Walt that the only thing to do if it put in, was to open up when it got very close and them make a break for it in the rubber boats. He nodded. A tense few minutes.

The silhouette did not turn it, but disappeared southward below the mouth of the cove to our left. We finished the job with considerable dispatch and set out back to the PT in the two rubber boats. When we were about 300 yards out, a light began to flash along the shore and then near the shore coming up the coast to the north past the cove where we had been! We still could not see the PT. Walt and the sailor in my boat began to row faster. I kidded the Englishman by telling him he didn't have to hurry, just pretend he was Oxford vs Cambridge! Our laughter was silent. When Tom and Walt were within 30 feet of the PT, it suddenly turned and its motors started up and it shied away like a skittish horse. Tom got on the handy talkie to call for Christ's sake to come back. When we arrived on the other side of the PT we were left sitting for three minutes and suddenly found a gun trained on us, a voice calling down, "Who is there?" I replied, "Nelson." "Okay." What had happened was that we had done the job faster than anticipated. The PT had spotted three small boats in the radar and thought we might be the enemy. Then it developed that the other boat was the French job and was in command of an English SOE expert who had gotten off his pinpoint from the north.

Something had gone wrong, but we did not know what it was for weeks.

Then we did not hear from the OP No. 2 team for four days, so I went over with Walt in the fishing motor sailer one day. We started at 11 A.M., reached there about 3:30. We went in on a rubber boat. (By the way, before this we had been informed that the air forces had not been briefed to expect this, and after what had happened once before to the ML, we were naturally a bit nervous. One of our Spitfire groups came along and circled us about 7 times. We fired recognition flares, and then got the guns ready as they continued circling, but the Spits finally went off toward Bastia).

The boys had been unable to make contact or get up the mountain. So I moved them down about 600 yards and personally carried one of their pieces of equipment up the mountain to show them it could be done, and left them a new radio. We left there about 5:30 and arrived back at 9:30. It had been a sunny day and loads of fun on this six-knot sailer, on which we crowded sail about 7:30 to increase her speed to about 7 knots. (I think I would like one of those jobs in the Adriatic where you get on one of these boats and spend 4 or 5 days leisurely doing the work. Probably it would get boring after a while, though.)

Then when I returned in the first place, everything had been bad luck. The Ginny job had indeed been wiped out — like this: The PT closed the shore, let off the boys in the rubber boats. Vinnie and Paul and 13 men. Another PT stood off shore to cover the operation. The outside PT stood off shore to cover the operation. The outside PT suddenly found itself in the middle of a German convoy, with E-boats, that was moving along the coast. Guns started popping, and then flares went up, right off the pinpoint, from a point on shore. The rubber boats were trapped just as they landed, and land patrols moved toward them. The inside PT took off, as did the other PT. They came back later. But at that time, E-boats were near and the outside PT had its motor jam. The inside PT went to help the other one and daylight broke and they came back. The next night they went back to the point and 3 E-boats were just patrolling up and down off the pinpoint. The next night they went back and found nothing. The Italian radio announced the capture of 15 American commandoes; the German radio announced that 15 American commandoes had been "wiped out."

The Scotsman, Dow, and Ginger (Italian MAS boat skipper with whom we often worked) were out with a French group on an operation similar to our intelligence jobs except that they carried ammunition. They found a few sticks floating around a place where the boat might have been. It is assumed that the boat blew up, whether from being fired on or not, no one knows. (Some rumors say that the Italian crew mutinied and went over to the enemy, after killing Dow, Ginger and the French. But this is just a rumor.— This latter rumor was later proved true!)

One of the Youngstown team was captured while I was away; the radio operator is carrying on and we were supposed to take him out this moon period (April). We could not for several reasons, including weather. He is "on the run," and has been for two weeks. On the night of April 27 we were going up for him (one attempt had been made while I was away — E-boats were found off the pinpoint — for some reason Tom tried the same Camogli pinpoint where we originally landed the team).

That afternoon I studied the new pinpoint intensely and got Mario in and told him frankly it might be a trap. The operator had never used his danger signals (signals to be used in case he was being forced to operate the radio by the Gerries). Therefore, he conceivably could have been captured and be leading us into an ambush under coercion of the Gerries. I will admit I was very ticklish on this job. I put the plain possibilities up to Mario frankly and told him he didn't have to go if he didn't feel "right" about it. Mario said if I was going to go why the hell shouldn't he — he liked Alfredo and Gianni too. So I told him what I felt we might do in certain contingencies, though I told him we had to admit the fact that if it was indeed an ambush we would have only about 1 chance in 1,000. Due to failure of radio contact it did not come off, and will have to do it the next dark period. So, of this writing, Alfredo's fate is still in balance.

Finally, as we approached the Cape, the boat was pulled around by stopping the port engine, pulling hard on the wheel and driving hard with the starboard engine. We cleared the rocks at the Cape and started down the east coast of Corsica. Suddenly I noticed planes. They were Spits. They came up the coast low over the water (about 150 feet) and rounded the Cape; then they came back over us and circled and then went back toward Bastia. I knew then that people back there had been worried about us and these planes had been sent out to see if they could find us.

We got back to Bastia about 11:30. All the brass we had up there were at the dock to meet us: Captain Dickinson (Navy chief); Major Croft, Commander Winney, K. Mill, and a bunch of others, including Pete and Joe. Well, the boys are put in, and now we have to sweat out the first contact, if any. I feel depressed about the prospects, but hope to hell it will work, for I really like those boys. (Maxted said, incidentally, that last night was the worst water he had ever gone through in a small craft.) Mario was standing, shivering and looking altogether miserable, when Tom came up into the wheelhouse, about 8:30 in the morning a few miles off the cape. Mario says, clapping Tom on the shoulder, "How are your feeling?" What a laugh!

7

Dark Moon Ops

"We frequently commented that the British taught us all we knew. They literally taught us the fine points of landing 'bodies' on the Italian and French shores using rubber dinghies. They taught us how to cope with phosphorescence in the water and how landing on open beaches in the dark of the moon was preferable to landing in hilly spots where observers might look down on us without our seeing them."*

Bastia, Corsica

June 2, 1944

Now for the operations during the May dark moon period.

Tom had learned that the French planned to take Elba, so he evolved a joint plan. It began with Tom and I going in with a group of nine of our boys along with five or six Frenchmen. We were to land eight hours before the big landing to set up a base to infiltrate through the lines. This would have been an innovative step forward for the organization, and damned interesting. (Just between you and me, it would have been a screwball operation, but it would have been so damned interesting.) In view of my knowledge of this large military operation, I was not allowed to accompany our ops for security reasons, although I was to plan and direct them all. (I was engaged in planning our side of it, particularly communications, which involved no little amount of detail. The security bug has bitten a lot of guys up here — guess it's becoming a "headquarters" like other places!)

The first job was getting Bob off Elba, where he had been for a month without communication. Apparently his radio busted. Walt and

*Peter Karlow, Targeted By the CIA

Joe went over one night, with Mario to row, and Walt in the bow. This was on May 16. They established handy-talkie communication with Bob, but while they were in the rubber boat near the shore, the PT's were attacked by three E-boats. The operational PT had to depart, leaving Walt and Mario on shore. They could not find the original pinpoint and could not find Bob. The PT came back later and managed to pick them up. But still no Bob.

I got special permission to accompany the next try, on the 18th — on the PT boat but not to land. Walt was to go in the bow with a British sailor rowing. They did not find the original pinpoint, but while they were on shore I noticed lights further up the coast. It seemed the light was flashing "N." I assumed this was Bob and called Walt and the sailor back. The PT then started for the place where the lights had been. When we were about three or four hundred yards from shore we were met by rifle fire. The familiar mosquito whine of rifle bullets over our heads and in the water near us induced an abrupt "about face" by the PT, which thought it was a snare. It looked like I had "bitten" on the trap, and I felt pretty foolish for a while, despite the fact that I was *sure* inside it had been Bob.

Later Bob managed to steal a rowboat and row back to Corsica (thirty hours of rowing). We then found that he really had flashed the "N" and the fire came from a Gerry road patrol that had just happened along the road on a shelf of rock above his position on the shore. We also found that, when we landed him, we had been north of our pin-point which explained why the French rubber boat came by us (almost piercing a serious "blow") and why we could not find the pinpoint in the pick-up attempts, since on the pickups we went to the *right* place, while Bob, of course, went right to the place where he was landed, as he should. We had never thought of questioning the navigation on the orig-inal job, since the man who handled it was the best there was at Bastia (he was later given a high decoration by the British). If Bob had not been so reliant we might never have known what really happened.

Youngstown was still a problem. On the 18th of May, Joe and Walt started to the pinpoint, but were turned back by weather after three hours. We selected a new pinpoint. On May 19, Walt and Joe got there but they had to wait for two convoys to pass and it was too late to let a boat down when the coast was finally clear. On May 22, I started out with Joe on the PT (having gotten special permission to go on shore in view of the circumstances of the job). We were turned back after two hours due to weather.

On May 24, we started again. This time we took the Reading team also. I looked on this job with a great deal of trepidation because of the negative possibilities. One member of the Youngstown team we knew had been arrested by the SS a month before; we had word that the other member had been arrested two days before but had escaped. Communications said the code must be considered "blown" in any event — it was DT and had been used too much; the whole thing could have been a trap. And I must admit I used to sit before the fire in the afternoons and try to drain my imagination dry, a system I found works for me — let your imagination wander where it will in the afternoon, and then when you get on the boat your mind is free and can be wholly applied to the job.

An English lieutenant was assigned to row me in. We were let down over a mile from the pinpoint, after having to wait for two F-fighters to pass the point (Cap Pomona, near Monerosso al Mare, southeast of Genoa). We got to shore (the Reading team, a replacement operator for Youngstown in the event Alfredo had reached the pinpoint, the English lieutenant, and I). I hopped out of the boat and pulled it to shore. The Youngstown reception was not there. Therefore, after the Reading team had disembarked, I told the replacement Youngstown operator to get back in. The English lieutenant was calling for speed — he was worried about those F-fighters, not more than a couple of miles away. Then, one of those embarrassing moments cropped up.

I previously had nothing to do with training the Reading team. The leader had been a young Italian officer — I did not doubt his intellectual brilliance, but I had always been distrustful of his self-reliance. Well, as we were there on shore, he picks that moment to begin to jabber that he would not stay there since there was no reception. (Tom had assured me he would stay whether there were a reception committee or not, and he, the team chief, had talked with me for an hour and a half on the PT about just what to do if no committee showed.) He went into a funk however. With an overloaded boat, and an inshore breeze it would have been near impossible to take him back to the PT. The English officer was undoubtedly thinking silently, "these Americans and their blundering way of training Joes." I never believed in being tough with Joes, but something had to be done. First I told him to shut up. He started to keep on talking, and I showed him a fist and told him if he didn't shut up I'd clip him. He fell silent at this. Then I went on as if nothing had happened, particularly giving words of encouragement to the radio operator, a young Italian (from Trieste) of great courage and patience. When we were ready to depart, I shook hands with both Reading guys. The former officer started to speak, obviously paralyzed with fear—I shut him up again and the Englishman, the spare Youngstown operator, and myself started out again.

I'm afraid Tom's judgment of this guy was not too good. He has a habit of *assuming* that Joes think as he tells them to. A Joe has to *want,* himself, to do the job—persuasion in training is the only way. I felt like a heel leaving Reading in this fashion, but it was the only thing I could do. A pinpoint on the enemy shore (especially on that Genoa-Spezia coast at that time) was no place to train or recruit. I've thought a lot about the right thing to do in a spot like that, but at that stage I still think I did the only thing possible.

We started back to the PT, battling the inshore breeze. When we were out a way, I contacted Joe on the handy-talkie. The PT had spotted us, but said they could come in closer. (At that point, we couldn't see them either.) Soon we spotted them. When I asked Joe if they had seen us, either by glasses or radar, he said, "No." They still had not seen us although they were very clear to us; this led to one of those moments when we wondered if we were approaching an E-boat. Finally they were coming directly at us. We started calling into the handy-talkie, "For Christ's sake don't run us down!" About thirty yards away they heve ho, and we got on board and came back to Bastia.

Youngstown was still in a spot, so when another operation for the French was going to the same pinpoint, we tried to get Youngstown to be there. I suggested that I leave money there if they did not show up. I went ashore to land the French team and get it on its way, and leave $2,500 in lire under four stones with two pieces of wood to mark the spot. We got back to the boat (a British seaman and I) and only ten minutes later as we were idling out, a convoy of six ships was seen coming right off the pinpoint. Boy! If we had been fifteen minutes later, we'd been right in the middle of the Gerries!

I laid on and Walt carried out an operation to the French coast. The military operation for Elba was put off. So that's the May dark period.

Pinpoint

Bastia, Corsica
June 18, 1944

On June 6 we received word that the invasion had started. The Sunday before, June 4, we had seen and heard nothing but planes, planes, planes for four or five hours at a time. You would wake in the morning to the constant drone of planes overhead, and this would continue, without break, until noon. Impressive as hell, but rather monotonous. When Walt and I heard of the invasion we felt, as everyone did I suppose — overwhelmed by the magnitude of it. At the same time we felt envious, and sort of cheap, at just sitting around while the big show was somewhere else. The cold figures were more than impressive: 11,000 planes, 4,000 large craft, and several thousand smaller boats.

It was at this period that Walt and I coined a little dialogue that was reprised by various parts of our outfit for some time: "What did you do in the war, Daddy?" "Aaah — shut up, you little bastard!"

The night of June 8 we tried a practice landing. We experimented with various communications and signal flashlights with colored filters. Tom and I went on the ARB out to twenty miles and came into a little sand beach north of Pino where Walt and Joe and the others were the reception committee. Before the operation we go to St. Florent to get on the ARB, Tom and I. Rather it was a house, or castle, slightly west of St. Florent, where the SIS representative, Captain Renton, had set up. It used to be Lord Chilcothe's place and had been the scene of a meeting with Lloyd George. It was beautiful. After a couple of Martinis, we had an excellent dinner. (God! The British know how to supply their people in a field with the elements of living — and I don't mean castles. I mean gin, whiskey, and good mustard!)

Then off to the pinpoint. A heavy wind came up, creating large breakers. Two British seamen and Tom and myself got in a rubber boat and started in. About 150 yards from the beach, the first really big breaker broke on us. It tore the third oar, which one of the men had been using as a helm, from his gasp. It broke one of the remaining oars in two, and we were swung about broadside to the breaker. The rower struggled valiantly with one oar to pull the boat around and just about made it. The next one hit us and the boat went absolutely perpendicular. We all thought it would capsize. (I remember wishing at this moment that I had learned how to swim!)

Finally, we were tossed out of the boat by a breaker, fortunately close enough to the shore to wade in after a thorough ducking. We arrived like a bunch of drowned rats. I realized after this how glad I was I had picked a beach instead of a rock landing for the mock up.

The Elba big job came off two nights ago. I was not on it — our whole part of it was washed out by Delattre de Tassigny.

Bastia, Corsica
June 21, 1944

On the night of June 19, I went up to the old pinpoint (Cap Pomonte) where I buried the money last moon period. It was a PT and I was to go ashore. It was our first operation to North Italy since Elba, the French invasion, Normandie, and the big push in Italy. We all wondered what would happen.

Of course, there were several possibilities that the pinpoint was blown. (1) The code had been used so much that it was not secure (and the pinpoint had been given many times in the code). (2) One of the men inside had been captured (and there was a real possibility that the radio operator was actually captured and being forced to operate for the Gerries). (3) The French team I landed when I left money might have been captured (while I was burying the money, those on the boat thought they had heard a couple of shots beyond the hill and thought they had seen flashes in that direction). (4) We had not heard from Reading, and they had been put in at the same pinpoint many weeks ago. (5) The pinpoint had been used so much in the past that it might well have been blown from many other sources. I was pretty much nervous inside about this job.

We reached the pinpoint and got about 800 yards off in the operational PT. The outside PT (which was about two and a half miles off) told us the radar showed "all clear." I had the bodies and equipment all at the stern, ready to go.

Just as we were picking up the rubber boat to launch it, Fergie Dempster spotted two corvettes coming around the point on our port beam. They were about 800 yards from us. We turned slowly to starboard to try to slip out. They challenged us with signal flares. We could not respond. A shot was heard (probably about a 40 mm.) We went a little faster. Then a signal light from shore. (At the shot, the bodies and

I hit the deck.) Two R boats (slightly smaller than E boats) were discovered to be off our starboard beam in the bay at Monterosso al Mare. They sent up more than half a dozen star shells. This made us feel like a virgin girl in the bathtub when the plumber enters. We went faster. More and more shots. I could hear a terrific whistle as one went overhead. (The destroyers mount four-inch guns and I imagine it was one of these.) We went very fast. The boats had opened up and we had been in close danger of being caught in a bad crossfire. (If we had gone another 200 yards it would probably have been all over. And if those destroyers had waited another couple of minutes we would not only have been another 200 yards, but down in the rubber boats, which would have been a whole lot of fun.)

During this melee, I got the bodies to crawl to the hatch and sent them down below through the officers' quarters. By this time, not only was the heavy stuff coming over and the star shells still lighting the area, but the tracer crossfire was crawling up on our wake. The PT skipper yelled at me, "tell them to throw a smoke can over at the stern." (He did not know whether I was a member of the crew or not, and didn't care.) I was a bit uncomfortable because I had no helmet. I crawled to the stern and said, "The skipper wants you to throw a smoke can over." One of the sailors back there said, "We've already thrown one over. Does he want another one?" Feeling rather foolish, I crawled back (raising up a bit at times and crouching as I went), and told him they had thrown one over, did he want another one? He said, "no." (By this time we were hitting about forty knots.) Someone in the darkness (we were outrunning the star-shell area and the tracer fire, but the heavy stuff was still coming) said to me, "Can you talk?" I said "Sure. What the hell d'you think?" This guy says, "Okay," and puts a rubber helmet on my head, which has earphones and a small mouthpiece. "This is a communication to the stern. Handle it for a while." I said, a little surprised, "Okay, sure." He said, "You press this when you want to talk," I said, "Check."

By this time we were several miles out and most of the firing had stopped, but the enemy was still sending up star shells and we had lost the covering PT. We pulled up some miles further out. I was still standing next to the bridge, by the forward starboard turret. I suddenly became aware that someone was on the phone. A voice said, thinking I was the regular crewmember at the post, "Is anybody on this phone?" Is anybody on this phone?" I replied, "Sure."

"What's the matter? Get scared and drop it?"

"I'm not the regular guy for this job. I didn't drop it: I picked it up," I said

"Oh. Say! That was sure close. There were five of them."

"I only saw four."

"Yeah. Guess that's right. Damned near got us, let me tell you."

"I don't think they like us," I said.

"You ain't just chopping your gums," came the reply.

"They were very inhospitable."

"What?" the voice said.

At this point in our interesting and cultural conversation, the regular radioman came along and took the onus of bow-to-stern communication off my hands — or ears.

We waited around for the other boat. It finally joined us. We were supposed to rendezvous with an ARB, which had another job five miles northwest, and escort it back. It did not arrive. I found out in the morning that the English had had a job in the ARB. They had had a rubber boat down and on the way to the shore when they saw the star shells and heard the firing on our show. Thereupon the ARB went away and returned later. They could not find the rubber boat, which meant that the occupants had left.

The next night we tried another pinpoint. When we were 600 yards off, we spied seven boats coming along and retired to let them pass. An F fighter convoy with E boat escort. We then went back in, and saw two other F fighters coming the other way. We pulled out silently and slowly again for them to pass. We then returned, and this time four E boats came along, going the other way. (I remarked to Walt at this point, with a certain amount of ironic truth, that they ought to have a traffic cop up there.) This time we went out again, and the ACF man, Boyle, said he did not want to try it again because it was too late. I thought differently; so did Walt. But ACF has the rubber boats, and had the rowers that night — so theirs was the power. We came on back.

The night of the 19th of June Walt took a French job (for which I did briefing and made the arrangements) out of Calvi. At 7:10 in Bastia we received word that one of the reception committee in France had been taken by the Gestapo and therefore the job was called off. It was imperative to get the PT back so the pinpoint would not be compromised needlessly. But the PT had left Calvi. A Beaufort night fighter went after them and caught up with them just about dark, at 10:30 P.M. The

PT, of course, called action stations as the aircraft approached. The aircraft came in directly — and from the north — instead of circling. The starboard .50 gunner on the PT apparently was a little trigger-happy, and, when the aircraft let loose a red and white flare signal (which the gunner nervously mistook for tracers), the gunner cut loose without a direct order. The bow 20 mm took it up. Then the piano near the stern (four .50s together). Then the stern 20 mm. The skipper (his exec had been on the bridge) came up out of the chart room yelling for the firing to stop. But few could hear in all that racket, particularly toward the stern. Finally it was stopped and the boat got the message and turned back. The plane had twenty holes in it — but fortunately no one was hurt.

A day or two later, we had the plane pilots from this incident to lunch, and also a couple of the officers of the PT.

The night after we tried three times to close the pinpoint without success, Walt and I decided (since there was no job that night) to go downtown to a new bar where we had heard they had a pretty good pastiche (the bar was intriguingly named The Okay Bar). We went there at four o'clock, intending to have a few before dinner (which was at 6:30). So we had quite an evening out on the town.

The next night we tried the job again. This time we took the ARB (no radar) with a PT to screen. The ARB closed to 350 yards off shore and Walt went in the bow of the first boat with an English rower and two bodies. The second boat carried an English sailor rowing, one body and equipment. The ARB shut off its motors and waited. About 15 minutes later star shells were fired by a corvette and R boat coming from the north. We started out. Walt was then about forty or fifty yards from shore. I was trying to get him on the Walkie-talkie to say we would be back, but could not make contact. We could see the tracer fire creeping up on us across our wake. The ARB only makes about thirty knots, and the tracer was gaining on us. I was in the open space between the turrets and the cabin roof. Finally, a green tracer came, or rather floated, across the roof of the cabin. I ducked back between the turrets just aft of the bridge. The next tracer came about two feet in front of me, about knee-high, across the deck. I was certain that the next would hit the starboard turret, and remember wondering what it would be like. Somehow they lost the range and we got out of it. All this time the radioman had been trying to contact the PT, desperately calling for it to create a diversion. Contact failed.

About ten miles out a boat was spotted on our stern at about three-quarters of a mile and gaining on us. At first we thought it was a German boat and would get us. It turned out to be the PT. Lt. Smylie, the ACF man, asked if I thought we should go back in the ARB, with the PT following all the way in, or whether we should transfer to the PT. I favored the latter, since it would be easier to maneuver with only one craft. So we transferred and went back, while the ARB headed for home.

We closed to about one-half mile in the PT. (Turned out that Walt had completed his job and was then about 150 yards back of us, but we didn't know it — water had got into the batteries of the handie-talkie and we could not communicate.) Just then several German boats opened fire from the east and we scooted, laying down a smoke screen for cover. We hit about forty-two knots and outran the tracer fire under cover of smoke. We slowed down about 2½ miles out. Then an 88 mm. landed about fifty yards off the starboard bow, so we speeded up again. We realized it would only call too much attention to Walt's party if we went to the same spot again that night, so we headed home.

(Walter had the two rowers in one boat with him. When we started off he was left just behind the line of fire. A German boat almost ran him down. They could hear talk on the deck. etc. Then he headed out to sea, battling the wind, and laid off the coast between three and five miles till the next night, when he came back to the pinpoint and waited for us.)

We got back to Bastia at 6:30 A.M., and of course the next day was one, not of sleep, but desperate (and in a very real sense, hopeless) preparation. We laid on air recess to look for the boys, but no luck. It was decided that we would have to go up prepared to fight to get them back. So three MTB's and two PT's were assigned to the job. Bill Sawyer and I went to handle TBY and handy-talkie. I had several conferences with Mac and others during the day to make arrangements. We started out about 7:30. Bill and I were on PT 305, which was to lead. We were to close the shore with the other four boats patrolling a mile apart, about two miles off. The British lieutenant, Bloomfield, who was in charge of the naval business, was one of the MTB's. He was to give commands for everything naval from that boat. The briefing, on the deck of one of the MTB's, was interesting.

Bloomfield stood like a lecturer at a rostrum giving the code words and the procedure to be followed — what was to be done in certain contingencies, etc. All the PT commanders and execs and MTB commanders and execs, plus Bill, myself, Mac and Smylie were present.

We started out in column with PT 305 ahead. At twelve miles off we slowed to nine knots. Bill and I made constant attempts to contact Walt with no results. "Wayne to Walt, Wayne to Walter. This is Wayne calling Walter. Calling Walter. Come in please. Over!" filled a lot of the radio waves the sets were on. No soap. When we got about one-and-a-half miles off it was realized that an E boat was sitting off the pinpoint. Later it was found there were seven boats around, including a couple of corvettes or destroyers. We decided (thinking that Walter was probably on shore) that it was necessary to get the E boat out of there. So the 305 idled in and turned to come out. The E boat obligingly followed, as had been hoped.

(Walt had been sitting about three-quarters of a mile out, waiting for us. We passed him on the way in, but did not see his light signal. We refrained from flashing the light inshore because he knew enemy craft were there and it might bring us under fire.)

As we were idling out, with the E boat obligingly, we thought, coming into the trap (the other four boats were getting into position to take her on), we observed Walter's light signal. We heve to. The rubber boat came over to us and the two English sailors climbed up the scramble net. Walt's legs did not function too well after being cramped in the rubber boat for over twenty-four hours. One of the PT sailors and I were helping him up, while two seamen pulled up the rubber boat when the pops that meant star shells were heard. Just as Walt reached the deck, the sky lit up brilliantly and firing began. We scooted after yelling "Locust" into the transmitter (which meant the pick-up was successful and Bloomfield could take any action he saw fit).

As the firing was on, and the 305 picked up speed, with the night air full of tracers, star shells and 88's and 40's, Walt and I were hugging each other on the bow of the PT. "What the hell kept you so long?" "For Christ's sake, you're getting snotty, refusing to ride back with us last night...." The PT skipper leaned over the bow and yelled, "Hey! If you two want to be alone why don't you go below till the battle's over?"

We went below, and for once in his life Walt preferred water, and lots of it, to bourbon!

Turned out Bloomfield's radio transmitter was hit at the beginning. He gave orders to attack (through the dead transmitter) and sailed in.

No one heard him and the other boats went the other way. He closed a corvette and fired two torpedoes, then retired, having had his boat hit several times. The firing continued a long time. As we were about three miles out (on the 305) a torpedo went right under us. Fortunately, though, although it touched some part of the stern slightly, it did not go off.

We got home all right, the other four boats continuing on an offensive patrol.

Two nights later the German radio announced that an engagement with five Allied small craft had been held in the pinpoint area and that four were definitively sunk, and probably the fifth. (Bloomfield told Walt and myself this in Florida Bar one night). I thought it quite interesting to have had the Germans announce we had been sunk. But, as always happens (somebody always has more experiences than you!), Bloomfield casually said it was the third time they had announced him sunk.

Well, now it looks like we may be washed up here on this type of operation. (The Fifth Army is now near Livorno. We can't operate between Genoa and the French frontier because of shore installations. In France the invasion has made moving around inside too tough and this leaves only the Spezia-Genoa coast for us — but that is where most of the Gerry traffic is.) As I say, since we have been washed up operationally here, after the end of the June period we received the personnel we have been yelling for for eight months — two conducting officers and three rowers! Oh, well — c'est la guerre!

En route Algiers to Naples
July 21, 1944

Flew down from Corsica to Algiers a couple of weeks ago. Had a quick talk with Henry and Dewitt and decided to go with the French Desk. Seems the job will be assistant to Dewitt, who will handle the operational aspects of the show going into Southern France. Naturally, I was let in on the fact that a landing in the south of France is planned (as who didn't know or guess?) and found that the forward echelon of our outfit would move on July 21. So I flew back to Corsica, turned things over to Walt Taylor, and then flew back to Algiers.

While up there, I handled some stuff on a Lysander operation that picked up an American flier who had been forced down in France. They got him out and I flew down to Algiers with him. His name is Herbert

Reed, from, I believe, Rochester. He had trouble with his motor (he was in a pursuit plane) about June 13 near Avignon. He had to bail out at 500 feet. He hid in the fields, and happened to run across an old peasant. This chap put him in touch with the right people (Reed is only 22). A month later he was to be included in an operation to pick up in France that our people had laid on in conjunction with the British. The first night the operation failed. The second night I was in Bastia and we received a cable at 10:30 containing important information for the fliers. I got in touch with the appropriate people in the British service and the planes were held up for about 35 minutes, while I got the rest of the message (it contained some garbles) and dashed out to the airfield in a jeep. The planes had their motors going, ready to take off. The message was read in the lights of a jeep and the planes took off immediately thereafter.

Well, I have been hanging around the French Desk since I returned to Algiers. All has been preparation for this operation, and I am writing this now on a transport in the Mediterranean.

This is a British transport — and, as usual, the officers have a wonderful time and the enlisted men have hell. We go first to Italy, I understand. Then we will go to a staging area and be held incommunicado until actually leaving for the landings to France. I understand that I am positively set for D plus 3, but Dewitt is trying to arrange it for the first day. I'd prefer the first day; but, since I came down late, I'll be glad to get on either. This is quite a colorful boatload — We have French troops, some of our French agents, several women, Indian soldiers (Sikhs), Moroccan Goums, Aussies, Canadians and Americans on board. This particular phase of the trip should be fairly short, not more than two or three days. Then will come the big trip.

The BBC announced today that there had been a revolution in Germany. It would be a shame to have the edge taken off the only landing I will probably have a crack at.

8

Operation Dragoon

On August 15, 1944, Allied troops landed in Southern France on the famed beaches of the Cote d'Azur between Marseille and Nice. This was the last large-scale Allied amphibious invasion of World War II in Europe.

Although Dragoon, replacement code name for Anvil, never received the publicity accorded the English Channel crossing, it did assist significantly in hastening the end of the war. After June 6, as Allied troops fought their way across Europe, OSS personnel in North Africa and the Mediterranean area had a sizable number of agents in place and in training, readying for a Southern European invasion, termed by General Eisenhower essential to the eventual defeat of Germany.

OSS Secret Intelligence (SI), working in Algiers, Algeria, in close liaison with the Allied Force Headquarters and the U.S. Seventh Army's Force 163, had labored long and effectively for the war's second major invasion, one of the earliest results of the Joint Chiefs of Staff approved North African mission, which culminated in Operation Dragoon.

It was an OSS as well as an Allied triumph. The spy organization had played a key role in the planning of the landings, providing intelligence of "extraordinary accuracy," including the location of German coastal gun emplacements and mine fields, to the operation's planning staff. Also, OSS communications in Algiers had "established mechanical transmitters which sent a continuous stream of dummy messages for some time prior to the actual invasion."

Wayne Nelson was one of the first five civilians and twelve military officers of the "First Lift" OSS Seventh Army Detachment (SSS-Strategic Services Section, G-2) who landed near St. Tropez on the following day, August 16.

Here are his diary notations beginning before the invasion.

August 7, 1944 (This is written at a staging area somewhere near Naples.)

Pozzuoli, outside of Naples

The last couple of weeks have been interesting, in the sense of being a prelude. We got on a troop transport in Algiers, and three days later we were in Naples. From there we went to Pozzuoli, a little town in the outskirts of Naples, where we were more or less confined, since, our next move, we did not know exactly when, would be toward a ship for France. While at Pozzuoli we took courses in practically everything: German army battle order, German guns, German documents, first aid, our own intelligence set-up, etc. We managed to get into Naples a couple of times. There is a beautiful officers' club there, overlooking the harbor (the Orange Club). Naples, in its natural layout, is a most beautiful place: large harbor, surrounded by hills, and Vesuvius in the background.

The city itself is dirty as hell, however. You can sit and sip a glass of wine, as we did, in a vast arcade (the Galeria), at an outdoor table. This arcade was sort of a "prostitutes' promenade." The first thing a man is struck by in Naples, aside from the town itself, is the size of the women's busts — and I do mean big. They are enormous. Therefore, the average group of anywhere from three to seven fellows, will sit, sipping wine and commenting on the various sizes that pass.

Finally, yesterday we found we were going this morning at 6 A.M. There was much trouble getting packs rolled, and getting everything you are to take in a musette bag, etc. Then, this morning, up at 4:30, breakfast at 5, leave at 5:45 in our own trucks. Stop to be picked up by Army trucks at a park in Naples. Two games of horseshoes while waiting, then into Army trucks and now sitting in a wooded park (Omaha), which is a staging area. We don't know whether we will be here hours, days or weeks. We are scheduled for "D plus 3," which will be close enough, though we all would have preferred D-Day. Some of the fellows had to come on the second lift, which will be D plus 5, and they feel absolutely sick.

What does one carry? Well, there is a web belt and harness, with a .45, two extra clips, canteen, first aid packet, and compass. Then there is the gas mask slung over a shoulder (I managed to get an extra carton of cigarettes into mine). Then the musette bag, in it are a mess kit, three pairs of socks, extra shirt, towel, handkerchiefs, two extra drawers and toilet kit. Also a couple of packs of cigarettes and cards and a few candy bars. Then the waterproof casing of the sleeping bag, with raincoat, field jacket, another towel and sleeping bag in it, rolled, horseshoe fashion, and tied around the musette bag. This is fastened on the web belt's harness. Then I have my brief case with papers, extra gun, cosh (a blackjack), about 20,000 in gold coins and francs, more cigarettes and candy. When you add it all up and start carrying it, your shoulders soon sag.

There's a helmet, of course, and, in August OD's. So here we all sit, leaning against our bags or trees, on leaves and dirt; some reading *Stars and Stripes*, some dozing, some checking over guns, some talking, etc. At any rate, it should not be long now, and the next entry should tell something of the show. All of us having wanted this show, and being in process of preparing for it when news of the attempted assassination of Hitler came, have felt almost afraid the war would be over before we went in on this. That is a pretty terrible thing to say, but it is only natural. It is not that we don't want the war to be over by any means — merely that we have all gotten set on this business of going in and we hope to get some action, I think.

August 13, 1944
Aboard the Darbyshire

(This is written on the ship "Darbyshire" (No. 509), lying off Castellamare, just south of Naples, waiting to set out for the invasion of Southern France.)

We came on board five days ago. After a night on the ground at the staging area (called "Iowa"), we put on full packs and got on trucks and were deposited near the docks.

The staging area was grimy, that is dirt all over, around and in you. We were in OD's, so the heat of a march with a pack like ours, which, in my case had a loaded brief case added, certainly raises a sweat. The pack, musette bag and roll, with belt, canteen, gun, first aid packet, compass, etc., must weigh about 60 pounds, and my brief case must be an additional 35 or 40. We marched down to the pier, — on the way a Red Cross girl had set up with large cans of lemonade and doughnuts and some stopped by the way for one or two, and then on board the ship. On her sides are hung many Higgins — boats (landing barges). She is an English ship carrying American troops and her crew, waiters, etc. are Laskars. She used to be in the Calcutta-Bombay run, I understand.

Our quarters are comparatively comfortable — upper and lower berths, service at the dining room — three meals a day and tea at 4 P.M. Breakfast at 8:30 A.M., lunch at 1 P.M., tea at 4 P.M. and dinner at 7 P.M. It is much better than any of us expected. But then, that is for officers. The enlisted men have, as usual, a hell of a time. They are crowded below decks in hammocks or swings; it is so hot and stuffy they can hardly breathe; their food is terrible. They allow 16 of them per night to sleep on deck. We have been just lying here for five or six days now. News is cut off. They announced to the officers yesterday that good news coming in might make the troops too complacent and therefore only an abridged summary would be distributed, instead of the BBC broadcast which we had been getting over the ship's public address system.

I sit now in the officers lounge: a large room which was formerly the main saloon. Windows lining the sides of the room give views of the shore of Italy, only 400 or 500 yards away. If you go up on the deck, Vesuvius stands out against the sky about one mile away. There are about 50 ships, loaded as we are, lying off here — waiting. We have on board with us elements of the 30th Infantry Regiment of the famous Third Division, which has seen everything from North Africa to Anzio.

In the officers lounge here, there are many tables, and bridge, poker, gin rummy, chess and checkers start about 9 in the morning and continue until 11 at night. There is a piano at one end of the room, in the center on a little raised dais. Occasionally someone will sit down and piddle, and I do mean piddle, around with the keys. This happened, as it does so often, the other day. A chap sat down and started to let his fingers wander over the keys. Several of us were playing bridge at the time. Then we slowly began to realize that this chap could really play — pretty soon he was well into one of Bach's toccatas and fugues, then a Beethoven sonata. Then others. This continued for about 40 minutes. The chap is small and dark, not bad looking. His eyes were kept on the piano; he was not looking for applause. He got none. But there was a hell of a lot of silent appreciation. Of course, the big long table in the center of the room, just in front of the piano, had its poker game continuing. The music was interrupted by loud laughter as a hand was won or lost, after heavy betting. Therefore, we may assume that there was a hell of a lot of lack of appreciation also.

We have a cross-eyed Laskar steward — I am in a cabin with the Red Cross Director of the Third Division. Each morning at about 7:30 this

Laskar comes in and lights the light and you open your eyes, which are at first blinded by the light, then slowly focus, if somewhat vaguely, on this cross-eyed Laskar. (It is a good thing there is nothing to drink on board.)

Each morning at 10 A.M. is the inevitable emergency station drill (or "parade," as the British say). Yesterday we had our first practice at getting into and out of the Higgins boats. Going down a scramble net with that pack of mine and a brief case will be an interesting job.

The characters who form the British officers are interesting. A British colonel is in charge of troops. He is a tired man, of about 53, tall, with a slight stoop. Typically British — slow speaking, indirect, but rather nice. This is because men of rank in the British Army can afford to be nice — they have others who can bustle around and do the dirty work. These include, the Colonel's adjutant, a British captain of about 40, red-haired, red mustache, bowlegged, and rather squat. He bustles about earnestly and anxiously. Then the British sergeant-major. This man is also squat, but has black hair and black mustache and carries himself as though he were Napoleon. He gives orders like a dictator. Then there is the mess officer whose shoulders are so square his head seems to be set into them at a rearward angle. He strolls about the dining room during meals, imperiously snapping a finger here or there for the Laskars to do his bidding. Of course, these officers transmit anything they wish through the American officers, which eases the situation a good deal.

On the whole, it is pleasant here. But yesterday we found out that an American armored column had reached Chartres, 40 miles from Paris, so all of us are anxious to be on the move to go in before the excitement is over.

It looks as if the war in this theatre will end soon — it seems hard to realize that some of those of this ship may get it, in the last, finishing touches on this Southern France job.

Well, if it finishes here soon, perhaps a rest at home and then to see what it's like in the Pacific — I understand the French Desk people have an offer to go out there — and I am now with the French Desk — so, perhaps.

August 13, 1944

Then, after five or six days sealed on this ship (2,359 men and officers), at lunch yesterday an armed Navy courier comes on board; at

2 o'clock we lift anchor; and by 3:30 P.M. we are on our way, the French battleship "Lorraine" following us, a heavy cruiser screening to starboard, and seven or eight cans protecting the convoy. Action stations are called, an announcement made that there is an important announcement to be made immediately following action stations. The announcement proves to be the reading of General Patch's* message to his troops — "You have set forth upon a campaign to liberate the sorely oppressed peoples of Europe; French and American soldiers, side by side, with the same equipment, will fight an inspired battle which *must* be won," etc. This drivel is listened to quietly; when it is over various poker players ask each other if they feel "inspired"—the reply is usually, "damned right. Raise two bucks." An abridged version of the news is given — never have so many words been used to express so little.

Then the first night under way — with the throb of the engines. A cockroach runs around the wall next to your bunk just before you put out the light — tantalizing your rest with wondering where he is, you settle back and it is hot, stifling. In ten minutes you are wallowing in your own sweat, and where is that goddamned cockroach now. Every bead or drop of sweat that rolls over your body in the dark becomes that damned roach. You would like to put on the light, but you have a roommate in the bunk below, and he is snoring soundly. So, finally off into a sweat stirred sleep, and maybe the cockroach is in the bunk below!

August 14, 1944

Then we go through the Straits of Bonifacio. For a couple of us, who have spent time in Corsica, this gives a bit of nostalgia. We are informed that we are the 12th convoy to pass through. An abridged version of the news is given us. It mentions good gains in Normandy, and then the three or four day bombardment of southern France. Several of us echo, "Why, daddy?" Then we are joined by other ships as we proceed up the coast of Corsica at reduced speed. We are apparently near the forefront now. To our port there are about 100 LCT's, a few destroyers and a cruiser. We are one of a single line of large transports in the center. Off our starboard stern we can see at least 100 other craft behind us. Destroyers encircle the whole business; there are at least four battleships some place around.

*Lt. Gen. Alexander Patch, Seventh Army Commander

A group picture of OSS civilians and military officers aboard the SS *Darbyshire* during Operation Dragoon.

We are called together by Colonel Gamble; we have a group picture taken on deck; Gamble says we must be ready to go in any time after we are alerted; the attack starts at dawn tomorrow; we play bridge, do odds and ends about tightening packs; collect rations. Each and every man and officer gets issued to him: three of K rations; three D rations; two packages of cigarettes; two boxes of safety matches; one little jar of halizone tablets; and one condom.

This morning we are issued the Army's little booklet on France. One of the chaplains organized an entertainment and sing on one of the aft decks an hour or two ago. It was all right. But not too much enthusiasm. It seems ironical that some of these guys will get it. I suppose none of us will get much sleep tonight. The naval shelling should start around 2 or 3 A.M. We also will have to watch out for night bombers; I suppose our shield of naval craft will protect the troopships from E boats and corvettes. Well, these waters are old stuff to me; I hope I have as much luck in big boats as I have had in little ones.

August 15, 1944

So for the rest of yesterday you hear announcements over the loud-speaker from commanders to their troops, generally — "ours in a glorious task — to liberate the tortured peoples — side by side with our French comrades — *I* will see you in Paris, and together *we* will march down the streets of Berlin — *we* must not fail — you are inspired troops," etc. ad infinitum.

So you play some bridge, and some clean guns, and some study maps, and some fix up packs — and everyone waits. Then I, personally, get a goddamned cold and my nose runs water all the time. Play bridge till 11 P.M., that guy plays some Bach and Beethoven and lighter semi-classics. Sleep.

The naval barrage begins at 5 A.M. The assault troops should be landing as I write this, at 8 A.M. We go in shortly afterward. No one knows exactly when. On the dot, at 5 A.M., the ship shakes with the rumble of heavy guns. Get up? The hell with it. The guns are faint in the distance now. But occasionally a heavy rumble shakes the ship. Finally, you get up at 6 A.M. The water is not on, so a handful of water from the canteen on the face, a drop on the hair — and topsides. Ships, plenty of them, around — large ships, small ships, medium ships. All types from the battleships, to the cruisers, to the big transports, to the patrol craft, to the LCI's LCT's, LST's, LSD's, what have you? Off in the distance, about four miles, we see the muzzle flashes of the heavy stuff— laying it into St. Tropez and vicinity. Our planes can be heard and seen — going and coming. But nothing as far as we are concerned.

Then, at 7, we have an air raid warning, which is shortly called off, without action. A Catalina flies down among the ships; wave after wave of our bombers go over, and for at least 45 to 60 seconds after each a rumble continues. Then another wave — then a ship barrage, then another wave of bombers — "Hate like hell to be on the receiving end of that." Nothing in return from where we are. Then at 8, we get an air raid warning — red — which means we have to clear the decks. This is H hour; and I return to the lounge and write this. Some of the boys are at the beaches now; others are going in; the ships are maneuvering for position; the planes are overhead — no enemy action of any consequence as far as we are concerned yet; and soon we will all be in. Seems, as the British say, " a good show."

August 15, 1944 — 10 A.M.

So you go down and have breakfast — and the haze is still on. You come up and go topsides immediately to see what is up. No raid, as yet. Then at 9:15 A.M. someone spies land. It is southern France, we know that; but a tremendous debate ensues as to just where (that is within a range of about 30 miles). Several of us think it is Cap Ladier (an old pinpoint of ours from Corsican operations), others think St. Tropez. It is probably one or the other. We are lying off now. The smaller landing craft have gone in. Little gunfire is heard. It is picking up just in the few minutes I have been writing this. Faint echoes of firing in the distance. We are probably about ten miles off. There goes a heavier rumble. Perhaps the Germans are pulling their old trick of landing, and depending on their ability to push it into the sea. Hope we can land soon.

And just a few minutes ago a PT came sailing by. It was one of those we had used from Corsica for jobs. It has about 15 German prisoners on board, probably picked up from some ship that was sunk. Certainly wish I were aboard that boat. We were just told over the public address system that we may expect to be in a state of yellow or red air alert all day, so everyone must keep under cover or be prepared to take cover at all times. Some maneuvers going on now — everyone is running to the port side of the ship to look at something — guess I might as well do the same — probably it is not worth running for though, so I guess I'll walk.

Incidentally, this should be exciting and I guess it will be in retrospect, but there just is not enough boom-boom to make it seem so at the moment. And I have a goddamned cold that has my nose running like a faucet! Damn it!

August 15, 1944 — 12:30 P.M.

And so it continues — rumors pop up — only one landing craft lost; two of the landings unopposed; etc. But no one knows. Everything proceeds comparatively quietly until noon. Then a terrific wave of bombardment rocks the ship. It is not hostile, but our own planes and warships which are apparently shelling and bombing positions on a hill around eight miles from us. Little landing craft scurry to and fro, to the beach and back, etc. I go down to my cabin at about 11 A.M. to shave and change my shirt; this latter involves sewing on a 7th Army patch. Outside the window of my cabin four soldiers are having an argument about horseracing. There is no excitement — red alert or two; but nothing serious so far. Probably 200 ships are visible, with glasses, from where we sit; but that can't be all, as several landings are proceeding east of us. None of us knows when we can land, or whether the German air force will have a recovery and give us some action; but it is possible we will land late today or tomorrow. It's a hell of a good break to be able to be here on D-Day anyway.

August 15, 1944 — 11 P.M.

So ends the first day of invasion — still on the ship. And everyone looking for the excitement to come. All day we sat out — first about 20 miles off; then 10 miles by 6 A.M.; then three or four; and by 4 in the afternoon we were about one half mile off shore near St. Tropez. At this point the landings apparently had been comparatively easy. But at 2 o'clock we could look east to where the 45th Division had gone in and see there was plenty of trouble down there. Reverberating rumbles testified to the power of the large ships that dotted the horizon, constantly battering the shore with everything from three to 16 inch guns. Intermittent hums of myriad motors bombing from the air. The coast at the point where the 45th was attempting to land gave forth puffs of smoke; fires started in the hills beyond.

Then came dinner. We had done nothing all day, but wonder whether we would get in to shore and land or have to lie out here. Many speculations were made as to the absence of the Luftwaffe. At about 2:30 P.M. I went down to the cabin and got out my only clean shirt, took the 7th Army patch off the dirty one and sewed it on the clean one. This must have been a half hour or forty minute job, slow and laborious — but, of, course, it was a good job (haw). Then came the job of packing my brief case, and musette bag and re-rolling my pack. This looked too formidable, so I climbed into my bunk and went to sleep. The gunfire could be heard intermittently. Then, about 5 P.M. I awoke and started the laborious job of packing. Things just wouldn't fit. I finally narrowed it down to the fact that my roll of toilet paper was too bulky to allow my brief case to close. So I spent at least 40 minutes rolling the roll into two smaller rolls of toilet paper so it would fit. Some way to spend the afternoon, or part of it, on D-Day. Then a turn on deck and dinner.

We had moved to within 500 yards of shore. The lighthouse on a hill stood off our port bow. Wisps of smoke at various places along the coast in front of us testified to the day's gunning and bombing. And still the planes came over and dropped their loads; and still the guns of the big vessels, the battlewagons and the cruisers, boomed and rocked the boat, and at times it would seem that the rumble, r-rumble, was shaking the earth.

We got the news broadcast, which said the landings had been made with 800 ships and 14,000 airmen participating. We had dinner. We kidded about after the war "What did you do in the invasion, Daddy?" "Shut up, you little bastard, I played piano in a two-bit whorehouse."

Then up on deck. Bang! A mine just went off directly off the shore, about 300 yards ahead of us. You can see the geyser of water about 40 feet high. A minesweeper scurries over, weaving its way among the LST's, the cruiser, the destroyers, the LCI's, and a pontoon that is all that's left of an LST which was destroyed earlier. It seems to have quieted down over there where the 45th was going in. No. There is another volley of big guns. "Lend me those glasses." You can see the silhouettes through the glasses of the large ships down there.

Then swing the glasses over to the shore in front of us. It is lined with people. Small landing craft are scurrying in and out. An LST looks as though it is practically up on the beach. You can see a road that leads, or winds, up the hill behind the beach. There are vehicles and men going up it. Then come two jeeps down — a couple of trucks up.

Another geyser of water near the beach. And another. Guess they must be shooting the mines off deliberately to pave the way.

Well, it's starting to get dark now. The first day is about over; it is still 8:15 P.M. The fires on the hills now glow dully in the twilight. The ships are enveloped, 10 by 10, 30 by 30, in the darkness. The gunfire is more sporadic. The hum of the planes comes at wider intervals. A large gun goes off now and then.

We won't get off this ship tonight anyway; so let's have a game of bridge. Fine. To the lounge, and a bridge game. A cold lemonade brought by the Hindu steward. War is hell department. Some fun, eh, kid? Well, we take one rubber. Your deal. What d'you say? Pass. I'll say — you contemplate your cards. Suddenly, at about 9:15 P.M., there is a burst of shots near the ship. Then the alarm bell ringing intermittently — clang, pause, clang, pause–clang. This means — air raid; take cover. All the people topsides can be heard hurrying down the stairs. Then all hell breaks loose outside as the ack-ack, including the large stuff, goes to work. Guess the best thing to do is to get a helmet. So you go down to your cabin and get the damned thing. Then back to the bridge game. The so-called raid is over. It was just a recce plane probably, or one or two planes that managed to slip through. If it was a recce, maybe we will have more tonight. So you finish the rubber; play another; and they close the lounge at 11 P.M. So you go down to your cabin and write this, while the sweat pours from your body into these wool OD's in the August heat, and your cabin-mate lies face up across the small cabin from you — snoring.

August 16, 1944 — 10:30 A.M.

So you get up to a calm sea at 7:30 A.M., and while you shave you hear the news broadcast from BBC reporting that all is going well and a lot of horseshit otherwise. Breakfast — you have slept soundly, but apparently nothing has happened during the night. A look topside and there is no change. Then at 10:15 A.M., as you are awaiting the emergency station inspection which never comes, they announce that debarkation will begin and call units. You are at this time in the middle of a gin rummy game, and since our unit is not called for the first lift, you finish the game and then write this. That good CIC pianist is at this moment playing a popular song, "I Can't Remember Where or When," and has just done the prelude to Ave Maria, and something else which you recognize as Bach but can't place exactly. You begin to notice that there was a bit of tension yesterday (perhaps "exhilaration" would be a better word); for now the relaxed attitude is apparent. We were wondering what has happened to Allan Stuyvesant, who went in with the paratroop units to Le Nuy. We hear that the Army has got up there and caught up with them, but Allan never jumped before and we have no direct news.

Well, we go ashore soon — certainly today — and then begins the march, and K and C rations and sleeping on the ground and all the rest of it; it should be quite interesting for there are hills and booby-traps and land mines and all the rest of it — land warfare that is new to me. And then our own work of taking people through the lines.

Well, I'll dash off now to see if I can get my pack straightened out — I guess we might get some action out of this soon — for if we get ashore and get a jeep we should be able to catch up with the advance units in a hurry.

August 16, 1944 — 12:45 P.M.
Beachhead at St. Tropez

So, as you watch Dewitt Clinton and another in a chess game, the
disturbing thought comes that you might get your damned pack fixed.
You go down to your cabin with this virtuous thought firmly in mind.
About 15 Hindu boys come in all saying, "Salaam, Sahib" and waiting
expectantly for tips. One, in particular, a little fellow and not the cross-
eyed boy of our cabin (the first sight I've seen each morning for ten days
now has been his startling phizz which just reaches the level of the upper
bunk in which I sleep), has been accosting me in the halls since yesterday. I have been avoiding him because I don't know what he is saying.
It seems like he is saying, "Badboy. Me Bad boy." The first time, yesterday, I said, "Okay, I'll forgive you" and walked away. As I entered the
cabin today and started wrestling with my pack, this elf comes in and
stands there looking at me. I said, fairly pleasantly, "Any suggestions?"
And he says, "Salaam, Sahib," evidently a greeting, a treat or a bridge
bid. So I say, "Salaam yourself." Well, he repeats this "bad boy" gibberish, me repeating "What?" at intervals.

Finally, I think I understand him to be the bar boy. So I tell him I
tipped the guys upstairs. And anyway the drinks were lousy. No liquor.
He keeps on repeating this gibberish of his, until I finally realize he is
saying "bath boy." Therefore, I say "Oh," rather dazed and worn down
by this time, and give him 20 francs to get rid of him. As I sit there con-
templating the wonders of Hindu stewards and how the hell I am going
to get this pack together, the public address system calls our unit "*immediately.*" I get to work and, fan on or fan off, sweat like a son of a bitch.
The pack reaches a state of seeming to hold together, however precariously, and then up to B deck and mill around with the others.

Finally I crowd into the bottom of a Higgins boat, between Dick
Crosby and Dewitt. You can see nothing, and the boat lowers and away.
After some ten or 15 minutes we hit a sand bar and then the beach. Off
the boat and up a sandy beach.

The beach at Pomplone. Off to the left on a little hill, is a lighthouse — Cap Cammarat, I believe. There is a sand bank log hut, which
is the Red Cross. A Sherman tank is wrecked directly ahead of us. Probably hit a mine. After about 40 feet of sand beach, there is a little pine
grove. Most of this is down already to build a road, etc. Up the pine log

road with pack and that goddamned 40 pound brief case and the helmet burning your head in the sun and that damned gas mask and all the paraphernalia. Up this road, with jeeps and trucks and other people's feet kicking dust into your sweat-soaked skin and clothes.

A couple of A/A guns are placed about. There is desultory gunfire in the distance up ahead. Several barrage ballrooms are moored close to the ground. Off the beach are many, many ships. Into the thin line of pines that are left, and a small house, knocked to smithereens. Up more dusty road. Around a hill, about one half mile away, are figures of soldiers, like ants, getting out their C or K rations. Stop along the road, "Hey there, don't get off the road. Can't you see that sign?" And signs, on either side of the narrow road which is faced with white tape, say "mines." So we stop along the road. Sit in the dust and release our packs; and then Crosby and someone else goes to see about transportation and we break out canteens and K rations. And then I break out this for a little note.

August 16, 1944
Near St. Tropez

So you sit by the road and eat a K ration. And you drop your pork loaf in the dirt and then dust some of it off and eat it. The dirt you didn't get off grits in your teeth. The hell with it. Christ, it's hot in these goddammned OD's. (Wool in the middle of August.) Then Gamble says we better get the packs off the road, and some of the guys have gone ahead to look for houses and cars, so theirs have to be moved too. So you get all sweated up doing this, and then you take off your shirt and sit down with your pack to your back for a cigarette. Just as you get settled, Milas returns and says if we can get all our stuff up to the next crossroads a truck will take it nearer to St. Tropez. We have found that our vehicle lifts (that is, the ships with our vehicles) apparently went in some place else, either Red Beach (Cavalaire) or to the east with the 45th and 36th. So we make five or six trips to get all the packs up to the crossroads. Then load them on a truck. Truck starts off, and everyone says we will meet it up the road. No civilian women come forth to give us wine or fruit — as we heard from the BBC was happening. No civilians are to be seen.

Finally, we stop at Battalion HQ, where a wireless message about the vehicles has been sent to Red Beach.

On the way up the road we can see a few shell craters, and places where mines have been dug up, or where signs warn mines are still in residence.

Battalion HQ is a house, half of which has been destroyed. Outside lie three stretchers with dead bodies bound in blankets. The wireless is in a dirt-covered log dugout. Then we walk up on the road to the quartermaster's dump where we draw C rations for tomorrow.

We listen to gossip about the landings — on our beach it was easy — eight casualties: two killed, six wounded; just east of us 45th and 36th had tough going and met some resistance; penetration is now apparently 10 to 20 miles; there are snipers around about a half a mile up the road; they just got one about ¼ of a mile from here — there he comes being marched down the road now; he is a civilian, claims he was helping our airborne troops; then the lieutenant at the quartermaster's dump says our own airborne troops were caught in bombardments by our own planes; one guy got 23 Germans in a little foxhole on the beach three hours after the landing. All this is the gossip of the first day of invasion here.

Off in the distance gunfire can be heard intermittently. On the road near us guns and vehicles and troops move up. We sprawl around under a few trees near the QM dump filling canteens from the water cans. Grateful, and I do mean grateful, for a bit of shade and the occasional imitation of a breeze that we might get.

August 16, 5:30 P.M.
Near St. Tropez

And so you wait around with a little group. Then you start into town. Someone says our packs are in the main square of St. Tropez. So we start up the road. There is about three inches of dust on the road and weapons carriers, A/A trucks, trucks and jeeps pass continually. The sweat soaks our wool OD's into clinging limpness. After about one half a mile scattered civilians come out to the side of the road to greet us — the V sign, bon jours and hand-wavings abound. Finally we enter St. Tropez.

We find our guys in the middle of the square with our packs. Bob Greene says there is a bar open across the way. So we go over, Bob Greene, Bob Thompson, Patterson, Walt Taylor and I. A few bottles of wine. They say there are still snipers in the town — one was shot and brought in about a minute before we hit the square. As we sit here in this bar, two or three mines go up outside someplace, shaking the building. It seems that they are clearing mines in the harbor. So we order more wine, the sweat pours down our bodies, and we sit here waiting for the next move. All the local people seem delighted we are here.

And by the way, that march was tough. The whole bunch are sweating like hell. Several of us have headaches and I feel like lying down and going to sleep. Like lying down anyway. (The OSS Gilbert & Sullivan Infantry — what those bards couldn't have done with our personal landing — briefcases, typewriters, civilians, marines, navy — Dewitt with a pack that looked larger than he; Jack Nile with a frying pan on his belt and his .45 slung directly front and center; Gamble limping; Crosby (as a result of the same jeep accident with Gamble in Pozzuoli) with a blackened eye and an adhesive patch on his nose.)

A good crack by Bob Thompson a moment ago: As he wipes the sweat from his face, and there is plenty of that (you have to be sure to wipe your face before lifting a glass or the sweat will drop in the wine): "What I need is four eggs and a salt tablet." Someone suggests there are no eggs. He says. "Guess I'll have to find me a girl with a farm." "What are you going to do for salt tablets then?" "Won't need them. Different kind of prostration."

We are in a typical small hotel-restaurant bar. Tables along the side of the room. The required menu regulations on the wall, with a couple of what seem to be water colors. A red, brown, creamy yellow wallpaper. Wall behind bar covered with shelves which are empty of all but wines and vermouth. Cashier's booth against wall at center of room. Several cut trees. A door to the street and one to the kitchen. A window and a couple of plain oval mirrors. Presiding is a woman of about fifty, stoutish, with several moles on her face. She is tired and would be just as happy if we went away (probably the effects of the several preceding days of barrage and bombardment). She takes it all with a stoic outward calm, however. She looks as though she has seen enough soldiers of every nation not to see any difference in them where a bar is concerned.

A picture of the Marshall on the wall.

August 17, 1944 — 9 A.M.
St. Tropez

We left one café and went to another where Dewitt, Jack, Gamble and I met several of the Resistance people. There was an engagement made for all of us to have dinner. We went with the truck to get Henry and Ponia settled, then returned to the café. Our people had gone and did not return. So we sat there and drank some pastiche (pernod or pastis) — Dewitt, Jack, Bob Thomson, Patterson and I. The doors of the café, fronting on the square, are massive with large glass panes. They were trying to close up.

Suddenly, no alert, no warning, the ack-ack started, a whining motor, and a bomb drops right in the square in front of the café. People were at the wide doors screaming and yelling to come in. We rush to the doors, open them, and I put my hand under the arm of a wounded French civilian to help him in. I literally get a handful of blood. I pass him on in to Pat, and they stretch him out on the floor. His belly and ribs have large chunks of flesh torn off. Someone says there is another chap, even more seriously wounded, at another door. I go over. I can see the man, huddled against a corner of the two steps outside the door, his legs covered with blood. The glass is blown out of the door, so I lean through to get a better view. I could see that he was pretty nearly gone — head and body hit in addition to his legs — but there are stretcher bearers on their way across the street to him, so I start to pull back.

Just then a large hunk of glass that had not been shattered comes down on my back. I go back to the bar where they have a couple more of the wounded stretched out on the floor. The stretcher bearers were getting to them. Dewitt reaches around to feel his behind, and says, "Look, I'm wounded." A glass splinter had scratched him. I feel my back a bit wet, and reach around to find a slight smear of blood. "Hey, I'm wounded too." Dewitt and I see this as good reason for the café people to get out the pastiche again, but apparently pinpricks and scratches will not dislodge a bottle in the possession of a panicky French café proprietor. So we go outside.

There is a car there with the motor running, and gas slowly leaking from a small hole in the tank. Someone says, "Look. Transportation; let's get it back before all the gas runs out." We hop in and start out for the place where the outfit has settled, just about a kilometer up the road. On the road, I get to thinking about how the guy who owns the car may have been blown out of it or scared by the bomb, and express a twinge of conscience. Jack Nile remarks that anyone around here must be a collaborationist. Thus rationalized, it seems simple, and we proceed to the billets and put a pan under the gas tank quickly to catch any that remains. No waste.

The car proves to be the first, and only for a few days transport, we have. But we don't use it until it has been painted.

Then we sit around and drink Cognac and sing songs. Then to bed. Dewitt and I are in a little house that was but a day before occupied by the Germans. It has two rooms, one bedroom and one dining room. Machine gun emplacements and fox holes are outside. The Gerries left in a hurry — their personal effects, etc. are still around. I slept on a Gerry blanket last night; as I look at it this morning, I have a hunch I would not have done so if we had had any more efficient light than flashes to examine it beforehand. One wall has been blown out, and the cool air awakens me in the early morning.

In the morning, we explore the place, picking up trifles here and there. I pick up some lush postcards (apparently favorites with the Gerries) and a Hitler postage stamp.

August 19, 1944 — 5 P.M.
St. Tropez

The day of the 17th, Don King and I set off on our first mission: Hitch-hike to St. Maxime in quest of a plumber, wine and vegetables. (The only water we have found in the headquarters is bottled carbonated water the Gerries left; we use this for everything from drinking (straight), drinking (mixed with cognac), washing for a day or two.) Rides were fairly easy to get on jeeps or weapons carriers. The road followed the coast pretty much and we could see the tremendous activity that was keeping men and supplies pouring on to the beaches. We could also see the bomb and shell craters that had been made by our pre-invasion barrage. The town was quite nice — here, for the first time since landing, a woman greeted us and pressed grapes upon us. As I had had no breakfast, I accepted them gratefully (wow!).

The plumber could not come today because (a) it was a fete day to celebrate the debarquement and everything was closed; (b) he did not have many helpers; and (c) he had a lot of work to do to make coffins for the resistance people who had been killed. He promised to come the following morning, however. The fact that it was necessary to go into the country to get wine or vegetables caused us to decide to go back (lack of transport). We went to the main road and got a ride with a chap who had been on the boat with us. We stopped at a little bar and had a pastiche and then back home. (The bar was named the Hermitage, and quite attractive — don't know how well "Old Hickory" would have liked it, however.)

A shave and brief wash in charged water, with helmet for basin, and C rations.

That night three of the chaps came back from Divisional HQ's and report the front moving so fast we would have to move ourselves or become rear echelon soon. General Donovan appeared briefly and made an observation showing both leadership and appreciation of OSS methods: "As far as I can see, you're doing a good job, and the best thing I can do is get out of here and let you do it. I borrowed this jeep from someone up the line, but if you'll have someone drive me down to the beachhead, why don't you just keep the jeep." We kept the jeep.

Staff meeting that evening to consider possibilities — much talk, no decision.

The following morning it was decided to send up an advance base and three teams for the three divisions: 36, 45 and 3. John Millas and I were the advance base — to be set up at a place Frank had found at Les Arcs. Third: Thompson, Ponia and Moretti; Thirty-Sixth: Justin, Walt and Sweeney; Forty-fifth: Frank, Patterson and Hoguet.

We went up late in the afternoon, past hundreds of parachute boys who were being withdrawn. Past the gliders which brought the airborne. Past the bomb holes, and the shell holes and the houses shattered, and the parachutist obstacles — posts, about 10 feet high, in the ground in rows, with barbed wire strung between. Past the mined areas. All of this in an hour and a half's drive. All these things, I suppose, will become customary in the future, but in war, each new locale, each sight of destruction, seems a never-ending occasion for wonderment.

The place at Les Arcs is a chateau — and it is really something, after the last few days: Running water (which can be heated), and linen sheets on the beds.

John and I went into town before dinner to get a drink and look over the place. The cafes had nothing, but a resistance member invited us to his home for a pastiche. It was good. He and his mother talked of the resistance movement here (principally FTP, leftist), of making pastiche, of times as they were, of the victory to come, and of the Germans (who, in the phrase that is found in every French speaking region from Africa to Corsica to France "sont tous pris. Tous! Tous! Tous!!)

Then John and I stood in the square at Les Arcs for a while. We saw people watching a road up the hill. We look. Coming down were several hundred people, following a charcoal burning truck, which had 12 plain wood boxes (serving as coffins) piled on it. They walked slowly; the men's heads bared. A sort of guard of honor walked in two files on either side of the truck: The Men of the Maquis — leather-skinned, blue denim pants, most of them, some blue shirts, some white; rifles, shotguns, Sten guns — anything that would shoot (and perhaps some that wouldn't) — slung over their shoulders; heads bared in tribute to the dead who had been most recently killed by the Germans in the mountain fighting (for near here the Germans had had to break off elements of whole divisions to carry on this hide-and-seek mountain and forest and bush and grass war), and who now rested in those plain, bare, square-cut boxes.

John and I removed our helmets and stood at attention as the cortege passed. We were the only Americans in town, except for one or two parachutists. We were moved by the sight, and the thoughts it evoked, for our business gave us more knowledge than the average person of the gallant fight these resistance chaps had put up. Moved more than a little bit; it is one of most impressive tableaus in my memory.

We returned and found that Frank had secured some brandy, some pastiche and some other concoction. So we had a few pastiches, and then dinner: C rations, tomatoes, and a few potatoes. And wine. And C ration crackers. In these surroundings the C rations seemed good. We dined in fine style.

Then Allan Stuyvesant came up from Le Muy. He was to have come with us, but had been selected as liaison with the Fredericks' Airborne and had parachuted in early the morning of D-Day. He had quite an interesting story to tell — naturally he has been the envy of all of us for a week or two!

This morning I went to Third Division CP. Found it up the line and had an interesting drive trying to find a gas pump. Finally found it and got 40 gallons of gas and 10 of oil. Went to Frassans, Videbans, Lourges and back to St. Maxime, then here again. (Les Arcs) Part of this country is still sniper country, but I saw none and heard none, though I saw many prisoners, and of course a tremendous amount of stuff moving up to the front (which is about 5 to 20 miles from here). It has been decided that we move up pretty soon to keep pace with the front. Well, let's go.

9

France: The Vosges Region

Wayne Nelson was the "SI Operations Officer with OSS detachment with the 36th Division of the 7th Army, August to December 1944 — recruiting, training and briefing French agents for infiltration through the lines to secure technical and strategic intelligence; planning and preparing such operations; conducting such agents through the lines; preparing and submitting reports of intelligence thus gained to 36th Division and 7th Army."[*]

As soon as our OSS unit debarked on the Riviera on August 16, it was apparent that the Seventh Army campaign in Southern France would be unusual. The army's lightning advance in the first two days caused plan and neatly conceived plan to be scrapped. Two days after D-Day, it was evident that the Strategic Service Section's (SSS) plan to work only at army level was ineffective, and on August 18 (D-plus-3), small SSS detachments were dispatched to the three divisions of the Seventh Army.

The experiences of the SSS detachment working with the 36th Division comprised two very different phases — the period prior to the crossing of the Moselle River on September 21 and the period of the advance from the Moselle to the Meurthe River.

After the 36th Division crossed the Moselle, the fluidity of the front decreased. Opposition became increasingly fierce as the division approached the Meurthe River in the Vosges region, and the relatively stationary German front became harder to penetrate.

There are no hard-and-fast rules of procedure for securing intelligence by infiltration through enemy lines. Recruiting, briefing and infiltration must be adapted to the peculiarities of the existing situation. Most of the agents our detachment used were locally recruited for specific missions in the region that the 36th Division was operating in at the time. Our main sources of agents were the various Free French Intelligence (FFI) organizations. France was rich in courageous men and women whose hatred of the enemy made no risk insurmountable to them.

---

[*]*OSS Field Report, May 22, 1945.*

For several days after the 36th Division crossed the Moselle in late September, the 3rd Division, operating south of the 36th, lagged behind and had not yet reached the river. This left the 36th Division's right flank exposed, and the division command was extremely worried that the Germans might counterattack on that flank.

The division needed information on German plans, but our recent experience with agents had not been good. The Germans were obviously taking greater precautions against agent activity, so there was a great need for agents with better 'cover.' Fewer intelligence operations with better planning were also a must.*

Here are experiences in this effort, including those about Joes, as the agents were called, that are related in the diary.

Chateau Prevalon (near Beaumont, just north of the Durrance)
August 21, 1944

Our first two daily reports were well received — the whole country south of Draguignan to St. Maxime I covered extensively in a little Citroen Frank "picked up."

Then we heard our troops had crossed the Durrance. John and I went up there, and we all decided our next advance base should be north of the river. I am now sitting in the garden of the Chateau Prevalon, slightly north of Beaumont. Quite a pleasant place — I suppose we will move again tomorrow or the next day. Got word yesterday that the 11th Panzer, or elements of it, were at Le Puy — so we hope the French can take and hold the ports of Toulon and Marseilles and that the Third will hold on the left. The right flank is now entirely held by the airborne Division; the 36th is up near Grenoble; the Butler Task Force is bounding ahead up there some place, instead of the 36th. For the moment our job is to keep close to the Third and 45th; and 36th is too far out for us to effectively cover it.

Last night drove from Perolles to Les Arcs, and then up here this morning. Just made it to Les Arcs by dark last night; was shot at by a sniper on the way down last evening. Varied speed and course for a couple of miles through the deserted part of the hills.

*An excerpt from Wayne Nelson's article about OSS spies published in *World War II*, July 1997

September 8, 1944
St. Hippolyte (France near the Swiss border)
(This covers from August 20 or thereabouts.)

John Millas and I established a sub-base at Les Arcs, near Draguignan, on or about August 19. We dashed all over hell trying to service the three divisional teams, but no go.

Trip to Mons (found Taylor missing) and then up Route Napoleon to Aspres. In Castellane the joy of the people unbelievable. Barmaid who practically raped Bill Duff in public. They had a member of Milice tied up in a chair in the center of the square. Were shaving his head. Dinner with a family at Sisteron. On to Aspres; couldn't find Justin there — so drive back at night to Pierrevert.

Got Citroen over an engineers' treadway bridge on Durrance — damned near scraped the guts out of the car.

Sub-base eliminated, and I assigned to Third Division team with Thompson and Ponia.

Putting two Joes through the lines at Pierrelatte with Thompson. We go out on a road about 150 yards from a German self-propelled gun, which opens fire. We dash back into scrub woods and spend three hours while the shells whine, whistle and puff (rocket shells) over us. We are about ½ mile from our own artillery and about 400 yards from Gerry artillery. Some day. It is quite a feeling when those shells go over and you hit the dirt — boy, do you hug mother earth! (Somehow entirely different from being under fire on the water.)

Stayed at deserted hotel all night. Next morning the Gerries have cleared out of Donzere. We try to get through to Montelimar — no soap. Outside Montelimar are 300 vehicles the Gerries have abandoned. Also their personal belongings, etc. that are strewn over the road. We capture one Polish German soldier who has been wandering around and 7 Todt workers (all of them quite willing to be prisoners).

Our Division moves up to near Flassans. We go there and stay overnight with a bunch of Joes in a broken down hotel. Then we move to Bourgoign. I go up to Lons Le Saunier with Dewitt, Ffoulke, Bill Clark and Rader. We receive a terrific ovation. I have a clipping from the local paper. We were the first Allies in town by four days. They crowded around the car, dragged us from it, and we were kissed by more men, women and children than a movie star. The Mayor boards the jeep.

Makes a speech. Tears in the eyes. One arm around Dewitt and one around me. We all sing Marseillaise. More speeches. More tears of joy. The Mayor embraces all Americans. We are paraded around town and then taken to a banquet at the Hotel Geneve. Cases of Champagne.

(On the way up we had an interesting trip. Passed 100 miles behind lines to get there. Very interesting, somewhat tense — until it started to rain, which it did, and we wound up soaked to skin. At this point, didn't keep alert look-out for Gerries; very uncomfortable; figure Gerries as uncomfortable as us if out and will stay indoors.)

Back down to Bourgoin again next day. Sullen looks of people in territory where they had never seen an American. They thought we were Gerries because of the helmet shapes. This at least proved that Gerries really did not get a, even token, ovation from the people.

Move up to Amberieu. Bob Thompson and I take a couple of Joes back up to Lons and put them in Chalon-Sur-Saone. We find a German armored column passing Louhans — some 50 tanks and accompanying vehicles. The resistance people stop us about 2 km. from Louhans and insist we have lunch. They take the Joes on. It is a little Maquis group and the lunch is good — omelette, meat, potatoes. Then, for dessert, creampuffs! It turned out the cook for this little group was one of the best pastry chefs in France. Head of resistance insists we accompany him to some nearby villages. We do. It is champagne, or particularly good local wine, here, there and everywhere. And everywhere there was an ovation. Our jeep smothered in flowers. We wind up in Lons and figure we will stay all night. Then we find the Division is moving up, so we go to work at 1 A.M. to find it.

I hitch-hike on a gasoline truck back to Amberieu, grab a car and go back up. We stay at Chateau Domblans outside of Lons. We move on up and try to get Joes through at Bescancon. Driving up the road in a civilian black car, no markings and no lights, with tanks, jeeps and army trucks driving at you the other way, on a dark night and dark as hell. Not even blackout slits on car. Sweat like hell.

Then transferred to 30th with Justin. Join it at Arbois. Put a Joe in Dole, going some 6 km. ahead of our advance units and then ½ km from Gerries. Then go up to meet the Joe near Besancon at Beure. Spend night at little road-house café. Much good wine; we manage to buy 12 bottles Vin Jaune du Chateau Salon, all bottled before 1920. Also 12 bottles Chateauneuf des Pape (1912); and some pretty good Jura wines. Back to Arbois in morning. There is still heavy firing at Besancon and Beure — particularly mortars and T/D's.

Justin and I came up to put a Joe in to Montbeliard yesterday — September 7. Found the French First Army in this district. They were stopped at Noirefontaine — a crossroads just north of St. Hippolyte. When we got there, five German tanks had come down the road just one hour before and knocked out the French A/T guns. We take the guy across the river on the railroad bridge — the other bridge had been knocked out — and then let him loose. (Did you ever drive a jeep on trestles?) I am now waiting here for word from him. Found this morning he probably did not make it, so contacted a resistance group here — including going up into mountains. Found the head of resistance is a "fraternity" brother, American or Canadian, Commandant Paul, sent from London, and am trying to get Joes to put through.

Staying at Hotel Les Terraces (Room 17). Beautiful country.
September 10, 1944

In these various little notebooks, I did not get a chance to say much about the detail of getting a team, or agent, through the lines.

Suppose you arrive at Pierrelatte, as Bob and I did about August 31. You contact the head of the resistance movement and he tells you about a couple of men who would be willing to do the work. You then go out and contact Regiment CP and find that they are held up at Donzere. There is gunfire all around, probably from about ½ mile away. You get your team of three men, brief them, and start out for Battalion CP or near the firing. At one road you are stopped, because the Germans have a road block just ahead. You go around another way. You are stopped by a bridge that has been demolished. (Later you are glad you were stopped, because the Germans prove to have been about 400 yards up that road with machine and A/T guns.)

Then you hear that another battalion is around the hill trying to get certain high ground. So you start around there. Pretty soon you see no Americans, but hear firing constantly. For all you know, you are ahead of the lines. There are five in the jeep — 2 Joes and Mack in the back, Bob in front, and me driving. At the crest of a hill, where the road is not lined with any trees or natural cover, and winds down around the other side — behind some trees there, one of the Joes suddenly called "Allemands." All those in the jeep hit the dirt in a shell hole at the side of the road, guns ready. You look and, sure enough, there are helmets to be seen over the fringe of low trees.

You get out of the jeep in a hurry and fall flat, your gun out and ready. It turns out to be an American patrol. They tell you the Battalion CP is up ahead "some place." So you pile back in the jeep and start out again. You come to a company CP; they tell you the Battalion CP is around the road to your left. You go sailing down the highway, when two soldiers step out of the brush on either side and say you can't take a car any further down the road, as the Germans are not so very far away. And where is Battalion CP? "Oh, it is on the other side of the road, but the colonel won't let any one go along the road even on foot, as the road is under observation. You have to go through the trees. You'll find it easy — it's just about 1,000 yards down, on the right." So you put the jeep in a clump of trees and we all start out through the brush on the right of the road.

We proceed carefully, guns in hand. We are challenged by a soldier — some place in the trees: "Birch." We do not understand at first. "Birch!," this time more emphatically. We remember the password — "Bark!," we reply. A head pops up from some small bushes. "Who is there?" Bob replies, "Lieutenant Thompson. Who's that?" "Lieutenant Schuyler. Can you tell me where Company I is?" "No, we don't know. Haven't seen it." "Okay." And the head disappears.

We continue for at least 1,000 yards, but can find no Battalion CP (With the firing around, one was reminded of the story of the General who commands the Third Division — when he called in all his battalion commanders one day. Kept them standing at attention for about 5 minutes while he finished with some papers. Then looking up and said: "Gentlemen — all good battalion commanders are dead." Well, this one certainly got his battalion up far enough!) Finally, we decide to take a look along the road. We proceed to the ditch at the side, and Bob sticks his head out. Bang! We duck back and hit the dirt. Bang! Whistle. Bang! We hug the dirt. Whistle. Silence. Turned out there was a self-propelled gun about 150 yards down the road. We go back about 500 yards and try the other side of the road. We can't find the Battalion CP, but run into a company that is going down in the gully to some woods down there.

The terrain is through a bunch of waist-high brush. We make our Joes take off their white shirts because they are too easily spotted. We

get down in a little clump of trees, after about 1 hour in the brush, hitting the dirt every two or three minutes as the shells go by from both
the German and our own guns. Then we see the charred remains about
us in this wood. Everything is black with the results of fire, for it has
been under a terrific barrage. We come across some things left by the
Germans as they got out. Rations still hot, personal clothes and effects,
empty champagne bottles. We finally let the Joes go about 400 yards from
the German artillery positions. It is getting dark. We find our way back
to the jeep and go to Pierrelatte to sleep in a deserted hotel for the night.
(A kind family heats some of our rations for us and we have a bottle of
wine before going to bed.)

Then up at 6:30 in the morning—no water in the hotel. We go
out, find Mac, who has been waiting for the Joes. They came back at
4:30 in the morning, but did not get much done. We then go over the
battle area of the preceding day, for the Gerries have pulled out. We start
up one road. At a bridge about 200 yards ahead, a sudden geyser of
smoke arises followed by the sound of an explosion. We go up to it and
stop. It was a jeep with three guys in it (which honked for us to let it
pass a few minutes before—thank God we did), which has hit a mine.
Three men were in the jeep—they are, when we get there, pieces of flesh
and meat around the landscape. The major portion of one poor chap
landed in a field about 70 yards to the side of the road. Part of the jeep
is a flaming hulk at the other side. Ghastly and grisly.

We continue on and find there is nothing we can do around there,
as it is now reduced to street fighting in Montelimar. We go to the line
of abandoned vehicles outside the city and get some German gas, and I
pick up several maps and documents that might be useful intelligence.
We pick up one prisoner and 7 Todt men on our way back and deliver
them to the MP's.

Then we go to Flassans and stay the night.

Then we go through the mountains to try to find the division. There
are plenty of Germans still in the woods we are informed, but no organized army. We find the Maquis organizing, about 3,000 strong, near here
to hunt them down. We find the division and it is about to move again.

Jack Nile and I go out, after the trip to Lons le Saunier, to put two
bodies into Lyons. We go into the outskirts of the City at Vanissieux
about 5 hours and 10 miles ahead of the advance units of infantry. The
Gerries are still further down in the city. The celebration and ovation

Jack and I received was simply fantastic and beyond belief. We were pulled out of the car and could not move because people were crowding around us to kiss us, shake our hands, pound us on the back, etc. Finally we sent the boys down into the city and got out.

War is really nothing but a series of uncertainties for the individual, I guess. I sit here now in a hotel, Les Terraces, at St. Hippolyte, near the Swiss border in the territory of the French First Army. Before me are the green hills of the Alps. It is peaceful and quiet, except for the occasional roar of army trucks and jeeps. The Doubs River flows by below the window in front of me. The Gerries hold Pont de Roide, not more than 10 kilometers up the road that disappears behind the hill in front of me. All, as I say, is peaceful. Yet the artillery at the sides of this town booms every 10 or 15 minutes. And the concussion shakes the building.

This morning I took a Joe I recruited here up to Villars where the French troops have some Goums and which is right on the Swiss border. I took him a little outside of town and told him to go ahead with the mission I briefed him in (to Montbeliard). The situation was intricate — A salient of Gerries here and there between FFI or Goum salients. I had picked a small road through a wood, and let him loose at the edge of the woods where it looked like he could get through.

Coming back, I was thinking about what a rotten business this is. This Joe was a hell of a good guy — he has a wife and 5 children, the oldest 14. He is 45 years old. I saw his wife saying goodbye to him just before I made the rendezvous with him this morning. His hometown has been liberated. Yet, he says, "Patrie first!" He is not a brainy man, but he knows this country, and he is the type that will do anything if it is diagrammed for him. I felt rotten about sending him on this mission which was dangerous as hell. As I say, I was thinking about this and following a road back, and forgot to take the shortcut to avoid a German salient. Fortunately, I was stopped by a Goum patrol of four soldiers just 300 yards before a German tank position. I quit daydreaming for the rest of the way back.

The Joe came back this afternoon about 5:30. He had tried and got through, but no go. I was, although it means failure from my standpoint, just as happy that he was back safe. He was very apologetic about it, and wanted to try again. I gave him some chocolate, 200 francs and several packages of cigarettes, and told him to go back to his family. (I also made a mental resolve not to watch Joes say good-bye to their families; and if I had to, not to think about it till after the war.)

September 11, 1944
St. Hippolyte

It's a funny way this business goes — up and down. You have a blank page and no ink; then somehow writing appears on it.

I came up here with Trinidad to see if anything could be done. The first guy I tried to put through couldn't make it. The French G-2's said impossible in this sector. It seemed that the guy Justin and I put through before Jus went back to the 36th had failed also. Yesterday, as I went to lunch at a little restaurant by the Doubs not more than a hundred yards from here, I was discouraged as hell and ready to give up.

Then I got word that the first guy was in Montbeliard on his way to Belfort. Then I got another source for recruiting Joes. Then a deal with the FFI chief north of here (a London fraternity brother, by the way, Paul) and made a deal to get a daily stream of stuff from him — he had some good battle order stuff, particularly on a new Panzer division coming in North of here. So I went down to the 36th CP and G-2 was interested as hell; Jus is pumping the stuff back to our 7th Army gang. Then I came back here and found a recruit ready and some more possibilities. (Particularly in the matter of sending Joes through Switzerland and out through Delle.)

Certainly variety anyway: one minute you are out in a jeep or on foot, wondering where the next shell will strike or when a Gerry will pop out of the bush at you; then you are in a comfortable hotel room, a little cold perhaps, wondering when someone will arrive with a new recruit or a message from a Joe already out.

September 14, 1944
Vesoul (Hotel Bourgogne)

Have been waiting here for some Joes to return since I returned from St. Hippolyte.

Yesterday received some wonderful news: Moretti, who was captured near Avignon, escaped and returned. They had him on a train going to Germany and he and two others jumped off the moving train. They apparently treated him correctly as a prisoner of war. He knows a little German, but pretended not to know any of the language. Therefore, he heard the Germans talking, and apparently they have a lot of our names. Whitney, who was captured with Moretti, also escaped and is back.

This morning, however, we received some tragic news: Pierre Yakes was killed last night. He had been putting some Joes through, or returning in a car, when some American soldiers opened up on him with machine guns. There were more than 130 bullets, Crosby told us when he came up today. He was a hell of a nice egg, son of an American soldier, who did not return from France after the last war, and a French mother. It was only four days ago that we spent the night together at a little café near Beure, just outside of Besancon, while the troops were trying to take the city. He had discovered an excellent wine cellar and we sat up with Sweeney waiting for some Joes who didn't make it until 3 A.M., drinking various wines, to sample them, of course.

I don't suppose one ever gets to the point where these things seem normal. The reaction one has is peculiar: There is shock, and a feeling that one feels badly. And yet one does not feel anything, and it is almost as though one had read in a magazine of the death of a stranger. There seems to be some sort of internal anesthesia which prevents any real feeling. When informed by other friends of the guy that he is gone, there are the clucking tongues and the cliché phrases, "Oh — that's terrible," "He was really a swell guy," etc. And faces screw up in an expression of sadness, but it's a mockery — because there is a cold blanket over any real feeling. The guy is just written off — "now you see him, now you don't." You saw him every day, you drank with him, laughed and cursed with him, and now his body is a mess — a bloody, broken mess. And he becomes merely another digit in the casualty figures — Mars' cash register rings again.

Then, since there is no feeling (perhaps it would be too personal to feel), the mind tries to reason it out, to rationalize it. Let us see — I saw him last there at the hotel — what was there about him that marked him for death? You try to think of something unusual, some indication that fate had put the finger on this particular guy. Naturally, you get exactly nowhere with this line of thought. Because there is no reason, or why, or wherefore to this whole goddammaned business.

And then, of course, when you talk with other friends of the guy, everyone talks about the last time he saw him. This is perfectly natural and happens all the time. But if you analyze it, it's pretty damned horrible — because, in a sense, though perfectly innocently, all try to share the sensation of the guy being killed. A guy goes out and gets knocked off, and he can't even have any real appreciation of what he went through on the part of others. How the hell can they know, or feel what he felt?

Then, of course, one has to listen and cluck over the gory details: "His neck was nearly severed by the bullets," "He was practically cut in two," "They left him there all night — bloody and gutstained," "He had gotten stiff and we could hardly get him out of the car. What a mess." And then the hushed tones, and clucks, and "horrible's," and "He was a nice guy," and probably everyone mentally amazed at the ever-new wonder that a guy is dead. And, for one person at least, the feeling of utter debasement that there is no feeling. It is precisely as though a character in a film had been killed — though I really think there is more feeling in watching a film story character die than a friend in this macabre play. This lack of real feeling inside is probably the basic degradation of war — not the mud, and filth and blood. Maybe I'm just tired.

However, since the war does seem to be in its final stages, there is a certain tendency to let down, not to be so full of piss and vinegar as when the war was difficult and not going too well for us. It does seem a shame that people have yet to die when the outcome seems so inevitable. It would be better in a sense if the Germans put up more of a fight; there is some fight, but it is a defensive, rear guard action for the most part. The hell with it.

I was impressed at St. Hippolyte, as I sat in a little restaurant by the Doubs and had dinner, and the French colonial troops were moving up on foot — the Gerries were only ten kilometers or less up the road. There is some sort of a sensation when you see the infantry moving — something personal in watching a guy on foot — that can never be captured by a man in a tank, on a plane, or a jeep. These boys of the French colonials had expressions of almost shyness on their faces, and smiles that were self-conscious. The smiles were for forced gaiety of any soldier going to battle. Then, of course, some looked at the officers eating in the restaurant with the spirit of "you lucky sons of bitches." Then the French officers marching with the Goums — more erect, firm, step, — noblesse oblige. Amercian GI's are not so shy or self-conscious. They are tight-lipped and stern generally when moving to battle.

Saw some girls in town here at Vesoul being marched off to have their heads shaved for having consorted with the Germans. It took on the atmosphere of a fete day — in some aspects it reminded one of the revolution as drawn by Dickens.

There is a rather ugly job to war: The job of going around in a truck collecting dead bodies that happen to be lying around. I was looking for a place to eat here yesterday — the troops had taken the town a few hours before — and a truck came by. The sergeant hailed me with "Haven't seen any dead Americans lying around here, have you, sir?" I didn't understand at first, and thought he was making a joke in rather poor taste. Then, he continued, "Or Krauts for that matter; we're looking for dead bodies." I told him I had only seen a dead Gerry in a ditch on the other side of town. He said, "Oh, that will be gotten by the other guys who are over there."

I'll have to stop trying to think pretty soon — the other morning when I put that Joe in near Villars-les-Blamont and was returning, I got to thinking about what a dirty business this was, etc., and him with a family and his fine, simple patriotism, and I damned near ran into a pocket of Gerries. Guess I'll just try to get some things down like this — and hope there will be plenty of time to try to figure it out later.

September 24, 1944
Remiremont

Don't know when I put anything in these notes last; but will start with an exciting day:

After a hell of a tough drive at night, with no lights, against tanks, trucks, etc., through muddy roads, arrived at the new CP at Luxeuil-les-Bains. This was about September 20. The next day, decided to take a Joe through as near as possible to Bains-les-Bains; the situation maps showed only that we had some recce elements as far as St. Loup. Mike Burke, although not part of our team (he had parachuted into France a week or two before and been overrun by the army) volunteered to go along as an observer. So Mike, the Joe (Georges Ruez) and I set out in a jeep.

We got to St. Loup, passed the recce elements at Vauvillers, then set out to get as close as possible to Bains-les-Bains (500 Gerries there at last report). We came to a canal where the bridge was cut, and found our way down one side and up the other (this was at Fontenoy La Chateau). We had only two revolvers and a carbine, and were a bit nervous at this extended period in plain view, and range, of any forces that might be on the other side. Nothing happened, however, and we reached a point about 5 km. from Bains les Bains. We were, of course, inquiring the way from kilometer to kilometer and taking the word of civilians as to whether they were Gerries around.

At a point in the road about 5 km. from Bains les Bains we found a small bridge had been taken out. It made a ditch of about two feet width across the road. There had been some boards laid across it in some disorder. There were tire tracks (not American) in the mud leading up to the boards, and on the other side, but not over them. None of us was qualified to tell whether the place was mined or not. In my mind there flashed a vision of the jeep which had blown up just two hundred yards in front of Bob and myself near Montelimar, and so we examined the place as carefully as we could — we could not tell, but it was possibly a plant.

We had more than accomplished the mission of getting the agent close to Bains les Bains, but somehow I had a hunch we could go further, if we could get over this spot. We inquired of a civilian if there was a way around through the woods. There was not. Finally I told the others to go off to the side of the road, out of possible range if anything blew. Then I got in the jeep and backed it up to a point about 75 yards away. I had decided to go across the damned thing, but I must admit it took all my will. I could see from the faces of the Joe and Mike that they thought the place was mined also. Then I put it into first, gathered speed and changed gears, pressed the accelerator to the floor and approached the "damned spot." I had to sort of lock my imagination and my emotions at the moment. Still half-expecting an explosion but nothing happened.

Mike came over not knowing whether to smile or not; the Joe was impressed (this was good psychologically, and he certainly did an excellent job when we put him through) — and we started off. I don't think, even in the boat days in Corsica I ever had a reaction like I did a few minutes later. As I was driving up the road, I began to be conscious that my arm was twitching. I stopped and looked at my hand, it was shaking like a leaf. I said to Mike, "Would you mind driving for a few minutes? I think I need a cigarette." He laughed, "I'll bet you do." I did. (I felt a bit foolish. Just goes to show that imagination is worse, sometimes, or as bad, as reality. Since nothing was there, it was anti-climax; I'm glad life has no regard for artistic form and indulges in anti-climaxes of this sort.)

Then there was the question of going on — we were about 35 miles ahead of our own Corps recce (which was holding this flank pending the cross-over of the 45th from right to left flank). I turned to the problems around us, but I have a hunch there is a corner of my mind that will be forever plastered with the emotions of that moment.

We got to a bend in the road about 2 kilometers from Bains les Bains. Here we talked with civilians, whose reports were confusing. There were Germans in the town — there were not — they had left the night before — they had left that morning (it was noon) — there were 100 Gerries left — 10-5-2-500. Finally, it seemed clear that there were probably only two or three Gerries in the town, at least there were two in a farm house about 1 km. down the road. We went ahead and parked the jeep so a portion of it could be seen from where the Gerries were supposed to be (and so it could go in either direction in a hurry). I stayed at the wheel. Mike kept watch on both sides of the road. I sent the Joe ahead on a borrowed bicycle to tell the Germans there was a large force of Americans coming and to surrender or else. He told them and they

Wayne Nelson and Mike Burke, the first Americans in Bains les Bains, France, being welcomed by the mayor and townspeople, September 1944.

looked out the window, saw the hood of the jeep down the road and surrendered. We took their arms, inspected their papers, and left them under a civilian guard to be turned over to the first Americans to enter the town after us.

Then we entered Bains les Bains. The town was hysterical. It developed that the Germans had left in force at 4 or 5 A.M. that morning. We were invited to the Mayor's house for lunch and had fine wine and champagne. (As always, the latter had been hidden during the years of occupation until liberation.) While we were lunching, a recce platoon of LeClerc's 2d Armored Division (from the Third Army) came in. The French were a bit miffed to find some Americans had gotten there before them. Some time later a recce platoon from our own Corps recce came in under Lt. Sims. He expressed wonderment that he was not the first, and then went on toward Xertigny. (He mentioned that they had been sending messages back all day about a couple of crazy Americans roaming around ahead of them.)

Mike and I were kissed by all the girls, had photos taken and given photographs. We signed more autographs than Frankie Sinatra. I received the Mayor's speech, and replied with one of my own — in what was probably the poorest French ever heard in those parts. (The Joe's father was a poacher in the town. I insisted that he have lunch with us in the Mayor's house, and the people began to look on him with a new and unaccustomed respect. I made sure, poor as my French was, that I stressed in most glowing terms the fact that the Joe was practically winning the war for us. The old man liked this; and the Joe damned near broke his neck for us on several missions thereafter.)

After lunch, we broke away and set out on the trail of Sims' recce toward Xertigny (by this time it had become part of a point of honor, or sport, for us to get ahead of them). We found them stopped at Chappelle aux Bois, 6 km. from Xertigny at a railroad crossing. They thought there were Gerries in Xertigny. We tried to find a way around, but could not. Therefore, we decided to go on toward the town. The recce leader advised against it, then asked if we wanted a couple of machine guns; we said "no" airily, and proceeded up the road (I heard one of the recce enlisted men muttering "screwballs" as we left them).

We approached Xertigny carefully — finally entered the town, about 1 hour ahead of the recce. Found the last part of the Gerries' column had pulled out 20 minutes before. Then we started toward Hadol; about 3 km from Xertigny we found the Gerries had passed only 10 minutes before (about 400 of them); they had taken all the bicycles they could find and a truck from the Fromagerie. They had also taken as a hostage the husband of a farm woman there. We proceeded a bit further, stopping the jeep while I walked around bends to prevent surprise, and let the Joe loose a short distance up the road. He had good wooded cover to the Moselle, not far away and with the Gerries in retreat, it seemed certain he could get there ahead of them. Mike and I went back, and received the wine, flowers, kisses and ovation of Xertigny which we had not had time on the way through. (The Joe got a courier all the way back to Luxeuil by noon the next day with important dope on the Moselle defenses.)

The next day I set out on the same route with Joes to get across the Moselle. Got to Hadol this time, and found the Gerries were about 2 km. up the road. I sent the agents off and told them I would wait, with Trinidad Vidal at a Café (au Centre, of course!) at Hadol for them. There was a recce platoon about 1 km. up the road engaging the Gerries in a fire fight, so we were covered. The Joes returned in a couple of hours. We had dinner with the kind people there, and I sent Vidal back with the jeep and the agents to give the intelligence to G-2 and got more Joes to put through this hole. A short time later, the recce platoon came back through Hadol and stopped to tell me they were falling back on Xertigney (since Sims' reports the whole recce regiment took an interest in our safety). I had to stay there to wait for the final agent, or his courier, to come back the following morning. I told Trinidad to tell Justin this was a marvelous opportunity to get Joes across the Moselle if we acted quickly and send up all he had in the morning, and I particularly impressed on Trin to come back soon for me as I had no transport.

I told the people in Hadol to keep quiet about me being there, since I was alone, and if the Germans came back into town I would not be able to help them. Some of the girls, however, got out the American and French flags and Crosses of Lorraine they had been hiding for liberation day anyway. I had dinner with the people there quietly, with shades drawn, and neighbors fearful about only one American being there. Where were the great American troops? They'll be along any minute. After dinner the man of the house got out the kirsch, and then, of all things, a campaign hat of an American officer who had been there in the last war. They had had it hidden, and well preserved, in the cellar for 26 years! I went to bed that night with my pistol at the head of the bed, after inspecting the window to see how I could climb out if necessary. It took a moment or two to get asleep, for every time you heard sounds outside, you immediately thought of the possibility of Germans. This got tiring, after a while, and I went to sleep.

In the morning some civilians from Arches, on the Moselle, came to tell me the Gerries had waded across the river the night before and the town had no Germans. I therefore set out on foot to walk the 6 km. to Arches in a drenching rain, leaving instructions for Vidal to follow with the jeep when he arrived. Near Arches a priest came out on a cycle to meet me. Then others. To all, my conductors said "il faux pas dire rien," for the Gerries had an observation post and machine guns in the church tower across the river at Archettes. I finally entered the town at 0900 after observation from a hill through glasses. There some civilians told me that, although the Gerries had left the night before, 40 had returned about 0830 that morning and were patrolling in the outskirts. M. de Carrelt, owner of the papeterie, suggested I take refuge and have lunch at his home, near the paper works. We took a little path there. I found his daughter wearing the "U.S." that I gave as a souvenir to a chap in Xertigny — turned out he was her fiancée. I had given it to him two days before, and he had gone through the lines to give her the souvenir of the "first American" in Xertigny.

She had been hiding it until the Americans came. The women of the house got into red, white and blue skirts they had been hiding against "the day." A good lunch was prepared — we had an aperitif first, very good. The owner was about 45 minutes in getting out the champagne he had well hidden for the years of occupation.

We were about to enter the dining room when a knock came at the door. Through the frosted glass of the door could be seen the silhouettes of three persons. They had on hats, which in shadow, looked like German field caps. The women rushed upstairs to be ready to take off and hide their red, white and blue things. I was led into a closet. I drew my .45, and the man of the house (Carrelet was an old French captain in the first World War) said, "Please don't shoot in the house unless you have to. I will try to get rid of them!" Then he went to the door. As it turned out, it was only three friends of the family who had sort of hunting caps on. They wanted to tell us that a group of six Gerries had passed by on the road below the house, heading for the woods. Then we had a good lunch, three wines, Charles Heidseck, and afterwards some brandy. Vidal did not come by 2 P.M. and an hour or two later the daughter's fiancée offered to take me on the back of his cycle to Hadol.

I thus rode back to Hadol in anything but a dignified position (and dignity would have befitted the taker of one city and three towns in the region certainly!) On the way I met American units of the 45th Div. approaching the town cautiously and gave them information that they could enter safely, but to look out for the 40 Germans in the woods and to realize they were under observation once they passed the hill in front of the town, from the other side of the Moselle. I also told them of the mined roadblock and the position of the German OP in the church tower at Archettes, as well as the positions of several artillery pieces which I had spotted firing from the second story of the Carrelet house.

I waited at Hadol for Vidal, but when he did not come by 5 P.M., I hitched back to Luxeuil from Hadol and found orders to go to the new advance CP at Raon Aux Bois that night since the crossing of the Moselle was planned.

Went to Raon through a blackout and a mass movement of tanks, infantry and artillery. Finally found Justin (physically bumping into him in the dark around the advance CP). Six battalions of artillery were already in place and the 141st Infantry of the 36th was to cross at about 4 A.M. I slept in the front of the Citroen; we were to be ready to cross with the first wave if desired, or whenever we were awakened. All night 105's and other large guns were booming within 100 yards of us — so did not get much sleep. The following morning I set out with two agents to try to cross the Moselle. Found that the 141st had crossed under cover of an artillery barrage and darkness but was pinned down on the other side of the Moselle. As we approached the river, mortar fire had the range and began dropping about 20 feet from us, so we turned around and tried another track. Got to Eloyes and found sniper and machine gun fire which stopped us there. One man had been hit in the mouth just a couple of minutes before by a sniper, and everyone was in the ditch or taking cover in houses. Therefore I took over from the driver and took the jeep back along the coast road like the proverbial "bat out of hell." One agent thereupon decided that he did not want to do this work, and would prefer to go back and join the French army attacking Belfort. I left him back at the CP, checked the situation map and decided to try at Arches. I went up there and found all the troops in town under cover and the people hiding behind closed shutters. I went up the road, but stopped the jeep behind a house in front of a cleared space. I proceeded on foot, telling the others to wait, about 30 yards beyond the house. Boom! Swish! Sounded like a 37 mm.—about 15 feet over my head. I hit the dirt and crawled back. After a wait of about 15 minutes for things to calm down, I noticed the Joe's morale was wavering (no blame to him), we got out of town. I went back to base.

The next day I crossed the river on a temporary bridge (which took four hours in the rain and mud and tank and truck traffic) and went up in the hills behind Eloyes to meet the local Maquis chief. He agreed to put three agents through for me. I could not get back across the river that night, so stayed with a family in Eloyes (well occupied by our troops) and the next morning went back to Raon.

10

Courageous
Women and Men Spies

Among those who rendered valuable service to the OSS in the days following the invasion of Southern France were a number of courageous men and women, especially two named Odette and Simone. Women were found to be valuable for short-range intelligence work. They attracted less suspicion in enemy territory than men, and although they usually lacked the necessary background for reporting technical data, they were often able to extract otherwise unavailable knowledge of German military intentions from enemy officers.

An interesting account of the "female spies" written by Wayne Nelson appeared in World War II *magazine, July 1997. In it he stated, "It takes courage to be a spy. The women who volunteered to be spies and came to the Office of Strategic Services (OSS) unit attached to the 36th Infantry Division with which I was serving in the Vosges Mountains of France in the fall of 1944—had plenty of courage." Given below in the diary are specific details about Simone and Odette who undertook a dangerous mission, returned safely and their report was particularly valuable because it warned of considerable troop movement in the forest region near Les Rouges Baux. They also brought back another excellent report from one of the chains of agents. These are among the tales of men and women who served their country courageously.*

Chinimenil (near Bruges, Vosges)
October 3, 1944

Don't know when I last put anything in these notes, but will cover the last couple of days here.

On September 30, I spent the whole day taking care of the agents, getting them installed here and "care and feeding" generally.

On October 1, it was decided to put two girls, whom we got from the FFI (Free French Intelligence) at Epinal, into enemy territory. The idea was to get them as close as possible to Granges sur Valonne. They are two remarkable girls, one has been helping the Maquis for two years and the other has been in the game for six months. Both are 29, the one who has been working for the Maquis longer is not too good-looking, but not bad-looking. The other is a platinum blonde and rather good-looking, though a little stout. They really get a kick out of crossing the lines and a life that is, naturally, not without danger. Damned good types.

I took them by jeep to Tendon, but there was a roadblock 500 yards beyond the town toward Le Thuly. I turned back and tried St. Jean de March. I was stopped at Faucompierre and warned that there were Germans just a bit up the road. I went back to Regiment CP, but could get no real info on the situation. Went back to the Division CP and checked the situation map. This showed that we had taken Lepanges, so I went up there with the girls. Proceeded from there by Neauville to St. Jean de March. Through all of this, I may add for the benefit of those at home who may read this, there was scarcely a minute without the sound of cannon and small arms fire. At St. Jean I found the last sound of cannon and small arms fire. At St. Jean I found the last outpost of the Americans. There were some infantry patrols in the hills to the right and to the left of the town. Down the road to Houx no American had gone. There were none who knew if there were Germans in the town or not, but it was assumed that there were.

I left the sergeant with the jeep at St. Jean and proceeded with the girls down the road to Houx on foot; we went to within 200 yards of the town, where I could see it. Here the road turned and was under observation from many hills beyond the town, to the east. Therefore, I left the girls there and returned. The girls were to circulate behind the Gerry lines and return to Lepanges that night — we made a rendezvous for the Hotel de la Gare there. I went to the hotel at Lepanges with Swede (the sergeant) that night at about 6:15. We secured two rooms and had the people heat up some rations, and sat there talking with the woman of the hotel and her daughter and the daughter's boyfriend until 11:15, when we went to bed. The Hotel de la Gare has been pretty well demolished by shellfire. It had one side completely blown out. The people slept in the cellars, as in all these towns when the war approaches and passes them, for nights.

At 12:30 Justin came in with Simone. Apparently the two girls had reached the town of Houx. There they found there were only seven Gerries in the town. The Germans were all enlisted men who wanted to surrender. Therefore, they surrendered to the two girls, who took their arms and locked them in a separate room and put the Germans in the cellar. Odette stayed there with the prisoners and Simone returned to our lines to get someone to go and take the prisoners. The Americans at St. Jean would not believe the story and said it was too dangerous to send anyone down that road. Justin was of course summoned by telephone, went and got Simone and came to Lepanges. Justin suggested that I wait the next day until the town was taken and then go find Odette, sending Simone to Chinimenil to wait there, and then we would make up another mission for them. He then went back to the CP. I gave Simone my room and went down to the Citroen to sleep. (I didn't want to disturb Swede, who was sleeping like a bear.) At about 4 A.M., however, it got too cold, so I woke up Swede and told him to move over and got about three hours sleep.

(I was really worried about Odette — as I had been about both of them during the evening — I still don't like the idea of putting girls in to do a man's work. You feel awful small when you leave them just beyond the lines. Or, as Justin says, maybe I'm getting soft.)

The next morning at 8 there was a lot of shelling. The family of the hotel were ducking into the cellar continually. (Swede was a bit nervous too, and said more than once he wished he were back at the supply room at headquarters.) As a matter of fact, some of the shells were passing within five yards of the house. I got some Nescafe out of the car and took a glass of coffee up to Simone, had some myself, and told Swede to stay there with the girl until I returned to the jeep (since the Citroen had a flat and we had no pump).

I went through Neauville — there was all hell breaking loose this morning in the region. Cannon, big and small, machine guns, planes buzzing unseen through the low clouds, and small arms fire. I nearly ran off the road when one shell passed through the trees above me and cut off a branch which fell on the engine of the jeep. (It was a pretty big shell and the falling of the branch just in front of me, combined with the rather "annoying" sound of a shell that close, startled me—to say the least—for a moment.)

I got to St. Jean where I had been the day before—and found it considerably altered by courtesy of German artillery. (In one house there had been six soldiers sleeping on the floor (Second floor, American style). A 150-mm. shell had passed through one wall and out another before it exploded; it only covered the boys with debris—no one was wounded.) No one had gone down the road to Houx. That town (being in a spot easily observed from all around the region) was a "hot spot." The infantry had taken high ground on both sides of St. Jean and to the northeast and southeast, but this damned road was supposed to be "b-a-a-d." I talked with a major there, and he said he "advised strongly" against trying to get down. I left the jeep and proceeded on foot down the road. You could not tell where the shells were coming from, or where they were going. Some whistled, some whooshed, and there was the intermittent crackle of machine gun and small arms fire.

I reached the turn of the road (where I had been the day before) and paused by a tree, from which point I could see the town and some of the surrounding country to the southeast. I spotted some high explosive stuff falling about 200 yards on the other side of the town; and some small arms and machine gun fire on a hill just north of it. In about a minute I heard the whine of a rifle bullet just over my head, followed by machine gun fire, so I ducked behind the tree and into the ditch at the left of the road. Rifle and machine gun fire continued in my direction, so I figured I was spotted and returned (via ditch) to St. Jean.

I tried again in about 40 minutes—no small arms fire this time, but I found mortars falling all around Houx, so it was not advisable to try to get through. So again I returned to St. Jean.

At about 10:30 I met a lieutenant from a cannon company, who had a radio jeep and two riflemen. He wanted to go down to Houx, if possible, to make some posts for artillery observation. I said it was inadvisable, but I would like to get there too—why not join forces? He said, "Okay, let's go." I climbed in the jeep and we took it about 200 yards down the road, behind a curve. The lieutenant left the jeep there with one of the men with instructions to wait and send a message as to his location. We then proceeded in the ditch at the left on foot.

We were spotted by an S.P. this time and they bracketed us, putting one over the bank to our left, and a couple in the field below the road at our right. We moved — fast — down the ditch. One hit the bank behind us. The lieutenant was marvelous — hell of a good crazy type. We joked about "The Gerries don't like us," and, "if they keep that up they are going to hurt somebody" and "I think they have seen us," which is followed by "You ain't just chopping your guns, brother." We played tag with this S.P.— about 15 rounds, none more than 20 yards from us — in the ditch, and thankful for the bank at our left. Then we were covered by the first house in the town.

The man and I crouched in the ditch at the left and covered the lieutenant who made for the first house across the way, entering by the window. Then we dashed over, and we all went through the house room by room, gun in hand, kicking open doors and jumping aside. We kept under cover, and leap-frogged each other from house to house.

The only human being we found in four houses was an old woman of at least 70 — who was sitting by a stove, wringing her hands and crying softly through toothless gums. Too old, too tired to care — and nearly crazy. We could not get her to speak coherently, so we went on.

The cattle in the town would sound off when a shell came close. A chicken or two would wander in the street. But these minor evidences of life only made the town seem more ghostlike. Finally, to add to the eeriness, we heard a bell ringing in a house across the street. It was a small store of general merchandise. It turned out to be a broken telephone — just ringing continually in this deserted village of, perhaps, 30 houses. I told the lieutenant to cover me while I dashed across to the store.

I entered the store, which was in semi-darkness and apparently deserted. I called out, and saw a door start to move. I turned to it with my Marlin, but it proved to be a woman coming out of the cellar. I asked her if there was a Mlle. Odette who had come yesterday, and she said, "Yes, she is in the cellar with the prisoners." I started down in the cellar which was black as pitch, and called, "Odette, Odette." Finally, I heard her voice, amid a strange babble, saying "Oh, bon dieu, le capitaine — il est venu." She rushed up out of the darkness and kissed me on both cheeks. Other shadows in the dark turned out to be the seven prisoners, and most of the local population, who had taken refuge in the cellar all the preceding night and that morning while the town was under shellfire. I turned the prisoners over to the lieutenant (and left him the problem of an old man who had gone stark mad during the night and thought he was Louis XIV, or something), procured a German revolver for Odette for a souvenir, and took Odette back up the ditch to St. Jean. The shelling had diminished a bit, and I was relieved when we managed to reach St. Jean.

We got the jeep and returned to Lepanges, got the others and went on to Chinimenil to get some coffee. When I saw Justin at the CP, I was again, of course, cautioned about taking chances. But, I replied, I did not literally enter the town until the Americans did (since the Lt. was with me). This merely brought "hell" as a response. It was quite an experience though — now that it's over.

The afternoon of October 2, I took my old friend from Arches, Dorget, to put him through to Gerardmer. I went to Tendon, thence by mountain road to a point about two kilometers southwest of Le Tholy, where there was supposed to be an American roadblock. The roadblock had pulled back when we arrived, so, since this was obviously beyond any point where the Americans would stop him, I sent him on.

That is about the story of all the excitement there was in the last couple of days. Only one can't put down everything, but I imagine every moment is exciting, or will seem so when one can look back at it. We are never more then five kilometers from the Gerries and shellfire has become as natural as the sound of a clock ticking (that is, except when they are very, very close — and when they are close, it is always an experience — a new experience and always tinged with a bit of downward pull inside a guy, in the region of the heart).

Docelles
October 15, 1944

On October 9 took the two girls, Odette and Simone, up to the Leclerc Division territory near Glonville to try to infiltrate them. To pass through the villages up there is to view a scene of desolation beyond description. Villages which had had, perhaps, 20 houses, have only three or four left any where near intact. It is one of the poor regions of France in any event, but, God, it will be absolutely wrecked, as it is now by the end of the war.

I found that it was too risky to chance the girls on an infiltration up there and returned to Rambervillers. Darkness caught up with us there, and in the absolute blackness, sans any lights at all, it was impossible to proceed further. Therefore, we put up at the Hotel de 'Est for the night. Stormy had a rather difficult time because he could not speak French, but he is good guy. We had C rations heated up — the hotel, of course, had no food — dinner becomes C ration stew, coffee and hard biscuit, a bottle of wine, and a bit of Kirsch.

The next morning I looked up Colonel Waller Booth and Mike Burke at Seconer, and found that they had been having a tough time and bad luck with agents also. They had three casualties among agents in the last week and it was estimated that a Joe had a one in ten chance of getting through in that sector. I therefore returned to the CP with the girls, not being willing to risk them on a chance such as that (particularly as my mind was still troubled with the news of the brutal killing of the men I put through several weeks ago in Tholy).

Finally discovered that people were again going in and out of Bruyeres by Fays. Sent two male agents in on October 11, and instructed their guide to come back as soon as possible on October 12 and, if he returned safely, he could take the girls through. He returned in the afternoon of October 12. I accompanied the guide and the girls through the forest just a little bit beyond the line parallel to the last OP. There was considerable machine gun fire to our left, and the Germans were but a hundred yards or so from our OP. I left them in the forest with the traditional *trois fois merde* and started back.

It was about 5:15. Then I proceeded to lose my way in the woods. This made a real dilemma. It was dangerous to approach the edge of the forest to ascertain one's location, because I did not know if there were Germans there or not. On the other hand, it was becoming dark and it was also dangerous to return to our lines after dark — since we had only a few recce troops holding this line, they all had nervous trigger fingers. Finally, guided mainly by the sound of the machine guns, I approached the edge of the forest and got some idea of where I was. Thereafter, I zigzagged back into the forest and to the edge again for about half an hour. At about 6 o'clock it was beginning to get dark, and I was just about to head up into the forest hill, find the thickest bush, and stay there for the night (it was also raining), when I remembered that the hill was full of land mines. No good. You walk through the forest and imagine you hear someone following you (this was an area full of recce and combat patrols from both sides each night). You stop; the brushing sound ceases. You walk again; again you hear the sound. You stop and look around, eyeing every leaf, tree and bush with a desperation born of an unmerciful imagination. Finally you realize that the sound is that of your own trousers brushing as you walk.

Losing the path, you claw frantically at obstructing bushes. Eventually I got a glimpse of a house, and in the gathering dusk, saw the outline of a Sherman tank near it. It was too dark to walk directly up, and I didn't know the password. So I got to a point about 25 yards from the house and then started openly down the path, singing "Mairzy Doatsy Doatsy." Got back to the CP all right.

Put several guys through the same place. Sat around waiting for them from time to time. Fun — with the recce guys who were stuck up there. And then watching artillery fire on a clump of woods in which there were Germans; more than 300 yards long; must have made them feel pretty sick.

Side note: You sit in a tent at the CP at the officers mess. You eat sausages, and corn, and sauerkraut, and bread, and cocoa, and some sort of cake. You talk of what the hell is going on up the line. And the shells boom, boom about two or three miles away. Occasionally the earth shakes as the big gun goes off near the tent. It is rainy and cold. And the lieutenant over there wonders when the division will be relieved; a captain nearby can't forget Anzio, talks about it all the time; but the lieutenant across the table, who has been in quite a scrap this same morning thinks, just for a minute perhaps, that the scrap this morning was worse than Anzio. But for us, I know that my job tomorrow is to try to find a hole in these goddam lines and, baby, it's getting tough as hell as they tighten up and they advance into the Vosges and winter comes on.

At night I will be in Chinimenil, eating with the Joes. Here there will be 10-in-1 rations, and some French fried potatoes (which Madame Marie knows I like), and coffee, and perhaps some horse meat (I am getting so I can eat it without thinking of it as part of "man's best friend"), and wine. For that meal, and just for that moment, I will be the king of all I survey. The Joes, who really do the job, will respect my slightest wish. And I will have to act out the part. Yet, inside, I know that it is I who should be kowtowing to them.

November 3, 1944
Chinimenil

Have not put anything in these notes for some time.

There was the operation to put in a radio team. Corbett and I took the team of four down to Jussarupt, a last outpost which could only be entered at night, and since there was too much moon, decided to wait until 1 A.M. before taking them on foot to a river about 600 yards out in no man's land. We knew the Gerries were about 300 yards to our right, and there was the possibility of being fired on by our own outpost at the left, because there was no telephone communication with it. We slept in a hayloft. One of the Joes had forgotten his papers, so we sent him back with Bob Faulls to get them. Bob came back at 11:30, but had had a jeep accident in the dark and the Joe had been cut in the head — would be out for about a week. Since this guy was the key member of the team, the operation was called off and we returned.

The next day I got an opportunity for a few days off in Paris. So I took the Citroen and drove up there. I spent four days — could not see the Comedie or Opera, as they had not opened, but did see the ABC (apparently the French equivalent of the Old Palace), ate several times at a little restaurant "Le Prince" on the Boulevarde Rochesouart that had much atmosphere — old metal ware, bidets, spinets, etc. hanging from the beamed ceiling — no other Americans there. I went the rounds of the cafes, and saw the usual sights. All very interesting and I came back finally, though, sooner that I had anticipated — found the rounds of places and the living (which was comparatively easy) much like New York in spirit at least and because anxious to return to the front after a couple of days.

When I returned, I found the operations had not gone too well. The front was still tightening — so we pitched in. I was up one night till 3:30 A.M. on the operation described above (at Jussarupt) and therefore slept late the following morning. When I awakened and went to the CP I found Justin had taken a Joe and had not returned. We were not too worried that day, but when he did not return that night, we did begin to worry. Corbett and I found he had gone to the third and went up to see Thompson first thing in the morning. Justin had gone through there and had taken young Hemingway with him. We went out with Thompson to check — and found they had not checked with 7th Regiment or Battalion CP. We found Stormy (my driver whom Justin had borrowed) and he showed us where he had left Justin and Hemingway, together with the Joe (a chap named Charlier), had taken to the woods from a road block and Stormy had waited all day and night for them. We could not go into these woods without a patrol, and therefore returned to CP.

Jacques Bacri came in about noon with a story he had gotten by going out with a civilian and sending him on ahead. Juss, Hemingway and the Joe had been near Gerbyfosse, a little village northeast of Bruyeres. As they approached a house, the Germans had seen them and thrown grenades. The body was wounded in the stomach. Then the Germans opened up with rifles — Jus was wounded in the foot and Hemingway in the shoulder. They were all captured and taken to a nearby house. The body died after a few hours. Justin and Hemingway were removed further back (to St. Die).

At the moment we are most worried that they may realize what they have and give them special treatment.

I went to the funeral of the Joe yesterday. (He had died a few hours after capture in the farmhouse.) It was a little church near the front. It was a rainy morning. As we approached, little groups of people — totaling perhaps 40 — stood in the rain outside. In front of the church was a cart and horse, held by a poorly dressed farmer, with long mustaches. On this cart was the plain wood coffin — a few straggly flowers (drooping, like the horse, in the rain) and a wooden cross that would eventually mark the grave. I was introduced to the mayors of the two nearby villages — one of them had put on a clean celluloid collar and ready-made tie. I was the representative of the Americans for whom the man had been working when he was killed. The priest came out in his black and white robes. The coffin was carried into the church.

Behind the altar in the church was a mural of the Madonna and Child. Daylight could be seen through this mural where rifle and machine gun bullets had pierced. Practically all the stained glass windows were shattered. The coffin was carried in and placed in front of the altar. The Mayor of Domfaing and the Mayor of Les Rouges Eaux followed. Then I followed with Jacques. We took our seats. There was a battery of 105's about 50 feet from the church on a little rise. (The Gerries were, perhaps, three kilometers away.) Intermittently during the service, these guns would be fired with a deafening roar and obliterate all possibility of hearing the service for a time. The little church would shake — and on one or two occasions the sound would be followed by the hesitant tinkle of falling glass remnants.

The coffin was in the center of the aisle in front of the pews. Behind this was an ornate (for this place) altar, and behind this the "stage." There the priest went through his incantations with the assistance of a little civilian who looked exactly like Barry Fitzgerald. The little guy would run for the water, tinkle the bell, chant the answers, and chant while the priest read. Nothing was repeated after gunfire — that part of the service was just a few words lost in the vacuum of war. Then all passed by the priest, kissed a little silver disc and placed some money in the box, passing then by the coffin where everyone made the sign of the cross with a little pestle from a silver mug. Then all were seated, the priest prayed, the guns continued to go off and shake the church and drown out the prayer — then the coffin was carried out, followed by us, to the cemetery. There we all passed it again, made the sign of the cross, and left it to be inserted in the hole that had been dug.

This ceremony was like a tragic-comic play. It had all the trappings of a play — and yet there was something grotesque. Accompaniment of the guns was fitting for this man. He left a wife and child, who could not come to the funeral since they were far away in Nancy. The war had been over for him — he was in friendly — liberated — territory, but he volunteered to do a mission in enemy territory. He had probably died in a pretty horrible fashion — for stomach wounds are not pleasant — particularly when it is the jagged little pieces of iron and steel that grenades dispatch. He had lingered in pain for probably five or six hours.... Well, we will give his widow some money, and a certificate signed by a colonel or something, which will say that her husband died gloriously for the war, and she can show this to the child when it grows up — or before.

Personally, I am now in charge of the team, but I don't like it. After the Bion-Utard incident (the two men I put in from Remiremont), after Levret (who was caught in Montbeliard), after the other one I put into Le Tholy (missing), I begin to feel like a murderer. I still don't mind risk myself, but a guy feels like a heel. He takes someone up a little beyond the lines and tells him to go on. And now the job will have to be done more and more by old men and women.

We have a CPA now at Bruyeres. The town is practically entirely destroyed. It rained yesterday and this little room in which I am sitting (which has practically all glass out and huge holes in the wall from shelling — almost three of the walls of the building are out) had more water in it than there was on the ground. It is cold here in the Vosges these days. I have not had a bath since Paris (and before that for three weeks — do I stink). It is not going to be easy this winter. I understand that the plan is for the Third Division to attack St. Die (crossing the

Meurthe as we (36th) crossed the Moselle) and then let the others pour
through as best they can. Then they are going to try to race through the
Vosges passes. It sounds crazy to me from what I have seen here, but
they may be able to do it. Hope they make it, but it's going to be real
tough.

Bruyeres
November 5, 1944

I must make a note on the domain over which I preside at the
moment. The SSS office, in combination with the SIAM (Signal Intelligence and Monitoring) office, is a little room on the 3rd floor of a
building, half destroyed by shells. The room is approximately 8 x 10.
There is a cot, two small tables, a field desk, a small stove burning wood,
and four folding chairs. Two of the walls are well cracked by shell-fire.
The window jamb is torn loose and all glass naturally gone (we have
inserted cardboard). Candles in wine bottles provide the light. The floor
boards are warped enough to make little hillocks on the floor. There was
once wallpaper in this room — remnants remain. Our situation map covers part of one wall. The plaster on the ceiling is about ⅔ gone, leaving
exposed lathes. The door is shakily on one hinge. Our big guns go off
now and then, and the concussion shakes a little plaster off the ceiling.
A slightly different sound occasionally — RFAD (Rural Free Artillery
Delivery), courtesy of the Gerries. More plaster down. On another cot,
which we put up only at night, I sleep. When it is cold — as it is always —
it is very, very cold. When it rains, as it is doing now, the ceiling leaks
a steady drip in 15 places — and that's no kidding — I just counted them.
This is our little corner of 36th Division CP at Bruyeres. Huh....

Chinimenil
November 10, 1944

And then there is the guy who went into enemy territory for us with
the Mayfair radio team. He was the most courageous of all the members
of the team — because he carried his death warrant physically — the radio.
He stayed in as a member of the team for a month and did terrific work,
reporting, and even correcting our artillery fire. Then the radio busted
as a result of one of our shells exploding nearby and they came out.

I arranged for one man to have his wife brought down from Bac-
carat. I arranged for another to go to see his family. And I arranged for

this particular guy to go to Nancy to see his wife, whom he had not seen for 15 months, since he was searched for by the Gestapo and had to leave and join the Maquis. He had been married 14 years and was about 39 years old. He was a little, wizened, leathery faced man — brave as hell. Used to be a poacher, and knew the woods like his pocket. He was happy as a young pup when he set out for Nancy, and I gave him 2,000 francs to give to his wife, along with cigarettes and some 10 in 1 rations.

When he got to Nancy he found that his wife had left, voluntarily, with a German officer two months before when the Gerries evacuated Nancy. (When he came back, I had already put him in for a Legion of Merit with the other members of the team, and I told him jointly with the others that before he or Jacques who was with him (on the trip to Nancy) could tell me what he had learned. Then they told me. What could I say? Even if I knew French well, the situation would have defied anything appropriate in words. I didn't say anything, just handed him a bottle.

11

Bordeaux Pockets

Wayne Nelson was the "Operations Officer of OSS Acquitaine Mission December 1944 to March 1945—recruiting, training and briefing agents for infiltration into German-held Atlantic coast pockets north of Bordeaux; planning, preparing and executing operations to effect penetration of the German pockets to secure technical intelligence."*

Neiul-le-Verieul (North of Bordeaux)
December 20, 1944

After closing out the 36th Division team about November 15, I went up to 44th Division for ten days in the vicinity of Luneville and worked with the 44th and 79th into Alsace until Strasbourg was taken.

Most of the time with the 44th was not too interesting. There were the nights in Saarreburg when the Gerries were throwing heavy, but heavy, mortars into the city and we spent from midnight to 6 A.M. in the cellar. The shells would arrive every five minutes like clockwork, and hit houses all around us (breaking our windows—we had an apartment in a house on Hermann Goering Strasse–formerly Avenue Poincare).

Then there was the time when two people who had done favors for us wanted to be taken to their home village of Vandenheim in Alsace. Since it was only 20 or 30 kilometers out of my way, I said, "okay." I asked if the village was taken by us and they said "Oui," so I did not check the situation map. When we got to the village, they took me around to the wine merchant's home, a really lovely place. We visited the "cave" and they gave me two bottles of Pommery Champagne and two bottles of very fine French vermouth. Then we had one of those three

**OSS Field Report, May 22, 1945*

and a half hour lunches that afternoon, a real meal. It was swell. I thought they treated me with a great deal of honor and respect, but, of course, thought this was just a natural expression of hospitality.

Then the young lady of the house asked if I would write in her autograph book. She said she had all the French officers who were there in the war of '40 and would like me to write in it as an American officer. I took another glass of Champagne and said, "Of course. Be delighted." Then I suggested she and her fiancée give me a photograph and write on it. They did. When I looked at what they wrote, it said, "In good memory of two young Alsatians happy to receive at Vandenheim the first American officer." I left as quickly as possible after that–the chuckles as I drove back were the result of the Cognac, wine and Champagne — I think.

Well, I returned to SSS Army base and continued what I was supposed to do before–write the history of the 36th Division team, since I was the sole surviving officer of the team not in German hands and wounded. In the course of this, I found out what Henry Hyde wanted me for: The memo which I left for [Captain Winthrop] Rutherford when I turned over the 36th to him had impressed [Colonel Edward Gamble, Jr.] Gamble and the others muchly, and I was supposed to write the history of the whole Southern France preparatory operation! (It's been a strange hegira I've made to convince somebody–anybody — that I can write!)

I spent a couple of weeks getting the 36th history in shape and was about ready to join Henry for the other report job. Then Frank [Schoonmaker] sent word that he needed a small boat operations expert around Toulouse for the three pockets, amounting to some 60,000 Gerries, north of Bordeaux–opposed only by the FFI [French Free Intelligence]. Of course I responded to this like an old fire horse and selected Don McAffee to assist me. We put a rubber boat and our packs in the old Citroen ("Old Betsy") and started out from Phalsburg in Alsace in the late afternoon of December 9.

Due to heavy military traffic and rain and mud we stopped in Luneville that night. We stopped at 6th AG to see Tom (then in Vittel) the next day and proceeded to Chalons sur Saone. Here the car broke down completely. The whole gearbox had to be replaced, which meant completely taking apart the motor. It was Sunday and you just couldn't get a French mechanic anywhere. The MP's (who were the only Americans in town and who were having bad relations with the FFI–which hurt Mac and me a bit, since we knew personally what the FFI had done for our boys and had worked closely with the FFI) take the car into their garage. That night happened to be the annual Kermesse — a sort of fair — and Mac and I found rooms in a hotel (the Central) and went to "the fair." There I ran into one of our former Joes with the 36th (Jean Claude). He was working with the SR and FFI. The result was that we soon had the whole FFI rebuilding our car. They put six mechanics to work on it for 24 hours and the following morning we set off again. Of course we had eaten with the Maquis boys and had, altogether, an interesting time, though we hated to be delayed.

We started out for Lyons. Had an accident on an icy and foggy road in the Col du Republique, which fortunately only destroyed a tire. Stayed in Lyons that night. Had a swell dinner at a black market restaurant (Chez Elle). The next day we reached Nimes where the car again broke down. We stayed there all night and had it fixed first thing in the morning.

The next day we went from Nimes to Toulouse, a lovely drive, passing through, notably, Montpelier, Beziers and Carcassonne (old walled part of town picturesque as hell).

In Toulouse we found King (Bayard) and discovered they had nightclubs there, at least one, with a swing orchestra and cognac! We went around there that night, and left to go to another place about 11 o'clock and ran into a cement signpost–shattering it. This put the quietus finally on "Old Betsy"— the Citroen that I had driven for more than three months at the front, in complete blackouts, across the lines, to and around Paris, and from Alsace to Toulouse. Kinda liked that car, but the cement post was really a bit too much for her "innards." Nobody injured, more than a scratch and a bruise, fortunately. Left Old Betsey's twisted remains in a garage and decided she could only be used now to salvage more parts. So to the hotel and bed.

It was apparent that we had to get up around Bordeaux. To do anything in the way of operations we had to get there in good time, and there was no transportation available. So Mac and I went around to the local FFI Army to ask for transport. We went through a captain, lieutenant, colonel, and finally to the general himself, stating that we had a mission of a commando nature to perform–in our combat outfits (the few Americans that stay in those parts generally wore dress greens) with

Marlins and knives, this story went over with a bang and we had a car and driver the following morning. So we went to a night club again that night, slept at the hotel and got off the following morning for Mirambeau. We found Frank installed in a Chateau near Neuil le Verouil and learned that there were 3 pockets of Germans: Pointe de Grave, Royan and La Rochelle.

The next day we started out with Frank to cross the Gironde Estuary to inspect the conditions at the Graves pocket. We had a custom-build Delage car which had to be pushed to start. It turned out that the car had to tow the motor sailer boat off the mud to get it started. So we had to push the car, which towed the boat, and row to the boat once it got started and was in the water–and off it went — at about 3 knots! Then the boat stuck on the sand bank, in the middle of the Estuary, but finally got off. Then the motor gave out! We landed, but found no telephone or transport (we were 10 miles from destination) and started to back up the Estuary. Finally, it started to rain and we could do nothing against the tide. So we sat in the boat for two hours with the sail over our heads, waiting for the tide to turn, whereupon we tacked up to the place and had lunch at 5 o'clock — after 6 hours on the water to make what was usually a 40 minute trip!

We got nothing really accomplished, since Frank was going off in all directions and would not really give us a priority on which pocket to work and we had no transportation (the FFI car had been sent back after our arrival).

Finally, we ran into this Captain LeClerc who had been doing coup des mains operations on the Ile d'Oleron. In one day we set up an operation, got Frank's approval and help, and then started out to land two Joes.

If our equipment, etc. for rubber boat operations from Corsica had been considered at times inadequate, this operation was paleolithic!

The big boat was a barge-like thing with a motor. It could make about 4 knots when pushed, and sounded like a squadron of planes. These FFI boys of LeClerc's were really something. We had no sooner started than I noticed little groups talking in a conspiratorial manner. Finally the chief, Sergeant Le Fevre, said "How would you like to do something active tonight." I said, "like what?" He said, "Oh, knock off a German outpost, maybe." I realized that it would be fun, but we had the security of the Joes to think of. On the other hand, these guys were like buccaneers and might mutiny if I said no. So I said, "Sure. Good idea." Then I waited till their pals, the two Joes who were to remain on the island were around, and remarked that it might be tough on them if we alerted the Gerries in the area and then skipped out, leaving them there. This fixed the idea all right, and when I added that we had already asked LeClerc to let us go with them on an action mission (which we had) sometime, they were convinced that we were still "right guys."

Well, things seemed to be going fine–this goddamned barge parading up the coast of the island making a noise like a bunch of planes. Weather was cold as hell, too. Then the Joes began to get nervous. Thought they would be all right if they could just get across the road. What road? Oh, a road about five km. inland, patrolled by Gerries occasionally. Finally, I agreed that we would escort them within 100 yards of the road and we took them to a point inland 100 yards from the road and 100 yards from a German outpost. Patrols were generally 18 Gerries. The Joes went on to cross the road and reach their destination. It was about 2 A.M. Don, LeFevre, another guy and myself, waited, as I (through some mental lapse, I'm sure) agreed, 45 minutes to be sure they made it. Plan was that if they were set on by an 18-man Gerry patrol, the four of us were to rush the patrol and save them!

We started the 5 km. trek back to the rubber boat — we had left another FFI to guard it. We found him all right–he was asleep in the boat! Paddled back to the "big boat," and started for home. They couldn't find the channel, so we had to lay off till daybreak. At 8 A.M. we found the channel and started in–shooting guns at ducks and anything else, just for the hell of it! (These guys are really okay–LeFevre told me on the way: "These Germans would surrender to the FFI if you had American forces down here. But they won't surrender to the FFI because they think we mistreat prisoners. I've been in the Resistance 3½ years and have taken many prisoners, but never mistreated one of them–I always shot them right away!" However, he said the last two milice he had captured had not fared so well. It seems they had been responsible for 40 or more of his friends being killed by the Gerries. So when he got these two, he tied them to stakes, put a lot of plastic under them, and tied a fuse to the plastic. He then lighted the fuse and told them "It is now 5 minutes to 4, at 4:20 you go to hell." And they did!)

Finally, we sighted a boat in the distance; the two machine guns we had (both light .30 calibre) were manned immediately and everyone lined the low bulwarks with whatever weapon he had–ranged from car-bines, stens, M-3's, to, .45's automatics. It was fantastic–just like old time pirate stories–here is this boat, 1-foot high sides lined with men with any sort of arm ready to attack anything that the boat might be (even if it were a corvette)! But the point is the spirit of these guys–if it had been a corvette, they would have attacked anyway!

Well, we got back, got a couple of drinks, and went to Fouras. The contact was made at 11 A.M. and perfectly received. This put us "in like Flynn." Frank was happy as a kid that he had a radio in. I was happy because it showed the old luck was still running and we had gotten away with it, and we were solid with the FFI boys since we had gone the dis-tance with them. All around, it was a good night's work.

In the periods before the op, I was feeling pretty moody. After all, I had done a lot of this boat business in Corsica and my luck held, so I thought I was through with that kind of business forever. Then came a period of different ops–through the lines, on land. And that was done. I was feeling that it would be just my luck to have played in the big leagues, and then come down to a Grade B war like this, and have the law of averages catch up with me. It was different after we started out though–there's a great thrill to a rubber boat job, and it takes hold of you once you're under way. But the more you do of it, the more you realize that there's a limit to luck. Like poker: You win for a while, some-times for a long while, and then.... I'm just getting moody. We'll see.

Le Mung (Near Saintes)
January 24, 1945

These last few weeks have been tiring, without having accomplished much. I have been traveling around a bit down here–generally between Marans and Le Neuil. Went down to Bordeaux one afternoon and spent the night, returning the following morning. They had a nightclub, Le Lyon Rouge, some music and a poor floorshow. It was interesting to note that apparently all during the occupation chocolate could be gotten on the black market at Bordeaux. Just returned from a five day trip with Frank, which took us to Toulouse and down to Perpignan, and over to Port Ven-dres and Banhul sur Mer on the Spanish frontier. On the way down, we stopped for dinner at a very good little place near Libourne: St. Emilion. Food was excellent — a good soup, pate, veal, potatoes, an excellent cheese, apples–and a very good red wine they have there "Cheval Blanc."

Perpignan was interesting, Port Vendres and the coastal towns lovely–as all the Mediterranean. I was supposed to return to 7th Army (which I wanted to do with the big push the Gerries are having on up there), a phone call from Paris stopped me at Toulouse and I'm back here until these ops are cleaned up. That may be several weeks, in which time I'll probably go nuts. Once the Ile de Re job is over, there will be probably only a few comparatively simple ops. I don't like it. I don't believe the job is terribly important here — or else they would send some decent equipment to these poor FFI guys. I'm getting a little tired I guess. I'd certainly hate like hell to get knocked off farting around some little pile of rocks like the Ile de Re–most of all where it would be for no particular purpose. However, it will have to be done, and I'll have to do it. So–what the hell.

After more than 12,000 km of driving since D-Day in Southern France, without an accident and under pretty trying conditions at the front, I've had three accidents down here. First, going through the Col de la Republique, on glassy-iced roads in a fog, when the car started to skid crazily as I was trying to avoid two French vehicles which loomed up in the mist–characteristically stopped at about the middle of the road. I pulled out with only a rear tire blown on that one by accelerating at the right moment. Then in Toulouse when the lights of another car blinded me and I smashed a cement post to bits–no one hurt, but the Citroen, Old Betsy, completely knocked out.

Then, the other day, when I thought the roads were merely wet, and it turned out to be about an inch coating of sheer ice. I was going about 75 km per hour, and started to pass a small French truck. I was blowing my horn, the truck went to the right and then–again characteristically — started toward the center of the road again. I touched the brakes and the Citroen was completely out of control. It took to the grass at the left of the road, danced crazily along for several moments, and then turned over completely, landing right side up. There were five full cans of gas in the back. Fortunately none hit me on the head. Three of them flew out the door, which shut itself behind them. I merely banged my knee against the steering wheel and had a stiff neck for a day or two, but was otherwise all right. The front right wheel and the steering wheel were knocked out, but the car worked again after five days in the garage.

All of this I'm putting down to indicate a state of mind and fatigue that is bad. It's true that everyone has been having accidents down here, but I believe there has been something in my personal make-up that is so tired that it had something to do with mine. I find that I don't think as fast as I used to. A heated discussion of some subject — world affairs, theater, art, etc.–merely finds me getting weary of the whole thing and lapsing into silence. My sense of humor is deserting me. I used to be the most equanimical guy, but I'm getting so I irritate easily. I have a hard time whipping up enthusiasm that I used to call forth as easily as turning on a light switch. I'm getting those pessimistic hunches that I had for a while about this time last year. As then, I do not fear death — not enough energy for it I guess. I merely acknowledge the possibility with a sort of patience — unpleasant, yes; but not particularly sad except in lack of purpose or reason for it. Sort of feel that it would be too bad if I never got to write the plays I want to — and follow this with the ever-present fear that when the opportunity comes, if it does, I'll not be up to it. Sometimes I've felt I was going nuts....

Above all, I feel at this moment that I'm not in shape to discharge my responsibilities properly. People have faith in me, and trust my judgment on pretty vital personal things: such as, "Will we try to land tonight, or wait till tomorrow night"; "will we land here — or there." On the answer to these questions depend several lives. This is a weak bit of musing. I realize it. And yet my mind refuses to get up and grapple with the questions that arise. I'm precisely like an old actor with a good record, who's becoming hollow and worn out. I'm living more and more in the past–in reverie. I just had to break this off to discuss where we would land with the job for Ile de Re. Another of those things where I have dissuaded the Joe from an alternative choice. Every time I have to do this now, I think of the time I decided against Walt Taylor's changing his pinpoint, and he was left. We got him back, it is true, but who knows what would have happened if I had agreed with the British to change the pinpoint at the last minute?

Yet I know my judgment was right–regardless of what the consequences might have been. I noticed just now, that I didn't hesitate to give my judgment on the Ile de Re job, and had no feeling of reverie — guess that's what the value of experience is. Despite such musings as these in off moments, you sort of feel back in harness when the op comes up and planning actually begins. Maybe that's part of it — there just aren't enough ops to keep busy on all the time, and you get a chance to realize how tired you are. Have to try to figure this out some time.

There's another thing — and that is the deadly monotony of war. I've been lucky in doing new types of things for most of this one–just being overseas, then when that became almost unbearable, the rubber boat jobs, and then something else that was new, through the lines stuff with the 7th Army. Now everything seems like a twice told tale. The only time down here I've felt like my old self was when we actually pulled the Ile d'Oleron landing — with plans going wrong, as they always do, and the thrill that comes on a job like that, it was really all right.

At the moment, though, I'm tired, unenthusiastic, and want to get this job over and get on to something new, or back home. I want the whole God damned business to be over with. The war's just a damned play that's running overtime and boring both the audience and the actors to death. Come to think of it, that might be a pun — a lousy, sardonic pun. Above all I want a rest. Yet I know, despite the hopes for enough money for six months to write after the war, that I'll get home (if I do), pay my income taxes, and, after one or two nights of spree, will be right back where I started. I don't know whether I'll have the energy to start again, next time, with hope.

Le Mung
February 15, 1945

The last few days have been quite something — in a minor way. Had another trip to Bordeaux and the Medoc country. Tom came down for a couple of days with welcome gossip of 6th Army Group and 7th Army crowd. Ran into Dennie Johnston, who had been in training when I was some years ago, — he jumped into France a year before the invasion and is now in Murphy's section of our outfit.

Over at Point de Grave, I slept in Madame Sans Gene's bed (many books and plays have been made about her–she was the wife of one of Napoleon's marshals). It's a tremendous affair — probably five feet by eight feet — brass — red canopy. The story is that she was very small, but her husband was a regular giant — hence the bed.

Came back here the following evening. Some of our boys had been arrested by mistake by the 66th Division up at St. Nazaire and Point de l'Orient. Ed, Howard and I rode about 200 km. between 10 and 1 in the morning to get their release. Got back to Lucon and stayed at the Hotel de Croissant for about 3 hours sleep and then came on down here.

Saw a rather terrible bus accident. A truck driven by Goums sideswiped a civilian bus and it turned over. Screams and yelling. One or more pinned under the bus. Howard and I stopped, but there was nothing we could do to ease the suffering of the poor devils. So we hopped in our car and went after doctors. Reported afterwards to the nearest FFI Hq and told them they would need something to lift the bus and many doctors. Gave them the time the accident happened and the direction the truck was going, which should have enabled them to catch it (It had not stopped and the thing looked deliberate) with a little calculation, since only 20 minutes had elapsed and there were many roadblocks in the region. Never heard anything more about it.

The poor son of a gun who worked for us at 36th and was shot by our own soldiers and then shipped to Montpelier, a French military hospital, came up in the form of a letter from his brother to me which caught up with me the other day. I just got the letter on February 12, it had been written on Jan. 21. The brother wanted to get to see him, and I had assumed that the people back at 7th Army would take care of that, had left instructions to do it, in fact. It had apparently not been done. The letter is a reproach and makes me feel like all hell.

Epilogue
by Kay Shaw Nelson

On May 2, 2009, hundreds of OSS veteran heroes, their lineal descendants and family members, active military heroes, and other honored guests gathered in the grand ballroom of the elegant Mandarin Oriental Hotel in Washington, D.C. The occasion was The OSS Society's presentation of the William J. Donovan Award to General David H. Petraeus, Commander of the United States Central Command.

The program for the event included a copy of General Donovan's farewell address that he delivered when the OSS officially was deactivated on September 28, 1945.

Men and Women of OSS:

We have come to the end of an unusual experiment. This experiment was to determine whether a group of Americans constituting a cross-section of racial origins, abilities, temperaments, and talents could meet and risk encounters with long-established and well-trained enemy organizations.

How well that experiment has succeeded is measured by your accomplishments and by the recognition of your achievements. You should feel deeply gratified by President Truman's expression of your purpose of basing a coordinated intelligence service upon the techniques and resources that you have initiated and developed.

This could not have been done if you had not been willing to fuse yourselves into a team — a team that was made up of scholars and research experts and of the active units and operations and intelligence who engaged the enemy in direct encounter, but also of the great numbers of our organizations who drove our motor vehicles, kept our records and documents and performed those other innumerable duties of administrative services without which no organization can succeed and which, because well done with us, made our activities that much more effective.

When I speak of your achievements that does not mean that we did not make mistakes. We were not afraid to make mistakes because we were not afraid to try things that had not been tried before. All of us would like to think that we could have done a better job, but all of you must know that, whatever the errors or failures, you have done an honest and self-respecting job. But more than that, because there existed an organization of solidarity, you must also have the conviction that this agency, in which you played a part, was an effective force.

Within a few days each of us will be going on to new tasks whether in civilian life or in governmental work. You can go with the assurance that you have made a beginning by showing the people of America that only by decisions of national policy based upon accurate information can we have the chance of a peace that will endure.

Major General William J. Donovan

Wayne would have perhaps been surprised by large numbers that gathered to honor the legacy of OSS on May 2, 2009 — almost sixty-five years after General Donovan recognized the organization's relatively brief official existence. He would have wondered at the proud and humbled faces of the OSS heroes, too few in number, that dotted the crowd. He would have been curious about the remarks of General Petraeus and other distinguished speakers that documented in no uncertain terms that the legacy of the men and women of OSS influences and serves as a model to be studied and adapted today and in the future.

Wayne's personal journey following the last section of the war-time diary continued shortly after VE-Day in the spring of 1945. After he had returned from completing his OSS assignment in Europe, in March he was asked by General Donovan to go on a special assignment as a member of the American Delegation, Allied Commission on Reparations. Given the assimilated rank of colonel by the War Department, he served with Edwin W. Pauley's Reparations Mission to Paris, Moscow and the Potsdam Conference, as a member of the Secretariat, reporting directly to Donovan, a trip that left in June and returned in September 1945. Only a small part of the trip was written about in the Diary.

On October 12, 1945, Wayne Nelson received a certificate that read: "To: Mr. Wayne Nelson With appreciation and commendation for your service to the Nation as a member of the American Delegation Allied Commission and Reparations at Moscow. Edwin W. Pauley, Ambassador, the U.S. Representative." In the accompanying letter Pauley added, "You are commended for your valuable contribution to the combined efforts of the American Delegation."

Previously, in April 1945, Wayne was presented by General Donovan with the Bronze Star Medal at a ceremony in Washington. The citation, said to have been one of the last documents to be signed by President
Roosevelt, read as follows:

CITATION FOR AUBREY NELSON'S BRONZE STAR MEDAL
    Mr. Aubrey W. Nelson, American Civilian, French Intelligence Branch,
Office of Strategic Services. For meritorious achievement in connection
with military operations in the Mediterranean Theater of Operations from
2 November 1943 to 25 April 1944. With headquarters on the Island of
Corsica, Mr. Nelson assisted in recruiting, training and thoroughly briefing
agents to be infiltrated into enemy territory for the express purpose of
obtaining information relative to enemy defenses, movements and communications. Menaced with being shot as a spy if captured, Mr. Nelson
nevertheless, beyond the call of duty and while in constant danger, voluntarily participated in numerous operations in enemy held territorial waters
and landed many times on enemy occupied territory in order to assist in
the infiltration of Allied agents.

APPROVED: Franklin D. Roosevelt

**Wayne Nelson (center) standing in front of General William "Will Bill" Dono-
van at Bronze Star medal ceremony, Washington, D.C., April 1945.**

In a letter dated January 2, 1946, from the OSS Citations Officer to Mr. Aubrey Wayne Nelson, he was informed about "General Order No. 196, announcing the award of the Croix de Guerre to you."

The award, dated 12 Juin 1945 read:

AUBREY WAYNE NELSON — Assimile Commandant de l'Armee Americaine

A fait partie d l'Office of Strategic Service depuis 1942. A effectue plusieurs debarquements clandestins dans le midi de la France, a organize et dirige les premieres operations d'Armee de l'Atlantizue. A debarque 3 fois dans l'Ile d'OLERON en Decembre 1944 et Janvier 1945 pour y faire passer du materiel radio. A fait preuve au cours de ces operations d'un courage et d'un esprit de decision exceptionnels."

After joining the CIA in 1949 and serving in Washington and overseas as an intelligence officer, Wayne was often described by his friends, especially OSS and CIA colleagues, with various portrayals. Notable among them are:

He always wanted to be a writer. He was a great observer. He was always a fast talker and writer. He loved big words, a lot of alliteration. He was an addicted reader, loved books, and arranged them by subject, never alphabetical. He was enthusiastic and eager for a challenge. He loved telling amusing and interesting stories. He had an aversion to petty talk, gossip, and had few enemies or hatreds. He had a photographic mind to remember it all, described as mind-boggling.

As a graduate of a dramatic school rather than a college, he compensated in full measure by reading everything and had the almost photographic memory to remember it all.

Wayne had the look of someone who was always having a great time but in private he was intimately concerned with world problems that he took seriously. He had no patience with those who criticized our country, his organization (OSS or CIA), or his family. As a stickler for hard work he had great respect for persons who kept their integrity.

As the late Peter Karlow, his friend, OSS and CIA colleague wrote on October 16, 1986: "To Wayne, the world was a stage and all in it were players. There were curtains for each scene, each act. And Wayne, as the hero, or the villain, or the butler, checking the stage sets and the acting, prompting. His shorthand notes right handed with the left hand, like Leonardo — wasn't he doubled in the 6th in 1938 with the Dodgers in Flatbush? Yes, number 36."

During his illness it was heartwarming to have the support of Wayne's former OSS and CIA colleagues and their families as he was hospitalized and his health declined. As the following obituary which appeared in the Tuesday, October 14, 1986, *Washington Times*, reveals, Wayne, until his death, led an active life and was respected for his many activities.

At a memorial service honoring Wayne two of his former colleagues stated that while his professional achievements must remain unpublicized, his personal life escaped no one's notice. He was remembered as "A Man of Great Self-Reliance and Courage; A Son of the Theater, and of American Life and Literature; A Master of Our Language; A Servant of his Country; A Man Who Gave Much and Asked Little; and Who Loved His Family and Took Enormous Pleasure From the Achievements of His Wife and Daughter."

AUBREY "WAYNE" NELSON, CIA VETERAN

Aubrey "Wayne" Nelson, 74, a former actor and playwright, retired operations officer of the Central Intelligence Agency, and a crossword puzzle composer, died Saturday in Sibley Memorial Hospital. He lived in Bethesda.

Mr. Nelson was born in Philadelphia and was a champion high school debater in Easton, Pa. He graduated from the Faegin Academy of Dramatic Arts in New York in 1932.

As an actor, he took the stage name of "Wayne" and was known by it ever since. After performing in summer stock and in New York during what he called the "Depression-ridden theater," he turned to script writing and writing plays, one of which was given a professional tryout in New York's Greenwich Village.

He joined Maj. Gen. William J. "Wild Bill" Donovan's Office of the Coordinator of Information in January 1942, serving as confidential assistant to Allen Dulles. He next worked for the Office of Strategic Services, the successor to the information office and a predecessor of the CIA.

In the OSS, Mr. Nelson served as confidential assistant to Gen. Donovan in New York and Washington from May until September 1942. He later served overseas with the OSS in North Africa, Sicily, Sardinia, Corsica and France. He was awarded the Bronze Star and France's La Croix de Guerre with gold star.

After VE-Day, Mr. Nelson was appointed to the staff of the U.S. Reparations Commission and served in Moscow, at the Potsdam Conference, and in Berlin.

He next worked in Hollywood briefly as technical adviser for "13 Rue Madelaine," a picture about the OSS, starring James Cagney.

He also assisted Allen Dulles, who became a director of the CIA, in his book, "Germany's Underground."

In 1947–48, serving on a Joint Chiefs of Staff project headed by Kermit Roosevelt, Mr. Nelson wrote the first volume and edited the second of the secret war report of Office of the Coordinator of Information-Office of Strategic Services, which was made public about 30 years later

Mr. Nelson began working for the CIA in 1949 and served in various operational positions in Washington, Turkey, Greece, South Korea and West Germany. He retired in 1970.

After his retirement he wrote a suspense novel and worked as a freelance editor. He also was a specialist in the origin and history of words and composed a great number of crossword puzzles that were published by The New York Times and Simon and Schuster.

His latest crossword puzzles, on political and historical subjects, were written for the new American Politics magazine.

Mr. Nelson was a charter member of the American Crossword Federation and Veterans of OSS.

He is survived by his wife, Katherine Nelson, who writes under the name Kay Shaw Nelson, and a daughter, Rae Katherine Nelson, of Washington

One of the most meaningful tributes to Wayne Nelson was a letter sent to his wife and daughter, Rae, from President Ronald Reagan at the White House where Rae served in the Domestic Policy Office from 1985 to 1992, including as associate director for education and drug policy.

THE WHITE HOUSE
WASHINGTON
October 21, 1986

Dear Mrs. and Ms. Nelson:

While I did not share with you Wayne's personal triumphs and moments of joy, I join you now in grieving his loss. Wayne left the world not as a CIA man, a writer, an actor, not as a father and husband, but as all of these. He was a good man, a true patriot in the very best sense of the word. His death leaves the world a poorer place, missing his bright mind, his gift with words, and the companionship he offered his family and friends.

As only you and Rae can know, he brightened and strengthened our world by sharing his spirit with you and those he loved.

Please accept my most heartfelt condolences.

God bless you.

Sincerely,
Ronald Reagan

Index

Africa, North 6, 8, 19
Ajaccio, Corsica 72, 75, 86, 87, 90–92
Algiers 2, 19, 21–31, 44, 108–111, 115, 132, 134
American Delegation, Allied Commission on Reparations 197
Arches, France 170–171

Bains-les-Bains, France 165–168
Barnes, Lt. Comm. Stanley 35, 37, 38, 50
Bastia, Corsica 42, 67–107, 121–132
Beaumont, France 155
Bermuda 114
Bethesda, MD 13, 200
Boar hunt 83, 84
Bonfiglio, Joe 75
Booth, Col Waller 179
Bordeaux, France 186–191
Bruyeres, France 183, 184
Burke, Mike 165–169, 179

Cambino, Tony 89
Capraia 35, 41, 46, 57, 78, 116
Casablanca 18, 112–113, 115
Central Intelligence Agency (CIA) 11, 13, 199–201
Chinimenil, France 173, 180, 181, 184
Clinton, Dewitt 68, 75, 108, 133, 146, 156
Coon, Carl 23–24, 31
Coordinator of Information (COI) 5, 200
Corsica 31, 67–94, 107, 198
Corson, William 7
Corvo, Max 32
Crosby, Maj. Dick 18, 146

SS *Darbyshire* 116, 136–146
Dark Moon Operations 116, 121–132

Donovan, Gen. William 1, 2, 5, 6, 8, 13, 31, 98, 104, 152, 196–198
Dragoon Operation 134–146
Dulles, Allen 5, 6, 12, 29, 70, 200
Durante, Pete 41
Eddy, Col. William 7, 8, 15, 19, 24, 69, 109
Elba 68, 70, 75, 77, 99, 102, 116–121
SS *Evangeline* 15–20

Fairbanks, Douglas, Jr. 29
Felsen, St. Milt. 24
Free French Intelligence (FFI) 154, 174, 187–190

Gamble, Col. Edward 69, 70, 140, 147, 149, 187
Garibaldi 2, 33
Genoa 53, 98, 99
Giannutri 40, 97
Gibraltar 18
Giglio 2, 36–48, 52, 55–65, 97
Glavin, Col. Edward 69, 70, 110–112
Gorgona 69, 70, 73
Greene, Capt. Justin 148, 157, 158, 171, 175, 178, 181

Hadol, France 169–171
Harris, Pinky 18
Higgins Boat 13, 86, 146
Hyde, Henry 109, 187

Ile Rousse, Corsica 68, 69

Joe 2

Karlow, Peter 11, 68, 73, 121, 199
Kent, Sherman 71

King, Don 151
Knight, Ridgeway 19

La Maddalena 32–66
Leavengood, Adam 16
Leger, Henry 2, 15, 18, 105
Livermore, Lt. Col. Russell 68, 94, 96, 97
Livorno 74
LST 32, 33
Mediterranean 1, 7, 18
Millas, Capt. John 156
ML (British Motor Launch) 66
Moscow 197, 200
Moselle River, France 154, 169–171
Motor Torpedo Boat (MTB) 37
Murphy, Jimmy 8
Murphy, Robert D. 8
Mussolini, Benito 33, 55

Naples, Italy 132, 135–136
Nelson, Aubrey W. 5, 8, 198–200
Nelson, Kay Shaw 5, 11, 196, 201
Nelson, Rae 14, 201
Nelson, Wayne 8, 14, 197–198, 200
Nile, Jack 150

Odette 173–178
Office of Strategic Services (OSS) 2, 5, 7, 12, 67, 134, 173, 196, 197, 200
The Office of Strategic Services Society 14, 196
Oran 18, 19
The OSS Society Journal 14

Palermo 32, 54, 55, 65, 71
Paris, France 181, 197
Patch, Lt. Gen. Alexander 139
Pauley, Edwin W. 197
Petraeus, Gen. David H. 196, 197
Pinck, Charles T. 14
Pinpoint 125

Potsdam 197
PT Squadrons (PTS) 35, 86, 142

Radar 39
Reagan, Pres. Ronald 201
Remiremont, France 165
Reparations Commission to Moscow and Potsdam 197
RON 15, 37
Roosevelt, Pres. Franklin D. 7, 198
Roosevelt, Kermit 201
Rounds, Leland 18, 19, 21
Rubber boats 37, 60

Sage, Jerry 8, 23, 24
St. Hippolyte, France 156, 161, 162, 164
St. Tropez, France 134, 143, 147–151
Sardinia 32–66, 86–88
Sawyer, Bill 130
Schoonmaker, Frank 187, 189, 191
Sicalzi, Joe 34, 44, 48, 50
Simone 173–178
Stonborough, Tom 32, 36, 94
Switzerland 6

Tangier 8, 23
Tarallo, Frank 32
Taylor, Lt. Walter 116–120, 122–132, 148
TORCH 7
Toulouse, France 188
Tunisia 71, 72
Tyrrhenian Islands 67, 108

Vesoul, France 162–164
Vierin 2, 38, 45, 48, 55–65

Washington, D.C. 8, 12, 13, 196
Wentworth, 1st Lt. Bo 94

Xertigny, France 168, 169

Youngstown Operation 105, 119–124